Kitty
Most Rev. Joseph H. Hodges, D. D,
Bishop of Wheeling
1300 Byron Street
Wheeling, West Virginia 26003
8/6/73

III - 13.1 - 9788

PRAYER
The New Testament

PRAYER
The New Testament

A. Hamman

Paul VI Center
667 Stone and Shannon Road
Wheeling, WV 26003
PLEASE DO NOT REMOVE FROM CENTER

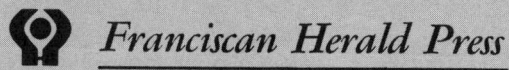 *Franciscan Herald Press*

PRAYER: THE NEW TESTAMENT, by A. Hamman, translated by Paul J. Oligny. Copyright © 1971 by Franciscan Herald Press, 1434 West 51st Street, Chicago, Illinois 60609. Library of Congress Catalog Card Number: 74-85507; SBN: 8199-0424-4. Made in the United States of America.

Nihil Obstat:
   Mark Hegener O.F.M.
   Censor Deputatus

Imprimatur:
   Rt. Rev. Msgr. Francis W. Byrne
   Vicar General, Archdiocese of Chicago

January 15, 1971

"*The Nihil Obstat and the Imprimatur are official declarations that a book or pamphlet is free of doctrinal or moral error. No implication is contained therein that those who have granted the Nihil Obstat and Imprimatur agree with the contents, opinions, or statements expressed.*"

FOREWORD

One might think that Christian prayer would be one of the most explored domains of Christianity, since it forms the very soul of Christian faith and is the very expression of Christian religion. The opposite is the truth. If we take a closer look, we are surprised to find that the studies devoted to this subject are very sporadic and that little attention has been paid to it in theology. There is not even one monograph on Johannine prayer. The five studies to appear in the last fifty years on Pauline prayer form a strange contrast to the numerous studies on justification. Such a situation has symbolic significance.

Our purpose, then, is to fill a particularly regrettable gap at a time when the faithful are returning to the Source. The welcome accorded our publication, *The Prayers of the First Christians*, is proof that the faithful are seeking what is authentic.

Prayer, therefore, is the subject of this book. The word is systematically used in its biblical sense, which includes personal as well as liturgical prayer. In a spirit of faithfulness to Scripture, we have not separated the two. Down through the centuries of Christianity, too many pseudo-problems, too many deviations have arisen from dissociating them. Why have we not always followed the advice St. Cyprian gives in his commentary on the *Our Father*: "The Master of unity did not wish prayer to be offered individually and privately as one would pray only for himself when he prays . . . The Teacher of prayer and concord, who taught unity, thus wished one to pray for all, just as he himself bore all in one."[1]

Our approach to prayer will be theological. There is no game preserve in the realm of prayer. Prayer is not the privilege of spiritual writers, as though there could be knowledge which does not lead to love and consequently to prayer. Prayer is a source of revelation and tradition. *Lex orandi, lex credendi*: this adage is more often quoted than taken into consideration. When the Adoptionists, at the end of the second century, threatened belief in the divinity of Jesus Christ, they were shown the Scripture, the writings of the ancients, and "all those canticles and hymns composed by the brethren of the first centuries, in which the early Christians sang the Word of God, Christ, and extolled him as God."

As a matter of fact, prayer plays only a silent role in theology. At times it is relegated purely and simply to the ascetic life, as if it were not the purest expression of faith. The time has come to react against a pigeon-holing which, in offending the very object of revelation and faith, gravely threatens to impoverish the domain and task of theology.

This study strives to analyze the texts of the New Testament without neglecting biblical and Jewish prayer. The stammerings of God's people are a preparation for Jesus' own prayer of praise, who always fulfills and transcends their prayers. Is not the Church herself constantly repeating the Psalms, the prayer of her infancy? Thanks to the gospels, we become conscious of the new aspects of Christian prayer, which continues but also breaks with the tradition of Old Testament prayer. The Acts of the Apostles and the epistles enable us to be present at the birth of this prayer which, from now on, is addressed to the Father through the mediation of the risen Lord.

Our bibliography may seem incomplete on many points. We do not claim that our documentation is an exhaustive one. We have made use of the works of others in order to stimulate our own thought and not to substitute the reflections of others for our own efforts.

It would have been possible to undertake this study from a

different perspective, but to choose is to reject, and therefore to limit oneself. Approaching prayer from a theological point of view did not facilitate the task, as the author knows only too well. He has benefited greatly from the suggestions and encouragement of ranking exegetes. Professors Martin Noth, Gerard von Rad and Father Albert Gelin were kind enough to read the introduction to biblical prayer. The advice and criticism of Msgr. Lucien Cerfaux and Father Mollat were most helpful in the study of the New Testament. Our colleague, Father Claude Macke, has read both the text and the proofs. Thanks to this help and that of others less well known, our book may perhaps be less unworthy of its subject.

Becançon, Notre-Dame des Buis,
Advent, 1956

Foreword
1. *Fathers of the Church, St. Cyprian,* Treatises, ed. R. Deferrari (New York, 1958), 36, p. 132.

CONTENTS

FOREWORD, v

PART I: INTRODUCTION
    The Biblical Basis of Christian Prayer, 3

Chapter I / THE HISTORY OF PRAYER IN THE OLD TESTAMENT, 5
From Abraham to Samuel 5, The Monarchy and Prophetism 10, The Exile and the post-exilix Period 20, The new prophets 21, The historical books 23, Wisdom literature 29

Chapter II / THE PRAYER OF THE PSALTER, 35
Genesis of the Psalter 35, Classification of the Psalms 41, The Psalms and cult 45

Chapter III / CHARACTERISTICS OF JEWISH PRAYER, 49
Prayer and faith in Yahweh 49, The God of Israel 50, The God of History 51, The God of the world 51, A personal God 52, The themes of prayer 53, Prayer and cult 55, Places of prayer 56

PART II: Prayer in the Synoptic Gospels, 61

Chapter I / JESUS AND THE PRAYER OF ISRAEL, 63
The Temple of Jerusalem 63, The Synagogue 66, Jewish prayers 72, The Psalter 74, The community of Qumran 76

Chapter II / THE PERSONAL PRAYER OF JESUS, 85
Surviving prayers 88, Jesus' confession 92, The prayer at Gethsemane 95, On the Cross 98

Chapter III / THE LORD'S PRAYER, 103
Context 103, The two versions 104, The Jewish roots of the Our Father 105, Structure 108, The doctrine of the Our Father 110, Our Father in heaven 110,

x   *Prayer — The New Testament*

May your name be held holy 112, Your kingdom come 115, Your will be done 119, Give us today our daily bread 122, Forgive us our debts as we have forgiven those who are in debt to us 126, And do not put us to the test, but save us from the evil one 130, Appendix: For yours is the kingdom 136, The text of the Our Father in Luke 136

Chapter IV / THE TEACHING OF JESUS ON PRAYER, 147
Semantics 147, Matthew 5, 44 148, Matthew 6, 1-6, 7-8 149, Matthew 7, 7-11 151, Conditions of prayer 154, The evangelist of prayer 155, Appendix: Luke's canticles 164

Chapter V / JESUS AND THE NEW CULT, 173
The Temple 173, Baptism 174, The eucharistic Last Supper 175, Jesus' last meal with his own 177, Conclusion: Jesus' prayer 181

PART III: Prayer in the Apostolic Community, 185
A. THE ACTS OF THE APOSTLES

Chapter I / EXPLICIT PRAYERS, 187
The election of Matthias 187, The prayer of the community during the persecutions 188, Stephen's prayer 197

Chapter II / THE PRIMITIVE CULT, 205
Description of the assembly 205, Religious meals and the breaking of bread 209, Meal and Passover 211, The eschatological banquet 213, The meals of Jesus 216

Chapter III / THE OTHER FORMS OF CULT AND PRAYER, 227
The imposition of hands 228, Prayer and charismata 230, Public and private prayer 231

Chapter IV / CHARACTERISTIC NOTES OF APOSTOLIC PRAYER, 233
Jewish fidelity 233, The newness of Christian prayer 234, The new cult 236

PRAYER
The New Testament

PART I: INTRODUCTION
The Biblical Basis of Christian Prayer

Israel's prayer is inseparable from her religious history and her spiritual message; it is the mystery of her election become the reason for her dialogue with Yahweh. The question of prayer, then, poses the very problem of the Old Testament.

We must guard against thinking of the Bible as composed of two erratic, irreducible blocks, the Old and the New Testaments, and imagining that the New has definitely superseded the Old. This concept, dear to the heretical leader Marcion, fails to recognize the continuity which, from Genesis to Apocalypse, constitutes the unity of history-salvation.

Scripture is one; it forms a whole. It is the story of salvation and of the world, the story of God who patiently, down through the centuries, has carried out his eternal design, and gathers dispersed mankind into one people. It is the book of God, who sets up a dialogue with man; at the same time it is the book of man, picturing for us a being of flesh and blood, whose passions and sins seem, on certain pages, to reflect back on God himself. It tells of the contract between God who offers, and man who refuses; between Yahweh, who reveals himself, at once close and distant, and man, who seeks him and prays to him.

The unity of Scripture is established by Christ. He it is who links all the pages of the holy book together. He is the meaning and the explanation of the two Testaments. He is the end of the Old in the sense that he arches it toward his Incarnation which fulfills all that had previously been foretold of him by the prophets and the Psalms.

Christian prayer must not be set against Jewish prayer. There is only one prayer, that of God's people, the prayer of waiting during the long period of the Promise, the prayer become thanksgiving for those who have seen the prophecies fulfilled.

Between Christian prayer and Jewish prayer there exist both continuity and break. The Church made her own the piety of her forefathers; but the New Covenant recast Israel's prayer in the crucible of Christ. In fulfilling the promises, Jesus threw the light of a new day on them. He fulfilled them beyond all expectation. The unique light Christ threw on the world and on history transfigured the epic of Israel just as it transfigured Moses and Elijah on Mount Tabor through the power of his coming and the splendor of his presence.[1]

Chapter I

THE HISTORY OF PRAYER IN THE OLD TESTAMENT

Jewish prayer presupposes the religious history of the people; the one is completed in the other. Israel prayed while meditating upon her history. It is therefore necessary to place piety back in the context where it appeared. The fragmentary state of the sources and the critical problems which they pose make it particularly difficult to follow the development of Jewish prayer and to go back to its origins.

Moreover, when accepting the order of the biblical books, we must never lose sight of the fact that this order does not coincide with the age of the texts. Down through the centuries each book has been enriched with new additions, and particularly with prayers, which are derived from different traditions. It is necessary to retrace the genesis of biblical prayers by taking into account the time of their origin, which often does not correspond with that of the writings which transmit them.

From Abraham to Samuel

The Pentateuch rarely speaks of prayer and we can only appreciate its place in the religion of the patriarchs in a very imperfect way. The story of Joseph makes no allusion to prayer whatsoever.

In Genesis, Israel's religious history begins with the call of

Abraham. He was the father of the Jewish people and the trustee of the divine promises. The God who spoke to Abraham is the God of the other patriarchs, the same who later revealed himself to Moses.

In the oldest traditions of Genesis, God spoke more often to man than man to God. God revealed to him that the sky was his tabernacle and the whole world his dwelling place. The familiarity of the relationship between God and man was, as it were, a reflection of the grace of paradise which brought God's presence quite close.[2] By his promise Yahweh bound himself to Abraham and to his descendants.

The religion of the patriarchs was more bound up with worship than with prayer.[3] Abraham carried out the priestly office: he offered holocausts (Gn. 22, 13) and sacrifices of communion (Gn. 31, 54; 46, 1). Certain places, such as the oak of Mambre were privileged ones (Gn. 13, 4; 18, 1). The patriarch offered a sacrifice of thanksgiving on the land he received (Gn. 12, 7) in recognition of God's ownership and dominion (Gn. 13, 4). He prostrated himself before Yahweh and prayed to him (Gn. 24, 52). He prayed that Abimelech might be healed (Gn. 20, 17) and asked forgiveness of the wicked in the name of the just (Gn. 18, 22-32).

The patriarch's prayer of intercession for the sinful town of Sodom demands special mention. The narrative (Gn. 18, 22-33) shows how the innocence of the just and the guilt of the sinners interact on one another, each group being taken collectively. Of the two, which will tip the divine scales, the innocent or the guilty? Abraham's prayer implies the conviction that a small number of righteous men can save the great number of sinners. Yahweh's replies admit the saving role of the saints, since God is more inclined to save than to destroy, to forgive than to condemn (Hos. 11, 8-9).

Abraham did not dare to ask for less than ten just men. The question of a smaller number remains open. Jeremiah and Ezekiel mention that God would pardon Jerusalem if he found only one just man there (Jr. 5, 1; Ez. 22, 30). The story of Genesis mysteriously leads up to the prophecy of the Suffering Servant who, alone, saves the whole people by taking upon himself the sins of the multitude (Is. 53, 5, 10).[4]

The episode of Melchizedek, king and priest of a city — like a later David — who blessed Abraham, remains mysterious. Melchizedek venerated the God of a cosmic religion which corresponds in the Bible to the covenant of Noah, by which God pledged himself to respect the changing of the seasons and to reveal himself through the laws of nature. This religion, which is found in the creation psalms, considers the universe as the work of God and the abode of his presence. Man is a guest there. The sacrifice of the first fruits was both a simple and eloquent expression of this belief.

Melchizedek invoked the "God of heaven and of earth." Throughout the defilements of humanity, he kept the purity of the covenant of Noah. He bore witness to this before Abraham, with whom revelation became more precise and, temporarily, more restricted. Through the simple elements of bread and wine, which bind man to the earth whose king he is, the two men communicated with a common and universal God and with each other. Such is the significance of the mysterious prayer of blessing and praise of Melchizedek, who foretold the High Priest of the new and everlasting covenant (Ps. 110).

The remainder of Genesis shows that Yahweh did not bind himself to one place but to a human family, that of Isaac, of Jacob, the descendants of Abraham. Jacob's prayer, doubtless of later composition, expresses in a striking manner the continuity of the faith which was rooted in that of Abraham (Gn. 32, 10-13). Despite their sin, their sons kept faith in the promises, as did their fathers. They invoked the Most High and built altars to him.[5]

Worship is explicitly mentioned in the patriarchal period; prayer is more implied than developed.[6] A few prayers to be found in the oldest documents enable us to catch a glimpse of the place filled by piety (Gn. 24, 12-14; cf. 42).

Moses is one of several persons who has most deeply left his imprint on the religion of Israel.[7] The God who spoke to him saw to its continuity with the patriarchs (Ex. 3, 6-16). Moses' encounters with Yahweh were frequent. Although they terminated after years of fidelity in an intimacy of which the Elohist speaks (Ex. 33, 11), in the beginning God kept his distance, impressed on him first of all the sense of his greatness and his justice, and of the absolute gratuity of his goodness[8] in the covenant that he was contracting with his people (Ex. 19, 3-6; 34, 10-28). His presence "by day and by night," represented by the pillar of fire (Ex. 13, 21), affirmed the divine transcendence.

Through the mediation of Moses, Yahweh made a covenant with the entire people whose ethnical entity from then on assumed a religious significance. The sacrifice of unleavened bread was, as it were, the sacrament of this belonging (Ex. 13, 3-10). By one and the same election, God forged unity and consecrated the religious mission of Israel. The departure from Egypt, before signifying their miraculous deliverance, laid the foundation of the mission the people had received to offer worship to Yahweh.[9] The passover was adoration as much as thanksgiving.

The religious character of Moses stands out in bold relief from this people of disparate Hebrews. Nevertheless, he remained united to his race both in the evil days of persecution as well in those of the betrayal of their trust. When God offered to raise up a new people, cutting off the old elements, Moses preferred to unite himself with the sinners; he preferred death to any break with his own (Ex. 32, 3-14). He brought the whole people under his charge to God in prayer; it was for their needs that he cried to Yahweh (Ex. 15, 25). He taught them to be faithful to God, while slowly, painfully, forging cohesion and unity.

The life of Moses contradicts the thesis that would see only a collective religion at the time of Israel's origins.[10] As much as any Jeremiah, Moses was a mystic who developed personal religion. His dialogue with God, in which he spoke to God "as a man speaks with his friend," the daring of his love, his lamentations when he was crushed by his responsibility (Nb. 11, 11-15), his gratitude when his prayers were answered (Ex. 15, 1-18; 17, 15-16), and his most exorbitant demand that God make his people his own (Ex. 34, 9) are more than ample proof of his personal religion.

The period of the Judges adds precious little to the history of prayer. Even when living among the Canaanites, the Hebrews remembered Yahweh despite their sins. They knew that his presence was not limited to one place, and that he remained faithful to his people. Samson's prayer was inspired by his awareness of the fact that he was defending the cause of God: the God of his people was scorned by his enemies. His victory was God's victory (Jg. 15, 18; 16, 28). It manifested God's power.

The Law of Moses survived; it was the portion of an elite. Even in dissolute living and in infidelity the people remained faithful to the Covenant. They knew that they were Yahweh's patrimony, the defender of his glory. Sin would never go so far as to make them forget God's beneficent presence, to which they turned in their defeats (Jg. 4, 3). If prayer did not hold a central position during this period, at least it expressed the faith of the generations of believers mentioned in the Epistle to the Hebrews (Heb. 11, 32-34) and showed that the Israelite people were aware of the fact that they were the bearers of a religious mission.

The canticle of Deborah and of Barak, which sings the praises of Yahweh after the defeat of the Canaanites, is one of the most beautiful prayers of ancient biblical literature (Jg. 5, 1-31),[11] composed when the events were still fresh in the author's mind. It proves that the worship of Yahweh remained the vital bond among the tribes of Israel. God had come to the aid of his people; the victory was that Israel was proud of her national God. She sang his boundless goodness, she exalted him and thanked him fervently. Deborah's canticle likewise attests to the development of Hebrew poetry and enables us to perceive, at a period when fear still held an important place in the religion of Israel, the tender feeling of the love of this people for their God. The role women played in the liberation of a people is an old theme; it served as a prelude to the song of Elizabeth (cf. Lk. 1, 42; Jg. 5, 24).

Gideon was victorious after he had first recognized Yahweh's sovereignty by offering sacrifice and after he had destroyed Baal's altar (Jg. 6, 25, 28). He attributed his victory to the Lord who had promised it to him (Jg. 6, 36-40).

The epic of Samson personifies to some degree the history of the Hebrews. His strength was the gift of God; even his birth signified divine power, since his mother had been barren. The child was promised to Manoah with the very same words which, according to Luke, the angel used in addressing Mary: "For you will conceive and bear a son" (Jg. 13, 5; Lk. 1, 31). Samson was punished for having broken his trust, but he kept his confidence in God and prayed to him in the midst of the Philistines. He knew that God was on the side of his chosen people despite their sin. He invoked Yahweh in the temple of Dagon: "Lord Yahweh, I beg you, remember me . . . " The answer to his prayer transcended his person. It consecrated the religious mission of Israel and was proof to the idolaters of the sovereignty of the God of the Hebrews (Jg. 16, 28-30).

The Monarchy and Prophetism

Our knowledge of the period which extends from the institution of the monarchy to the Exile is more extensive, for the simple reason that the sources are more abundant. The historical framework can be reconstructed with the help of the books of Samuel and of Kings, which utilized documents of the highest value: the History of Solomon, the Annals of the Kings of Judah, the Annals of the Kings of Israel, and the Lives of distinguished men of God.

The richest documents for the study of Israel's religion are the writings of the prophets: in the eighth century Amos and Hosea in Israel; Isaiah and Micah in Judah; in the following century, Jeremiah, Nahum, Zephaniah, Habakkuk; at the beginning of the captivity, Ezekiel.

The historical and prophetic writings enable us to understand that religion is not simply a relationship of the Israelite people to Yahweh. This impression could arise, because those who belonged to the group of Israel were vividly conscious of their solidarity. The individual, "while remaining united to the other members of the nation and while serving a common cause, pursued, in the domain of religion, a special task, distinct from the national task."[12] We need only cite the very old use of theophonic names[13] to see how little the individual was sacrificed to the community, but rather how rich he was because of his personal vocation. God's influence manifested itself both in the big and little things of everyday life. Yahweh was the "Alltagsgott," to use Wendel's word.[14]

The books of Samuel contrast with the book of Judges. They are dominated by the strong personalities of the prophet Samuel and of King David. Samuel made his appearance just as this new era was about to unfold, as John the Baptist did when the messianic promises were to be fulfilled. Both were sons of women who until then were barren, a fact which underscores God's goodness (1 S. 1, 6; Lk. 1, 7) and the transcendence of grace over nature.

Hannah, the wife of Elkanah, is one of the most beautiful figures of the Old Testament. She was an Israelite according to God's liking. Her prayer, with its threefold repetition of the word "servant" which she applied to herself (1 S. 1, 11) already preluded that of Mary (Lk. 1, 38). She expressed her confidence by her self-effacement and by her completely interior way of praying. Eli, the priest, interpreted her prayer in a blundering fashion because silent prayer such as hers was not yet a current practice in antiquity. Hannah asked God for a son in a spirit of faith: he would belong solely to Yahweh; she would consecrate him from his birth to the service of the altar. When he was born, she called him Samuel, which means son of prayer (I S. 1, 20).

She expressed her gratitude by offering a sacrifice in the Temple.

The canticle which the editor attributes to Hannah (I S. 2, 1-10), even if it is of later date, is characteristic of the way in which the people interpreted the figure of Hannah and deepened the theme of her prayer. Her canticle is the prototype of the Magnificat, which is obviously inspired by it. It extols the providence of a wise and powerful God who prefers his faithful, the feeble and the poor, to the rich and powerful of the earth. The poem ends in a cry of hope with an evocation of the King — Messiah (vv. 9-10). This relates it to Psalms 2 and 18 and places the books of Samuel in their true perspective. Hannah's song shows how the people meditated on their history; personal prayer emanated from the life of God's people.

For those who can discern the economy of God's promises and the meaning given to the history of their people by the judges and prophets under the operation of God, David appears as a first fulfillment who rounds out the previous stages. With the capture of Jerusalem, the conquest of the promised land and the work of Joshua was completed. Stronger than Samuel, David brought Samson's activity to final victory. Better than Samuel, he restored the national and religious unity of the people.

His prayer, both simple and profound, was expressed in his reply to Michol, who spoke ironically to him regarding his dance before the Ark of the Covenant (2 S. 6, 21-22): "I was dancing for Yahweh." His religion spontaneously involved him with the crowd. David, too, was the type of the prophetic times. Nathan told him that he would be the royal ancestor of the Messiah. This prophecy constituted the summit of the history of the dynasty. David replied to this unheard-of promise with a song of praise, one of the finest in Scripture (2 S. 7, 18-29).[15]

The prayer overflows with love for Yahweh, with admiration for the manifestations of his goodness, and with overwhelming humility. It exults with joy while it abounds with the promised fulfillments. It was man's Amen to God's word, to his eternal

Covenant irrevocably bound from now on to the race of David (cf. 2 S. 23, 5).

The same book of Samuel relates the solemn transfer of the Ark to the city of David. The religious festivities were accompanied by sacrifices offered by the king-priest and by blessings. There is no question here of prayer (2 S. 6). The text alludes to a hymn sung by the people during the sacred dance (2 S. 6, 15, 22).

The canticle attributed to David (2 S. 22, 2-51), which is found with many variations in Psalm 18, raises the question of the Davidic authenticity of the Psalter. The tradition is too well established to be doubted. Difficulties begin when it comes to specifying the portion of the psalms composed by the king-poet. Dom Calmet admits no more than forty-seven Davidic psalms. The heading "Of David" and the ascription made by historic colophons (2 S. 22, 1) do not ensure authenticity. The problem is complicated by the difficulties inherent in the entire sacred text, which was in part transmitted orally before being committed to writing and which over the centuries has undergone important revisions. Moreover, the insertion of liturgical texts and prayers characterized the work of later scribes. For example, Psalm 18, according to Kittel, would date from the time of Jeremiah or of Deuteronomy except for verses 8-16, which might be by David.[16]

The books of Kings recount the prayer of Solomon to Yahweh in the midst of the holocausts at Gibeon, the high place of Israel. It was the song of the king's gratitude for the divine goodness shown toward his dynasty, particularly towards his father, David. In his turn Solomon prayed to obtain wisdom in the governing of his people. The Lord found the king's prayer pleasing and granted him, in addition to wisdom, power and glory (1 K. 3, 6-14). This prayer was to inspire the one which the book of Wisdom placed on the lips of Solomon (Wis. 9, 1-18).

The prayer attributed to Solomon (1 K. 8, 12-13), of unquestionable authenticity, is a poem composed on the occasion of the solemn transfer of the Ark and the tables of the Law from the city of David to the Holy of Holies of the Temple.[17]

During the reign of King Ahab, one of the first prophets of Israel made his appearance. Elijah appears as the man of prayer: "Then the prophet Elijah arose like a fire, his word flaring like a torch" (Si. 48, 1). He sought communion with Yahweh in solitude. His prayer was permeated with respect and intimacy (1 K. 18, 21, 36-38). He was "the man of God" in every circumstance, obedient to his will and the defender of his majesty. Before the sensual cult of the Sidonian baals, established in Samaria, Elijah defended the purity of Yahweh's spiritual religion.

The grandiose setting of Mount Carmel indicates that the monotheistic faith was at stake in this rivalry. The drama of Israel, God's people, was the drama of all mankind; as to Baal, the false God, and Yahweh, the living God, the question arose: which was definitely the true God? The silence of the false gods was oppressive. Elijah began by piously rebuilding the overthrown altar, he took twelve stones according to the number of tribes that the schism and sin of Jeroboam had partitioned and profaned (I K. 18, 31). The prophet's wonderful prayer, at the time of the ritual offering, revived the tradition of the fathers in all its purity: "Yahweh, God of Abraham, Isaac and Israel, let them know today that you are God in Israel." The efficacy of Elijah's prayer contrasted with the impotence of the cries addressed to the baals. The whole people, faces to the ground, acknowledged the true God.

Elijah shows in the same episode how prayer and worship interact. The man of prayer restored the true worship in Israel. One supported the other, one continued the other. In this way he established the role of the prophets in regard to the priesthood and the laity.

The second book of Kings (19, 15-19; 20, 2-3) relates the piety of king Ezechias. It was the time when King Sennacherib was invading the kingdom of Judah. His message to Ezechias was an insult to Yahweh. The king began to pray. He knew that the case transcended his person and his kingdom and the honor of the God of Israel. Judah's drama played the drama of God as well as the salvation of other nations. The king's prayer indicates how greatly the horizon of the Hebrews has widened.

If, at first sight, prayer does not seem to play a predominant role among the prophets of the eighth century, their action was decisive for the religion of Israel and would exert its full influence on the post-exilic period.

Amos, the first in time among the prophets whose writings have been preserved, imbibed in his long, solitary meditations the understanding of God's greatness, of his sovereignty over the world, perhaps also the spiritual significance of the desert for God's people.

In a period of prosperity and false security the prophet proclaimed the time of misfortunes and punishments, because Israel had violated the laws of righteousness and humanity. Amos vehemently attacked liturgical prayer that was not linked to the righteousness demanded by Yahweh. "I hate and despise your feasts, I take no pleasure in your solemn festivals. When you offer me holocausts, . . . I reject your oblations, and refuse to look at your sacrifices of fattened cattle" (Am. 5, 21-22). This was the first protest against wholly external worship; it was to be followed by many others.[18] On this question the New Testament furnishes definitive statements.[19] Cult has no value unless it involves the soul and transforms it (Am. 5, 21-27; cf. 8, 10). Israel's sin was aggravated by the fact of her election. In some way it compromised God whom the disloyal Jews invoked (Am. 5, 14).

Twice God let himself be moved by the prophet's prayer (Am. 7, 2-6). In blunt, monolithic expressions Amos recalled the purity of Yahwism, which he wished to restore in its integrity. Though he remained affiliated with the Mosaic tradition, he ushered in other prophets such as Hosea, Isaiah, and Micah.

Hosea's basic theme was that of Yahweh's unrequited love

for his people. The Covenant was compared to a marriage which united Yahweh and Israel. The chosen spouse was laden with blessings. However, instead of returning love for love, Israel showed only ingratitude. She went so far as to form an alliance with strangers instead of trusting in the might of her God; she prostituted herself to pagan divinities, Baal and Ashtaroth.

Through the personal trial of a love intensely felt for an unworthy woman, Hosea discovered how the heart of God feels toward disloyal men. Worship became a sham, which made God say: "What I want is love, not sacrifice; knowledge of God, not holocausts" (Ho. 6, 6). From now on, sin took on an infinitely more tragic significance; it was infidelity to love. Yahweh therefore cannot allow any sharing; he demands a complete return. Israel's prayer would only be true on condition that it expresses conversion of heart.

If Amos introduced the nuptial metaphor (Am. 5, 1-2), Hosea developed it and gave incomparable importance to this theme, which expresses the union of God and man in both Testaments. It will be found in the prophets,[20] in the Canticle of Canticles as the very fabric of the song, and again in St. Paul and St. John.

In the year 740, when King Uzziah died, Isaiah received his prophetic mission in the Temple of Jerusalem. The same vision, during a liturgical solemnity, revealed to the prophet Yahweh's transcendence and holiness and man's sinful condition. Like Elijah, whose vocation he revived, Isaiah taught a triumphant monotheism, flashing like lightning, and even frightening, when Yahweh appears as the "Holy One," the "Strong One," the "Mighty One" (cf. Is. 2, 17-21; 8, 13-14).

Among the various acts of worship Isaiah mentions prayer (Is. 1, 15) of which God is weary because of sin. If he attacked the insincerity of their cult, he never put in doubt the legitimacy and holiness of the rites. The prophet vilified "lip-service" which does not convey the feelings of the heart (cf. Is. 29, 13-14; cf. Mt. 15, 8, 9). Prayer has value only insofar as it expresses a purification of the heart. If the prayers and hymns inserted in the text of the prophet are of late date, they at least bear witness to a sense of God's holiness which the prophet impressed on the religion of Israel and the preponderant influence which he exercised on post-exilic piety.

Micah, a contemporary of Isaiah, continued Amos' rugged preaching. He attacked the disloyal leaders of the kingdoms of Judah and Samaria. On the day of judgment they will call to Yahweh in vain for help. He reprimanded the cult of Samaria (1, 7) and that of Judah (Mi. 1, 11-13); he denounced social injustices (Mi. 2, 1-2, 8-10; 6, 10-12) and pleaded for a pure worship, for a sincere faith and, above all, for the unity of God's people. In addition to punishments, he announced the splendid reign of the Day of Yahweh for the remnant.

In 722 Samaria was besieged and taken. It was the end of the Northern Kingdom. The monarchy had encouraged a real religious syncretism. From the days of Manasseh, the Temple had been transformed into a crossroad of idols (2 K. 21, 1-9; 23, 4-14); moral decadence had kept step with the baalized religion.

A century later Jeremiah was born in the vicinity of Jerusalem. At that time young King Josiah took up the tradition of his ancestor, Hezekiah, purified religion and morals, and reformed the Mosaic cult.

The second book of Kings relates how, in 621, the high priest Hilkiah discovered "The Book of the Law"; certainly this means Deuteronomy. The influence of this book was considerable for the reform of the cult; the Covenant was renewed, the Temple purified, and the Passover celebrated (2 K. 22, 3-23, 25). The effect of this book is reflected in the editing of the history of the Kings, and likewise in the thought of Jeremiah (Jr. 11, 1-14).

Like Hosea and Deuteronomy, Jeremiah had an understanding of historical retrospection. He went back to the origins, to the time of fidelity, when God concluded the Covenant with his people (Jr. 6, 16). This "resulted in failure."[21] The prophet did not break with the traditional framework. The Covenant with the people of Israel would endure (Jr. 24, 7; 31, 31-33). But it would be renewed, interiorized in rebuilt Jerusalem. No other prophet has given such importance to interior religion, in which the Covenant would be engraved in each man's heart (Jr. 31, 33). The prophetic appeals were addressed not only to the group but to the individual. Yahweh was not only the God of Israel but also of every human soul. Jeremiah was the prophet of personal religion.

The core of his doctrine is his interior life, which he reveals particularly in prayer. The latter emerges spontaneously, as in St. Paul and Origen. No other prophet allows us to penetrate so deeply into the secret of his communion with God. His "Confessions," which alternate with his prophetic messages, give us his dialogue with Yahweh. From him comes the admirable saying: "When you seek me you shall find me, when you seek me with all your heart" (Jr. 29, 13).

Suffering, which is expressed in his prayer by lamentation and struggle, gives him a more pathetic tone, which preludes the piety of the *anawim*. He turned toward Yahweh when he was despised, torn, crushed and when, under his very eyes, the prosperity of the wicked posed terrible questions to him. Although he suffered on behalf of a faithless people, although God himself forbade him to pray for his nation (Jr. 7, 16; 11, 14; 14, 1-14), yet Jeremiah renewed his efforts and interceded for the sinners for whom he, like Moses, remained jointly responsible (Jr. 10, 23-25; 14, 7-9; 14, 19-22).

When Jeremiah's enemies triumphed, he dared question Yahweh on the incomprehensible mystery. He appealed to God's judgment because it seemed to him that justice must be accomplished here below (Jr. 17, 12-18; 18, 19-23; 20, 7-18).

The experience of his interior struggles helped Jeremiah understand and teach the people that trials do not mean that God has forgotten men but rather that they are the crucible of the new creation. On the very brink of the old Covenant and until the catastrophe, the prophet laid the foundations for the religion of the new Covenant. His prayer, with its deeply human overtones, introduces into Scripture an authentic spiritual experience which makes it at the same time heart-gripping and real. It constitutes a peak of the mystical life. "Jeremiah is the father of true prayer."[22]

Tradition attributes the Lamentations to Jeremiah. Whatever the critical value of this opinion, these poems fixed Israel's spiritual attitude in the face of the most painful catastrophe in her history. The laments which are expressed there do not stifle hope in God's design; they attest a keener consciousness of sin, thus preparing the conversion of the heart preached by Ezekiel.

Like Jeremiah, Zephaniah in the same period announced a spiritual religion; it was necessary to seek Yahweh and to remain submissive to him in humility. As a witness of the first great humiliation of Judah, he called his contemporaries to the spiritual poverty which would enable them to welcome salvation with faith and love (Zp. 2, 3).[23] The two Psalms (Zp. 3, 14-18 and 18-20) which express the joy of Sion and the return of the dispersed, seem truly the prophet's work.[24] They celebrate the joy of Jerusalem which has again found its savior king and Yahweh's presence. They prelude, with Nahum, a lyric style which was to have a great success after the Exile.

Habakkuk[25] ends the alternation of prophetic messages and laments with an ardent prayer of supplication (Hab. 3, 1-19), in which the prophet asks Yahweh's intervention, evoking the memory of the past. This final hymn remains an apple of discord for critics. Did the author take it from the liturgy of the Temple, or did the sacred service take possession of it later? Either way the whole book of Habakkuk appears to be a dialogue between the prophet and God.

The unjust demands of the Chaldeans which tore Israel apart pose the painful problem of the retribution of nations. The prophet asked for light in order to see clearly. In prayer Habakkuk discovered with certainty that the oppressor would perish, but that the just man would live because of his indefectible attachment to Yahweh. The hymn which closes the prophetic messages contracts, by its trust in God's might, with the somber colors of the first two chapters. It takes up, in the form of Babylonian poems, the theme of God, the Creator, conqueror of the rebel elements (Hab. 3, 8-15), and sings the triumphal march of Yahweh, at the head of his people at the time of the new Exodus (Hab. 3, 3-7). The cosmic struggle ends with an anthem of hope in Yahweh.

Ezekiel's message is contemporaneous with the conclusion of the book of Jeremiah; it covers the period which preceded the capture of Jerusalem (587) and ends with the vision of the rebuilt Temple (571). He was therefore witness to one of the most troubled and also one of the most decisive periods of Israel's history. If punishments swoop down on the faithless people, Ezekiel underscores personal responsibility with a force never before attained (Ezk. 18, 33).

Paradoxically, the prophet proclaims that Yahweh is not bound to any certain place (Ezk. 11, 16); he is present everywhere to his faithful. At the same time Ezekiel describes with scrupulous care the future reconstruction of the Temple and the organization of the cult. In the restored cult the sanctuary will become once more the abode of the untouchable and formidable God, the place where Yahweh is, as it were, isolated by his holiness. On the return of the divine glory into the Temple the prophet no longer crosses the threshold of the "Holy One." God speaks to him from within (Ezk. 43, 6-12).

This splendid isolation of God and of his own, which protected the cult and the priestly office from any idolatrous encroachment and from all familiarity, was to characterize postexilic Judaism from then on.

The Exile and the post-exilic Period

The Exile was of short duration. Nevertheless, it marked a decisive turning point in Israel's history; something died within the political structure. The event deepened the faith and the religion of God's people by sorting out the faithless Jews from the faithful remnant.

The seed sown in tears by the prophets will rise in new harvests and prepare a religion "in spirit and truth." Under the influence of the prophets the poor of Yahweh will know the promise of future fulfillment.

The new prophets

At the beginning of Cyrus' great victories, about 546, the Spirit of Yahweh took hold of an unknown prophet. He spoke of consolation and of hope. The second part of Isaiah resumes, beyond Ezekiel, the tradition of the old prophets, particularly of Jeremiah.[26] In the land of exile, independently of the entire liturgy, Israel had an extremely spiritual and personal religion.

As vehemently as Ezekiel, the second part of Isaiah attacks idolatry and proclaims Yahweh's final victory. "I am Yahweh, unrivaled; there is no other God besides me" (Is. 45, 5, 6, 18). His religious universalism was broader than that of his predecessors. His sense of the Covenant that bound Yahweh to Israel, his veneration of Abraham and of the great memories of the Exodus gave a new and inimitable accent to his messages.

We find hymns scattered throughout the text, rich in poetic sensitivity, rich, too, in religious fervor (Is. 44, 23; 42, 10; 49, 13); they recover the tone of liturgical praise. These songs, which may have accompanied the exiled Hebrews, thrilled the prophet with the thought that they would soon return to the rebuilt Temple.

The exile made it clear that sin was the obstacle to intimacy with Yahweh. Sin prevented Israel from finding in the cult the first overtures of the soul in its quest of God and from rising up to true prayer (Is. 43, 22-24). To characterize this interior religion the second part of Isaiah recovers the tender accents of Jeremiah (Is. 49, 14-16, 54). Is not "Servant of Yahweh" the primary description of Jeremiah?

The third part of the book of Isaiah contains the liturgical hymns that were perhaps recited during the religious assemblies.[27] Here, as in Ezekiel, the calamities of sin are laid bare; sin effects a break between man and God. The confession of sin prepares the heart for conversion and creates intimacy with God.[28] Repentance reestablishes dialogue (Is. 58, 9; 65, 24).

The anthems of the Servant of Yahweh depict the perfect disciple, who preaches the true faith, dies a martyr, and is then glorified by God. The doctrine of the expiatory suffering of a righteous man appears for the first time. Christian tradition recognized in these anthems, for which Moses and Jeremiah served as models, the perfect worshiper of Yahweh who not only interceded for his people but lived and died for them. In him prayer and cult, sacrifice and life were reunited and merge. He completed the interior transformation of mankind with no restriction.

The second part of Isaiah preludes the entrance of pagans into the universal community. This preoccupation would from now on find expression in prayer and worship. This missionary theme became a leitmotif among the post-exilic prophets.[29]

Jonah, like Malachi, is clearly to be interpreted in the light of a decentralized universalism with regard to the Temple of Jerusalem (Ml. 1, 11). In the book of Jonah we find pagan sailors invoking Yahweh (Jon. 1, 14). Once converted, they offered a sacrifice to him on the ship without being obliged to go to Jerusalem (Jon. 1, 16). Like Joel, Jonah recommended the prayer of penitence to the Ninevites; it would bring them salvation (Jon. 3, 8-9). The canticle (Jon. 2, 3-10)[30] whether it be prior to Jonah or his own work is constructed after the pattern of thanksgiving psalms; it recalls past afflictions and recounts deliverance from them. It lets us glimpse how pious Israelites, in their personal sorrows, made use of liturgical prayer.

God replied to Jonah's headstrong prayer by showing him the mystery of his forgiveness and of his goodness. The universalist perspectives of Jonah's prayer place this little book among the most exalted expressions of the religion of Israel.

History of Prayer in the Old Testament

In the purifying trial of the exile the Jewish community was born. The last prophets laid the foundations for the transition from the old to the new order by emphasizing religious values and the spiritual mission of Israel. In Zechariah, as in Ezekiel, the Temple was the center of the spiritual regrouping, first for the Jews, than for the nations. Zechariah effected in his own person the union of priesthood and prophetism. He prepared the way for the dominant influence of the priests in the post-exilic period, when prophetism came to an end.

The book of Joel gives us an example of prayer in special circumstances, on the occasion of an invading swarm of grasshoppers. The public calamity instigated a liturgical assembly in the Temple, where the priests in the name of the people raised their supplications towards Yahweh. The liturgy of mourning, which we have already met,[31] comprised two calls to prayer and penitence, the second being of a new religious character, illumined by the hope that Yahweh would let himself be moved.

Prayer in Joel is conceived in the communal and hierarchic framework. The prophet speaks to the people more than to individuals (Jl. 2, 15-17). The Israelite found his salvation and the granting of his prayers in and through the liturgical assembly. This insistence, which departs from the prophetic tradition, rejoined it when Joel links the efficacy of prayer to the repentance of a broken heart (Jl. 2, 12-13). The most powerful argument of the prayer of the people remained the Covenant which bound Yahweh to his heritage and which enlisted him against the nations that derided his silence (Jl. 2, 17). We meet this argument again in Psalms (42, 4-11; 79, 10; 11, 2).

The book of Daniel, in its present editing, is contemporaneous with the Maccabees. Inserted in it are prayers of various dates. It bears witness to the liturgical customs dear to the dispersed Jews: to turn toward Jerusalem, to pray three times daily, morning, noon, and evening (Dn. 6, 11).

The historical books

Critics place the redaction of the book of Chronicles, of Ezra and Nehemiah in this same period of the restoration. The author, who wrote between 350 and 200, was familiar with another historical period, which we call deuteronomic history (Deuteronomy, Joshua, Judges, Samuel, and Kings). David, to him, was the central figure of the entire Bible and his influence made itself felt even in prayer.

The Chronicler, living at the time of Israel's downfall, intended to comfort his contemporaries by reminding them of Yahweh's Covenant. He developed religious fervor among the post-exilic Jews; this alone could give them unity and cohesion. He strove to describe the liturgical and messianic significance of David, whose theocracy preluded the reign of Yahweh in the days of the Messiah. God here appears as the Ruler of all the nations (2 Ch. 20, 6); he opens his Temple to the prayer of the foreigner as well as to that of the native (2 Ch. 6, 32).

The religious service, the levites as well as the cantors, took on importance. They were appointed "as ministers before the ark of Yahweh" (1 Ch. 16, 4). The Chronicler gives us some songs of praise, as the Asaphites still rendered them in his time (1 Ch. 16, 7-38; cf. Pss. 105, 1-15; 96; 106, 1, 47-48). All the people answered in chorus: "Amen! Alleluia!" (1 Ch. 16, 36).

If we were to compare Chronicles with prior historical works, it is evident that prayer had gained ground. Thanks to this book we can measure the deepening brought about by the Exile. Following a literary usage that was held in high esteem at that period, the Chronicler attributed personal prayers to David, Solomon, Asa, and to Manasseh (1 Ch. 29, 10-19; 2 Ch. 6; 14, 10; 33, 12, 18, 19). The invocation "my God" seems to date from this period and characterizes the course of piety.[32]

Following Chronicles, the books of Ezra and Nehemiah relate the return of the exiles and the reconstruction of the Temple, the solemn promulgation of the Law by Ezra, and the renewal of the Covenant. Ezra tells how, after the erection of the altar, priests and levites sang their praises to Yahweh, which were taken up in chorus by the crowd (Ezra 3, 10-11). Touching, too, is Ezra's prayer to God in which he confessed the sins of the holy nation, caused by mixed marriages which were shaking the community; he wished to put an end to these abuses (9, 6-15; 10, 2-3).[33]

The book of Nehemiah attests the progress achieved through prayer and the importance it assumed in the religious life of the restoration. As in Jeremiah, whom he reminds us of in many ways (Ne. 3, 36-37), prayer here almost grows out of the text. Nehemiah was a man of prayer; prayer to him was second nature; it entered into the very texture of his narrative as of his life. God's will was the light of his path. We should note the progression of the *Remember*, which marks Nehemiah's second mission and ends, like the book, with "Remember me, my God, for my happiness."

Moved by the news he heard of the misfortune of his country, Nehemiah wept, prayed, and fasted (Ne. 1, 4). His prayer, inspired by Deuteronomy, confessed Israel's sins. He united himself with the faithless people (1, 7). He based his trust on the mercy, the promises of Yahweh, and on the wonders of the past. Strengthened by these proofs of good will, Nehemiah asked God to support his petition before the king (Ne. 1, 5-11). He prayed before presenting his request (2, 4). His undertakings were placed in God's hands, who directed the events. Work and prayer went together in the construction of the Temple (3, 36-38; 4, 3). Nehemiah motivated the people in this atmosphere of fervor (4, 13-15; cf. 8, 6).

The solemn promulgation of the Law included anthems of praise (8, 6; 9, 5), and the confession of sins (9, 2) inspired by the Pentateuch and more particularly by Deuteronomy. The psalm quoted makes a strong contrast between the kindness of Yahweh, who chose Abraham and guided his descendants, and the accumulated sins of the people. Nehemiah invoked the Covenant and divine mercy so that God might take pity on the distress of his children. The influence of this penitential prayer is shown in the prayer attributed to Daniel (Dn. 9, 4-19), doubtless composed in the Maccabean period. The same applies to Dn. 3, 26-45.[34]

We might compare it to the prayer of Galuth, quoted by Baruch (Ba. 1, 15-3, 8), which enlightens us on the piety of the Dispersion. Far from Jerusalem, the exiles maintained ties with Sion; they avoided contact with idolatrous cults and, in the liturgy of the synagogue, retained the memory of their religious past. Their prayer was composed of confession and hope; it asked for conversion as strongly as return and liberation, and attested the religious mission of which the exiles became conscious upon contact with the pagans. Another text, preserved by the book of Daniel (Dn. 3, 52-90), shows the place gratitude held in the prayer of the synagogue.

Although they are later than the writings of the Chronicler, we can compare the books of Tobit, Judith, and Esther. The spiritual deepening of Israel and the progress of prayer in the post-exilic community gives them a new character.

The book of Tobit[35] is a jewel of Hebrew literature and of the religious life of post-exilic Judaism. As in Genesis, God was close to man and was the master of events; his mercy tempered the rigor of his punishments. Through the care of angels, whose role is singularly developed, he watched over his faithful and guided their expeditions. Messengers and intermediaries of God, the angels were also commissioned to carry the prayer of the saints to God.

Tobit's life was guided by the fear of God, which inspired him in all things to observe the divine law scrupulously and to help his neighbor, more particularly the poor and the needy.[36] The Dispersion of the faithful among the pagans was providential; it provided the opportunity, through the praise of the believers, to make known the true God, the Father (Tb. 13, 3-4).

Prayer, fasting, and almsgiving were three constituent elements of Jewish piety. Prayer occupies an exceptional place in this book. Tobit, tried by his misfortune, mocked by all, even by his wife, turned to God. He did not rebel as much as Job, for God is just and merciful despite the sins of the people; Tobit confided his bitterness to God as well as his distaste at having to go on living such a life. His sadness reminds us of Moses (Nb. 11, 15), Elijah (1 K. 19, 4), Job (7, 15), Jonah (4, 3, 8), and Baruch (1, 15-22; 2, 4; 3, 8).

Sarah, exiled in Media, turned toward Jerusalem and sought refuge in God. She began by glorifying God's greatness, then spoke of the trial which made her wish for death (Tb. 3, 15). The angel Raphael, who was sent to Sarah as to Tobit (3, 16) had first been the intercessor before God of the prayers of both of them (12, 12).

Tobit and Sarah began their married life with a prayer of praise (8, 4-7). The book ends with a poem composed of two hymns. The first is a song of gratitude for the great goodness of God. God is Lord and Father. This devotion to the Father appears for the first time in post-exilic prayer and in the official prayers of the synagogue, for example, in the eighteen blessings which prelude the *Our Father*.[37] The second prayer is an address to Yahweh in the style of the prophets (Is. 60); it foreshadows the Apocalypse. In the land of exile the Holy City crystallized the hope of Judaism; it would be the regrouping place for the exiled and the nations. The Psalm lets us see how prophetism became prayer and how prayer contemplated the messianic promises.

In the book of Esther, God directed events without ever being mentioned. Mordecai offered proof of an unshakable trust in Yahweh's protection and in the salvation of his people. The two prayers of Mordecai and Esther are additions of the Greek text. The source of both was Old Testament prayer, but concerned with personal justification, which hardly appears in earlier prayers.

Mordecai's prayer (4, 17b) is a praise of God, Creator, King, Master of all things and all-powerful in the accomplishment of his designs. It evokes the promises made to the fathers. Esther's prayer repeats the classical themes: God's goodness which has chosen Israel, the sin of the people which calls forth God's justice, and the impiety of the pagan nations who attack God by persecuting his people.

Esther asked that the pagans be punished. The Jews conceived the realization of God's design and the reestablishment of order only through the extermination of the wicked. The prayer of the suffering Servant had not lifted the people to the plane of universal charity. Esther's two prayers, touching yet vindictive, do not mark a progress in Israel's religion.

Contrary to the Hebrew book of Esther, that of *Judith* is clearly and deeply religious. The God of the fathers, the God of battles was ever present in the history of his people. Beyond the betrayals that merited chastisement, Israel's destiny involved the Most High. Behind the scene of human enterprises, God was faced with enemies. He manifested his power by triumphing with disarming means.

Judith's prayer (Jdt. 9, 2-14), which echoed the prayer of the entire people (4, 9-15; 7, 29; 13, 17), repeats the theme of trust based on the events of the past. We find a strong indication of the religion of the "poor" (9, 11) who, crushed by a hostile state, confided their anguish to God.

Judith's anthem of gratitude, which recalls the Psalms, took up the theology of God's sovereignty at creation as well as during the course of history; along with the entire book, it entered into the current of pharisaic piety, which was strong in its attachment to the Temple and to religious institutions, as well as in its faith in divine Providence.

A completely new element appears in the second book of Maccabees; it explicitly teaches the resurrection of the body (2 M. 7, 11-14; 12, 43-44, 45, 46). The value of prayer for the dead (12, 43-46) is evidenced, as is intercession for the living (3, 31-34; 15. 12-16).

It must be noted that this late, more formal prayer gained in application what it lost in spontaneity. In order to measure the difference between two types of prayer, we might compare

Daniel's Canticle of the Creatures with that of Francis of Assisi. The same may be said of many prayers which, at this time, were inserted in the older books of the Bible.[38]

Wisdom literature

The sages of Israel exercised an influence on the religious life of the people comparable to that of the prophets and priests. Their literature is the fruit of an intellectual and moral movement which sinks its roots deep in Egyptian heritage.

If wisdom appears in numerous texts of this category with characteristics that are at once profane and universalist, it is no less true that it remained amply receptive to religious inspiration.[39] It found in God the solution to the great problems posed for man's reflection. Primed with the first traditions of the patriarchal families, wisdom literature replaced prophetic literature, and the scribes collected the legacy of beliefs and of the past in order to bring Israel to a spiritual unity.

First in date, the book of Proverbs remains true to the faith of the fathers in God and in man's relations with him. If its doctrine resulted from a reflection ripened by experience, it is not entirely unlike the message of the prophets. Yahweh created the universe which he rules, as he does in all that happens, with unsurpassing wisdom. Justice is the norm of his conduct toward men. The concept of retribution did not reach beyond earthly horizons. Man's fundamental attitude toward Yahweh was fear inspired by consciousness of the difference that separates creatures from their Creator, a fear blended with trust (Pr. 14, 26-27; 19, 23).

Too clear-minded to believe there is any power of magic in sacrifices, the author of Proverbs prefers the just man's prayer (Pr. 15, 8, 29) and the observance of the Law (28, 9). Penitent prayer and works of mercy gave hope of forgiveness for sins (16, 6; 28, 13). The teaching rejoined that of the prophets.

Men of thought and guidance, the sages wrote down their statements within the religious framework of the Jewish people. "Where there is no vision the people get out of hand; blessed are they who keep the Precept" (29, 18). The sage's religious actions, far from separating him from the common effort, was associated with two other religious forces of the nation: the prophet's vision, the priest's Law. The experience of life was put to the service of God.

In the book of Job the doctrine of the sages evolved in the direction of dialogue. Perhaps contemporaneous with Malachi, the book of Job treats of the mystery of God in terms of earthly retribution. The speakers vainly tried to see in the trial Yahweh's punishment; and Job could admit that a god of revenge might be the true God (Jb. 13, 7; 19, 2, 21, 28). Despite his calamity, he did not become hardened in revolt. His faith was stronger than the dialectics of his friends. He appealed to the just, good, and kind God (10, 8-12; 14, 7-15), rather than a vindictive God (16, 21).

Although he was plagued, tormented in spirit, and disfigured in body, Job prayed. His condition, because of the very burden of his trial, drove him toward God. Even if events separated him from God, he had to find him again. Job's piety was but the expression of his faith (12, 1-10; 16, 17, 20-21). Although he moaned and groaned in his sufferings, although he spoke immoderate words (6, 3, 26), his complaining ended in prayer: spontaneous prayer, which constantly surfaced, as in Jeremiah; but in Job it was more closely bound up with the personal drama which gripped the just man in its vise. God was the only escape in his pain.[40]

Although God dwells in an inaccessible sphere, Job found him in his baffling mystery. He was constantly haunted by his presence. He met God at every step he took, at every moment of his life. God enveloped him with his throbbing presence. Despite adversity and his mounting destitution, Job kept touch with the living God. He was ready to accept everything, suffering, yes even death, provided God appeared on his side as his defender and friend (19, 25-27). After God had manifested the mystery of his transcendence to his servant by revealing his goodness to him and the distance which separated them, Job humbly returned to the stammerings of prayer before the grandeur of his God (42, 2-6).

Ecclesiastes makes no disclosures on the spiritual life. Here we find no prayer, no allusion to any precisely religious experience.

The book of Ecclesiasticus[41] loved Jerusalem's religious life, but it preferred the piety of the heart and observance of the commandments. The author's prayer was that of a sage (Si. 23, 1, 4-6). It shines more for its conciseness than for its verbosity (7, 14). The two prayers cited (36, 1-17; 51, 1-12 Heb.) open on messianic vistas. In the first, the author reminds God of his past favors and promises; in the second, God is praised not only for creating and governing the universe, but for having redeemed Israel, reassembled the dispersed and made his might flourish in the house of David. Both prayers, related to the Psalter (Pss. 78; 136) resemble the eighteen blessings.

Last in date, the book of Wisdom opens a new perspective on Jewish religion; God has made man for immortality. After death the soul of the faithful leads a life of endless happiness with God (Ws. 3, 9), provided man, while on earth, seeks God in the simplicity of his heart (1, 1).

If explicit prayer hardly appears in the wisdom literature, the entire doctrine of the sages is taken up by the Psalms. The book of Proverbs contributes its vision of the world and of life: the vanity of human activity, the blessings of family life, the beauty of brotherly understanding.[42] Psalm 49, in its use of apostrophe, as in its teaching on the precariousness of riches, is wholly inspired by the literature of the sages.

The problem of retribution is found again in the Psalter where it reflects the wisdom style (Pss. 1; 37; 112; 128). The mystery of God, which rent Job, is likewise found in Psalm 37. Psalm 73 analyzes the same question on the basis of an experience which makes its rendering more dramatic. The whole biblical heritage is ultimately found in the Psalter.[43]

Introduction & Chapter I
1. H. de Lubac, *Histoire et Esprit* (Paris, 1950), pp. 436-446.
2. Abraham is God's friend (cf. Is. 41, 8; Dn. 3, 35; Ne. 9, 8; 2 Ch. 20, 7).
3. Cf. Gn. 12, 7-8; 13, 4.
4. G. Von Rad, *Das erste Buch Moses* (Göttingen, 1952), III, pp. 181-182
5. Cf. Gn. 26, 25; 31, 54; 33, 20; 35, 1, 3, 7.
6. Gn. 30, 6; 17, 22.
7. F. Heiler, *Prayer: A Study in the History and Psychology of Religion*, trans. Samuel McComb (New York: Oxford Univ. Press, 1932), p. 121.
8. Cf. Ex. 24, 1-2, 10-11.
9. Cf. Ex. 9, 1, 13; 10, 3, 8, 24; 12, 31.
10. Thesis of the rationalist critique of B. Stade, *Geschichte des Volkes Israels* (Berlin, 1887), I, 507; particularly that of J. Wellhausen, *Israelitische und jüdische Geschichte* (Berlin, 1897), p. 69.
11. Even the authors who do not admit the authenticity of the ode affirm that its composition is "contemporaneous with the events. The participation in the event is so authentic and so intense that it is difficult to admit that anyone else could have described the situation so exactly." (O. Eissfeldt, *The Old Testament, An Introduction*, trans. P. R. Ackroyd (New York: Harper and Row, 1965), p. 100.
12. J. de Fraine, "Individu et société dans la religion de l'A. T." *Biblica*, XXXIII (1952), p. 328.
13. M. Noth, *Die Israelitischen Personennamen im Rahmen der gemeinsemitischen Namengebung* (Stuttgart, 1928), p. 133.
14. A. Wendel, *Das freie Laiengebet im vorexilischen Israel* (Leipzig, 1932), p. 97.
15. Cf. 1 Ch. 17, 16-27. For the question of authenticity, see L. Gautier, *Introduction à l'A.T.* (Lausanne, 1939), I, pp. 270-271.
16. R. Kittel, *Die Psalmen* (Leipzig, 1929), p. 66.
17. It was first preserved, like David's elegy on Jonathan (2 S. 1, 18), in the Book of Canticles or Book of the Just, which is now lost. On the other hand, the prayer of the Dedication (1 K. 8, 23-61), written in a clearly deuteronomic style, develops the theology of the Covenant and reveals the highly spiritual character that the religion of Israel was to attain in post-exilic times.
18. Cf. Ho. 6, 6; Is. 1, 11-17; Mi. 6, 6-8; Jr. 6, 20.
19. Lk. 11, 41-42; Rom. 12, 1-2; and especially Jn. 4, 21-24.
20. Cf. Jr. 2, 1-7; 31, 3, 22; Ezk. 16; 23; Is. 50, 1; 54, 5, 8, 10; 62, 4-5.
21. A. Gelin, *The Key concepts of the Old Testament*, trans. George Lamb (New York, N.Y., and Glen Rock, N.J., 1963), p. 67.
22. J. Wellhausen, quoted in F. Heiler, *op. cit.*, p. 122.
32. A. Gelin, *The Poor of Yahweh*, trans. Kathryn Sullivan, R.S.C.J. (Collegeville, Minn. 1964), pp. 29-31.
24. Jerusalem Bible, *ad loc.* p. 1525ff.
25. H. Bévenot, "Le cantique d'Habacuc," *Revue biblique*, XII (1933), 499-525.
26. T. Chary, *Le culte dans la littérature exilienne et postexilienne* (Tournai-Paris, 1954), p. 119.
27 Cf. Is. 59, 1-14; 63, 7-64; 11; compare with Pss. 44; 80; 84; 74; 79.
28. Cf. Is. 59, 12-14; 63, 6-64, 11; especially 64, 5-6, which announces Ps. 51, 5.
29. Cf. Is. 45, 14-17; 45, 20-25; Zp. 3, 9-10; Zc. 14, 16-17; Ml. 1, 11; Jon. 1, 1.
30. For the problem of critique, see O. Eissfeldt, *The Old Testament, An Introduction, op. cit.*, p. 406.

History of Prayer in the Old Testament

31. Cf. Is. 1, 21-28; Lm. 2, 13-22; Jon. 2, 3-9.
32. See O. Eissfeldt, "'Mein Gott' im alten Testament," in *Zeitschrift für die Alttestamentliche Wissenschaft* (1945-1948), pp. 3-16). From now on we shall refer to this work as *ZATW*.
33. H. Gunkel, *Einleitung in die Psalmen* (Göttingen, 1933), p. 64.
34. Th. Chary, *op. cit.* pp. 259-264.
35. See A. Lods, *The Prophets and the Rise of Judaism* trans. S. H. Hooke (London, 1937), p. 346; cf. also p. 16.
36. Cf. Tb. 4, 7, 16; 1, 17; cf. Is. 58, 7; Mt. 25, 35.
37. See below, pp. 67-69 and 105-108.
38. A. Greiff, *Das Gebet im A.T.* (Münster, 1915), p. 49.
39. *Ibid.,* p. 119.
40. Cf. particularly Jb. 7, 7-21; 10, 2-22; 13, 20 - 14, 22; 17, 2-16; 30, 20-23.
41. W. Baumgartner, "Die literarischen Gattungen in der Weisheit des Jesus Sirach," *ZATW* XXXIV (1914), 169ff. Cf. also H. Gunkel, *Einleitung in die Psalmen,* p. 50.
42. H. Gunkel, *Einleitung in die Psalmen,* pp. 381-384.
43. We shall study prayer in the time of Christ in our study of the prayer of Jesus. See *infra,* pp. 173-183.

Chapter II

THE PRAYER OF THE PSALTER

The Psalter contains the richest material in Hebrew and human prayer. The prayers scattered through the books of the Bible, spread out over centuries, are found grouped together in the collection of one hundred and fifty Psalms: a final result, in the third century, of what originally were detached selections.

The very richness of the Psalter makes its inventory and understanding more difficult. The loose and archaic style, the genre proper to Hebrew prosody, the various influences which came into play during its long elaboration, the revisions it has undergone from generations of faithful who prayed them, the work of adaptation for liturgical use, the vicissitudes of a stormy history which corrupted a text in daily use, are so many difficulties which bristle through the text of the Psalms.

We will first take up the genesis of the Psalms and then proceed to study their diversity and spiritual doctrine.

Genesis of the Psalter

The Wellhausen school dated most of the Psalms from post-exilic times. Since then, a great many commentators have returned to more traditional opinions. The Psalter contains a good number of pre-exilic prayers, and the literary style goes back to antiquity in Israel (Am. 5, 23; Is. 30, 29). As we have seen, David occupies an exceptional place in the musical annals of his people. Even in his youth he was noted for his lyrical talent (I S. 16, 18).

We have seen him welcome the Ark with dances and songs (2 S. 6, 5). The Chronicler ascribes a preponderant role to him in the organization of the liturgy and of sacred music. He tends to glorify the psalmist-king, but one only lends to the rich.

Around the year 740, Isaiah took it for granted that liturgical chant had been hallowed by long usage. Deborah's anthem is still older. Thus we can state that Jewish hymnology had a very ancient origin and that it had reached maturity as early as the monarchy.[1]

The Psalter is not the fruit of any spontaneous generation. Various influences of unequal value have marked its development. Gunkel has applied the method of *Formgeschichte* (history of forms) to the Psalms, trying to explain their development by comparing them with similar parts of the Bible and with apocryphal literature, especially the extrabiblical poems.

What influence did Mesopotamia, Syria-Palestine, and Egypt, whose literature is now better known to us, have on the Hebrew Psalter?

The most significant similarities are to be sought in the structure of the poems, in the choice of style and literary themes. We find obvious resemblances between Akkadian literature and the Psalter. Relations between Babylonia and Israel were continuous. Abraham was a native of Ur in Chaldea. From the ninth century Assyrian invasions were frequent in Palestine. The long exile put the Jewish people in contact with the old and sumptuous cult of Babylonia, which was to leave a deep mark on the exiles. Yet Babylonian influence is only rarely direct. It is usually exercised through the mediation of Canaan.

There exists an affinity of styles, at least for the hymns and lamentations, which are met here and there. Nowhere, however, has it been possible to cite a Psalm which plagiarizes a Babylonian poem. The resemblances end with general expressions, such as: *Until when . . . ? Tears are my food . . . I mourn like a dove.* It is possible to point out several allusions to Akkadian myths. The structure follows the rule of parallelism and of stressed syllables; we meet with strophic groupings, refrains, and acrostic poems.[2]

The Psalms contrast in their freedom with the monotony of Babylonian poems. Though the Exile had been a powerful stimulant to Hebrew lyricism and even an enrichment, progress was achieved in the direction of and in the deepening of Yahwism.

The land of Canaan was noted for its musicians. It had furnished players and instruments to Egypt and Assyria. The cantors of the levitic guild, Ethan, Heman, and Korah, seem to bear names of Canaanite origin. From the fourteenth century Canaan possessed a flourishing lyric style. Letters addressed to the pharaoh contain expressions very akin to certain biblical texts: "When shall I see the face of the king, my lord?" (Letter 147; cf. Ps. 17, 15); "If we ascend to heaven, if we descend to earth, our head is between your hands" (Letter 264; cf. Ps. 139, 8).

The poetic texts discovered at Ras Shamra, dating from the fifteenth century, are close to biblical literature; the vocabulary is often identical, with a related poetic structure, although less rich. But there the resemblances end. The subjects treated are always mythological. The poems which describe the first day of the year, the role of the dying and rising god whose perspectives are strictly naturistic, cannot account for the origin of the Psalms of the reign of Yahweh, whose perspectives are eschatological.[3]

Contacts between Israel's sages and Egyptian wisdom are undeniable. In this roundabout way Egyptian literature could have had some influence on the lyric work of the inspired scribes. Egyptian poetry, too, follows the rules of parallelism. Litanies and repetitions are frequent. But, for the rest, comparisons are forced, except for Psalm 104, which is clearly inspired by Akhnaton's great hymn to the sun, composed in the fourteenth century. The biblical work, however, refers to the creation narrative of Genesis, as though to emphasize in a similarity of form the difference in doctrine separating Jewish monotheism from Egyptian literary compositions.

The "literature of the poor" of the New Empire, prior to 1100, is composed of tablets found in a Theban necropolis. They include supplications and hymns of thanksgiving in times of trial, sickness, and oppression. The attitude of the supplicants is so unusual in Egypt that we could infer a Semitic influence in their composition.[4]

As to doctrinal content, a comparison of the Psalms with pagan literature shows no relationship except for the obsession with sin which, among neighboring peoples, did not necessarily go beyond the domain of introspection. The Psalms continually extend beyond this scheme, affirm faith in the living God, and express the obsession of those "who seek God."

Within biblical literature itself, the most diverse influences have marked the genesis of Hebrew psalmody. Exegetes are not in agreement on the influence exercised by prophetism. It would seem that Jeremiah may have been strongly influenced by the prayers of the cult.

The Exile was a time of prayer and meditation. Conditions were different; the Israelites found themselves in a hostile land (Ps. 137, 4), where they had neither temple nor sacrifices. In a foreign country, the people and the nation of Israel became a community which acknowledged the same God. Belonging to the people of Yahweh now depended more on free will and free choice than on soil and race.

The experience of the Exile had shaken God's people by internationalizing them. Religion became more spiritual; the trial made them discover what was essential: prayer, hymns, Scripture. The pious Israelite could build a house of prayer any place, could turn toward Jerusalem, for God is everywhere; he is the king of the universe.[5] This experience of life underlies many Psalms.

The post-exilic anthems were deeply influenced by the second part of Isaiah. The expectation of Yahweh's parousia, spoken of by the prophets, developed upon return from the Exile. Already Israel had been cruelly deceived in her temporal hopes: subject to pagan kings, disquieted by her neighbors, humiliated in her national pride, she projected the grandiose promises of restoration into the future, promises that were so poorly fulfilled up to now. Isaiah's influence enabled Israel to widen her horizons.

The psalmist drew from the most recent as well as from the most prophetic messages of the past; their work was one of anthologizing.[6] Allusions to history are frequent. The epic of God was the foundation for hope.[7] Certain Psalms contain Israel's history in miniature, according to the tradition of the Hexateuch.[8]

The horizon extends from creation to the monarchy. But attention was concentrated on the events of the Exodus and on the entry into Canaan, already dear to Jeremiah and to the second part of Isaiah. In their turn the psalmists sought comfort in meditation on the great series of events which gave them hope for new and marvelous manifestations in the messianic era.

After the Exile, the influence exerted by the sages was no less profound. "The psalmist-sages knew the prophets better than we suppose. This explains why there are so many prophetic elements in the Psalms. To their authors poetry was a sort of prophecy. The second part of Isaiah and Job had so prophesied."[9]

This statement by Ludin Jansen, a Norwegian, is valid not only for late Judaism but even for the golden age of the Jewish Psalms, the beginning of the fifth century. Isaiah had been raised in the school of the scribes which had existed since Solomon's time in Israel, Mesopotamia, and Egypt. Jeremiah, despite the clashes he had with the too artful scribes, drew from the sources of their morals and monotheism.

In the Persian epoch there existed veritable schools of scribes which enlivened the Jewish communities, maintained, and developed the study of the Scriptures. Most of the Psalms were composed in these surroundings. This accounts for their similarity to each other despite the variety of styles. The quintessence of the Bible passed into the psalter, which became the book of meditation and of prayer for the Jewish soul.

The psalmic style allowed the scribes to spread their teaching. The rhythmic transcription as well as the mnemonic system facilitated the work of memorizing. In the "new" canticles, the sages imitated the old while propounding traditional doctrines drawn from the Law (Si. 15, 10; 39, 8, 15) and from the prophets.[10] The poems of the scribes, more scholarly in workmanship but less spontaneous, inculcated respect for the Law, understanding of the harmony of the cosmos, and developed universalist perspectives.

Even in the works of the sage-psalmists the drama of God's people is manifested. National and religious structures had foundered; the Israelite was forced to ask himself the essential question, that of faith. Prayers were no longer words to accompany rites, cries wrung from need; they were the expression of a faithful soul asking itself the reason for its own spiritual existence and discovering in the life of the patriarch and in his tragic destitution the drama of faith.

But, while the learned scribes discussed the Law, others, the *anawim*, were involved in the tragedy itself. Daily life constantly raised the question: *Where is your God?* Living in more modest circumstances, they were the victims of the wicked dealings of the great and mighty, mingling with a paganized or pagan world, face to face with a carnal, materialistic environment dominated by "the pride of life." The *anawim* constituted the "pious core of the nation,"[11] unified by a common fervor more than by social or intellectual relationship.[12] Their communal life was the very antithesis of the secret assemblies of the scoffers and the impious. Two spiritual worlds confronted one another, each isolated from the other.[13]

The prayer of the *anawim,* which is found in the Psalms (Pss. 34; 37; 9; 25), is linked with the teaching of the prophets.[14] It proclaims fidelity to Yahweh, trust in the God of their fathers, for whom they suffered and in whose hands they left their fate. They were aware of being God's true people, the "remnant" announced by the prophets, sole inheritors of the promises, impatiently awaiting their fulfillment. Their prayerful symphony preluded the song of the *Magnificat.* From their midst came John the Baptist and Zachary, Anna and Simeon and more especially, the Virgin Mary.[15]

Classification of the Psalms

The religious poetry of the Jewish people had its laws just as it had its literary genres. Four fundamental tonalities predominate in the Psalter, leaving room for multiple variations, for polymorphic types ranging from prayer, properly so called, to meditation and religious exaltation. We find these types occasionally outside the Psalter, and sometimes even in pagan literature; their form continued even into the New Testament (Lk. 1, 46-47, 49-55, 68-79).

The Psalms can all be reduced to two categories: Psalms of praise and Psalms of supplication. Praise and supplication are the two poles of the Psalter.[16] This classification shows immediately that, properly speaking, there are no Psalms of thanksgiving, because Hebrew does not even have a word to express this sentiment. This was to come to birth in the New Testament, especially in St. Paul.

Praise always has God for its object; it emanates from him in order to sing his greatness or his actions. It always implies an assembly before which the believer proclaims the divine favors: "Then I shall proclaim your name to my brothers, praise you in full assembly" (Ps. 22, 22).

With Westermann[17] we can distinguish:

Descriptive praise (God is . . .), corresponding to the Hebrew *hillel*. It is a global, ontological praise of God, of his being, of his action: *Great are the works of the great God!* These Psalms make no allusion to any particular fact or event.

Narrative praise (God has done . . .), corresponding to the Hebrew *'ôdâh*. This is the act of recognizing, with the ambivalent meaning of the verb "to confess," of proclaiming the favors of God, but also of recognizing and confessing man's defections.[18] This praise comes at times from the community, at others from the individual.[19]

The other Psalms are *supplications*. These are rarely prayers of petition in the modern sense of the word (*sâ'al*). Usually they are entreaties, calls in time of need to be rescued from danger or want. Their object is the actual situation of the person praying. This supplication is now collective, now individual.

The *hymns* are exhortations to praise God; the just, the nations, the universe, or the poet's soul are incited to do so. The motives for praise, for joy or fear are detailed; they are taken from the manifestation of God in creation, in profane and sacred history, especially from the time of the exodus from Egypt. Two acclamations sum up these anthems: "Alleluia," "Amen."[20]

Among these Psalms, some are eschatological or didactic; others, while not hymns properly so called, develop hymnic themes in the supplications or the narrative praises, particularly at the beginning or the end.

With these hymns are associated the *Canticles of Sion*,[21] which exalt Jerusalem, the goal of the annual pilgrimages.[22] We find very ancient traces of them in Isaiah (2, 3), Micah (4, 2), and Jeremiah (31, 6). We can compare them to certain prophetic messages of Isaiah (26, 1; 33, 20). These canticles are often eschatological, particularly in the second part of Isaiah, where Sion appears as the bride of Yahweh toward which the procession of nations ascends.[23]

The Psalms of petition are the most important portion of the Psalter. They include lamentations in the midst of communal or individual trials, songs of trust and of thanksgiving. Often the three intertwine in a unique composition. The Psalms of suffering, derived from the *Qinah*, known to the Babylonians, may have passed to Israel through the intermediary of Canaan.[24]

Taken individually or collectively, these Psalms have a somewhat identical structure; they utter a call to God, describe trials, implore a hearing, confess sins, protest innocence, remind God of reasons for being merciful, and hurl curses at the enemy. They often end in a song of victory or gratitude while promising God sacrifices and praise. The various themes interact according to a uniform plan.

The collective *lamentations* had their appointed place on days of fast and penance,[25] as the historical and prophetic books relate. The style is pre-exilic and is already found in Hosea.[26]

After the Exile the collective supplications referred to the catastrophe of 587.[27] The sacred elegy is profoundly influenced by the prayer of Jeremiah. The lamentations were doubtlessly recited on the anniversary of the fall of Jerusalem[28] and on days of national mourning.

Although we do not intend to systematically interpret their "I" in a collective sense, it seems that several individual lamentations were interpreted and used as national elegies.[29] This collective "I" was placed on the lips of Israel.[30]

Individual supplications are among the most numerous and the most varied. Here we find every sentiment of the one praying, manifesting his virtuosity and impetuosity. They are related to the lamentations of the prophet Jeremiah[31] or of Job.[32] We can also compare Isaiah 52-53 with Psalms 22 and 69. Psalm 51 is related to Ezekiel, Psalm 39 to Ecclesiastes.

Trials are described in a series of images and hyperboles; the suppliant is surrounded by snares, attacked by warriors or by savage beasts (dogs, lions, bulls), calumniated by lying lips; he is drowning in the waters, descends to Sheol. In addition to persecutions, exile, and old age, three kinds of ills are most often envisaged: sickness, calumny, sins. Trials are looked upon as punishment for sin (Pss. 38, 11; 41, 5); hence the ignominious accusations of which the sufferer seeks to justify himself before God.[33] Elsewhere the suppliant confesses his sins and implores God's forgiveness, which is for him the condition of salvation (Pss. 22, 9; 32, 1; Si. 38, 9-10). Before the insults and blasphemies of the pagans and the impious, the psalmist hurls curses and cries for vengeance, in conformity with secular usages of the ancient East.[34]

The Psalms of trust and of praise bear some resemblance to

the Psalms of supplication. The Psalms of trust sing a simple and ardent faith, the joy of the Temple, where the believer is Yahweh's guest (Pss. 15; 24; 42, 3; 63, 3). The Psalms of praise were known in Mesopotamia and Egypt. Collective specimens are rather scarce, but the Bible has preserved some beautiful texts of individual prayer.[35]

The structure of these Psalms includes an invitation to praise, followed by a recital of the perils endured from which the divine assistance has delivered the beseecher; gratitude from the humble, who are exhorted to rejoice and perhaps to repeat the anthem: "Give thanks to Yahweh, for he is good, his love is everlasting (Ps. 118, 29). The presence of refrains presupposes a liturgy and the presence of a choir alternating with the psalmist (Pss. 67; 107, and particularly 118). These chants were apparently recited at the sacrifice of thanksgiving solemnly offered in the Temple (Jr. 33, 11), or they accompanied the ritual sacrifices (Ne. 12, 43). All these chants are universalist. As for the portions which are not prayer properly so called, they are an elevation of the mind, meditations on the Torah. The scribes composed them according to the rules of rhythmic sentences (Si. 44, 4-5) in order to apportion the teachings drawn from the prophets and the Law. The Torah is presented as supreme wisdom; it distinguishes between good and evil, guides the just, as Psalm 1, frontispiece of the entire collection, teaches. Psalm 119 is the most finished expression of this cult of the Law on which the psalmist meditates day and night.

Other Psalms are lessons in ethics: they recall the conditions requisite to please God: fear of God, uprightness; they draw the portrait of the just man, as opposed to that of the impious. The history of God's people, taken up in the form of a litany, throws light on these teachings. Among the other subjects for reflection, we find the problem of man, his origin, his dignity, and his destiny (Ps. 8). The question of retribution is often evoked, particularly in view of the insolent prosperity of the impious. This problem remains all the more thorny, since Jewish eschatology long remained rudimentary and mingled the good and the wicked in the same somber Sheol.

The *prophetic* and *eschatological* Psalms made capital of the writings of the prophets and especially of Isaiah. Alongside the prophetic messages which use the metaphors of cup, of fire, of the crucible, and proclaim the proximity of salvation, the Psalms of the Kingdom extol Yahweh's universal royalty, the splendor of the new Sion, and the advent of the messianic era for all nations. These Psalms draw their inspiration from second Isaiah, from Ezekiel, and Zechariah.

The royalty of Yahweh, already implicit in the Mosaic theophanies, is expressed in a temporal manner in the theocracy of the Jewish kings. After the failure of this "empiric kingdom,"[36] there matured the idea of an entirely new kingdom, whose King would be the Anointed One, where Yahweh's work would be both justice and mercy. This new kingdom would be open to all the people of the earth. Three Canticles of Sion (Pss. 46; 48; 76) draw their inspiration from the prophecies of Isaiah[37] and proclaim the future glory of the city of the great King, the summit of the universe, the gathering place of the exiles, where Yahweh will be enthroned.

The messianic Psalms (Pss. 2, 72; 89; 110; 132) provide the purest expression of Jewish eschatology. The expectation of the Messiah rests on Nathan's prophecy to King David (2 S. 7; I K. 8, 25; 1 Ch. 17). Throughout its history the house of David is exalted. Priestly prerogatives are attributed to the kings of Judah. The Exile only intensified the messianic hope all the more. The Psalms, in their turn, orchestrate this waiting by glorifying the Davidic descendant, king and priest at the same time, who was to hold his authority directly from God and establish the kingdom of Yahweh. The Church was to strive to find this messianic meaning throughout the Psalter.

The Psalms and cult

Starting from the principle that cultural, collective piety has always preceded individual piety, Gunkel has endeavored to discern behind each of our Psalms the concrete liturgical situation which forms its historical and social context, and which he calls *Sitz im Leben* (life-situation). Gunkel's classifications in regard to all the Psalms take into account parallel biblical and extrabiblical works, as well as the place they occupy in the cult:[38] those who prayed were the spokesmen for the entire community.

Gunkel's views have reversed the theory of the collective "I"[39] which attempted to find in this "I" only a literary fiction to express the sentiments of collectivity.[40] What is this position?

In antiquity any prayer, including individual prayer, was molded by the language of the cult, by its vocabulary and concepts, which were somewhat stereotyped. Though the prayer of the pious layman is by no means lacking in the Old Testament, its spontaneous outpouring was modeled after conventional forms. The petitioner speaks of a journey into the underworld to express his need or the threat of his enemies. This dependence shows the intimate bonds which unite all the members of the community.

Certain Psalms have a liturgical character (Pss. 24, 118, 136; 150). Others swarm with allusions (Pss. 42, 43; 95; 98; 99) which attest the existence of a lyric liturgy. Weiser has endeavored to point out the cultual inspiration which explains the themes developed in a number of Psalms.[41] The liturgical-musical titles, even if they are later than the composition of the Psalms, follow an older tradition which must have existed from the time of the monarchy. The guild of Asaph was founded before the Exile, since Nehemiah cites it among those repatriated (Ne. 7, 44; Ezr. 2, 41). It is not likely that it was formed during the time of trial.

A great number of Psalms were used in the cult; others have undergone modifications and were adapted to their liturgical function. Besides these, there exist anthems which could be used for the cult (Pss. 78; 119) but which were used more for individual meditation.

On the whole, the fact that Psalms having a collective sense are less numerous than those with an individual tone proves that the cult, like the influence of Jeremiah, played a determining role in the development of personal prayer.[42] The finest prayers of the Psalter, although in a form that remains archaic, indicate the newness of an authentic spiritual experience and prove that during the post-exilic period a religious deepening took place; the influence of the prophets was bearing fruit. We have but to compare these Psalms with Babylonian songs to see the difference between them and the progress made.

Nothing is more erroneous than to think of cult and the individual as opposites. They are "twins," to use Greiff's expression.[43] Far from expressing any opposition or tension, the Psalter shows how cult developed individual piety, and to what an extent the personal experience of prayer served to prepare for a cult "in spirit and truth."

Chapter II

1. E.g., Pss. 20; 21.
2. Cf. Jerusalem Bible, "Introduction to the Psalms," pp. 779ff; A. Robert, *Les Psaumes* (typescript), pp. 23-24.
3. H. Gunkel, *Einleitung in die Psalmen*, pp. 154-155; 160-165. An excellent analysis of the sources is to be found in H. Weiser, *The Psalms* (Philadelphia, Westminster, 1962), pp. 23-35.
4. A. Barucq, "Péché et innocence dans les psaumes bibliques," *Mélanges Vaganay* (Lyons, 1948).
5. L. Köhler, *Old Testament Theology* trans. A. S. Todd (Philadelphia, 1958), p. 79.
6. E.g., 2 S. 12, 13; Pss. 2; 89, 132; 2 S. 7. A. Robert, *Les Psaumes*, p. 15.
7. E.g. Pss. 44, 2; 60, 8-10; 68, 8-28; 74, 12-15; 77, 11-21; 80, 9-11; 81, 5-17; 83, 10-12; 95, 7-9; 99, 6-7; 135, 8-12.
8. Cf. Pss. 77; 78; 105; 106; 114; 136. A Weiser, *Die Psalmen*, pp. 27-28.
9. H. L. Jansen, in A. Robert, *Les Psaumes*, pp. 26-27.
10. Compare Jr. 8, 8-9 with Ps. 45, 2; Pr. 25, 1.
11. R. Kittel, *Die Psalmen* (Leipzig, 1929), p. 287.
12. A. Robert, *Les Psaumes*, p. 63.
13. A. Gelin, *The Poor of Yahweh*, p. 410.
14. E.g., Zp. 3, 11-13; Is. 2, 3; 49, 13; 61, 1-2; 66, 1-2.
15. A. Gelin, *The Poor of Yahweh*, p. 98.
16. Here we are following the very forceful study of C. Westermann, *Das Loben Gottes in den Psalmen* (Berlin, 1953).
17. C. Westermann, *op. cit.*, pp. 21-22.
18. F. Horst, "Die Doxologien im Amosbuch," *ZATW*, XLVII (1929), 45-54, has shown in the text of Joshua 7, 7-9, that doxology and confession constituted the same juridical act.
19. We can find the same distinction in the names of persons: Elnathan,

Johanan (narrative) or Abraham, Tobias (descriptive). M. Noth, *Die israelitischen Personennamen* (Stuttgart, 1929).

20. A. Greiff, *Das Gebet des A.T.*, p. 75.
21. Pss. 46; 48; 76; 87.
22. Pss. 84; 122; cf. 1 S. 1, 3, 21; 2, 19.
23. Cf. Is. 60, 11; 62, 10; compare with Ps. 68, 30; Tb. 13, 11.
24. Cf. 2 K. 1, 19-27; 3, 33-34.
25. Cf. Jg. 20, 23, 26; 1 S. 7, 6; 1 K. 8, 33-40; Jr. 36, 1-10.
26. Cf. Ho. 6, 1-6; 14, 3-9; Jr. 3, 22 - 4, 2; 14, 7-10; 14, 19 - 15, 5; Pss. 44, 60, 74; 79; 80.
27. Pss. 60; 123 129; 137.
28. Zc. 7, 3; Is. 58, 3; Jl. 1, 13; 2, 12-14.
29. Pss. 22, 28; 59; 69; 71; 102.
30. Ps. 129, 1; Jr. 10, 19-21; Lm. 3.
31. Cf. Jr. 11, 18-23; 12, 1-3, 5-6; 15, 10-11; 15, 21; 22, 7, 14-19.
32. Cf. Jb. 6; 7; 10; 14; 17; 19, 30.
33. It has been supposed that the accused, in order to prove his innocence, submitted himself at the Temple to the judgment of God and there pronounced a ritual oath. We have no precise information on this kind of ordeal. Cf. H. Schmidt, *Das Gebet der Angeklagten* (Giessen, Switz., 1928).
34. Cf. Jr. 12, 3; 17, 18; 18, 21; 20, 11; Pss. 109; 40, 15; 58, 8; 69, 23; 120, 3; 129, 5; 137, 8-9; 140, 10.
35. E.g., Is. 38, 10ff.; Jon. 2; Jr. 20, 13; Jb. 33-27.
36. A. Gelin, *The Key Concepts of the Old Testament*, p. 41.
37. Is. 11, 9; 25-26; 49, 14; 51, 17; 60; 62.
38. H. Gunkel, *Einleitung in die Psalmen*.
39. R. Smend, "Uber das Ich der Psalmen," *ZATW*, VIII (1888), pp. 49-147.
40. O. Eissfeldt, *The Old Testament, An Introduction, op. cit.*, p. 115.
41. A. Weiser, *The Psalms*, pp. 23-35.
42. Cf. J. Herman, *Euchomai*, in *TWNT*, II, 782-799.
43. A. Greiff, *Das Gebet im A.T.*, p. 91.

Chapter III

CHARACTERISTICS OF JEWISH PRAYER

The Psalter, like the scattered anthems, translates Israel's history, the drama of salvation, into prayer. It extols the deeds of God in the midst of his people; each individual becomes conscious of being part of a whole and of being united in his suffering and hope with God's designs, which is slowly being fulfilled. The entire religious doctrine of the Old Testament is found in the Psalter in the form of prayer and meditation: "theological" prayer, that is, or more exactly "theological" prayer, not in the sense of abstract, dogmatic formulas but in that of an "existential" faith which seeks God, and of a spiritual experience which knows mystical intuitions.

Jewish prayer, then, expressed the faith of the Jewish people and sums up the whole of Yahwism by deepening its history and the meaning of the prophetic message.

Prayer and faith in Yahweh

The fundamental element of Jewish religion was the worship of Yahweh. "I am Yahweh your God . . . You shall have no gods except me" (Ex. 20, 1-3).[1] All prayer was centered on the one and only God, the living God. Beside him pagan divinities were mere nothingness; adoring them was the gravest of sins.

The true God is eternal, transcendent, changeless, everywhere present and close to us; no one and nothing can escape him (Ps. 139). He is the Lord of the universe which he created with a word. He governs the world and guides history. While remaining invisible, he manifests his infinite perfections in action. If the psalmist had recourse to anthropomorphisms, he deeply believed that God dwells in an inaccessible citadel.

The God of Israel

The one and only God was the God of Israel. He it was who sealed the Covenant of Sinai and chose Israel for his people from among all the other nations. This pact rested essentially on one condition, the people's obedience to Yahweh, an obedience which involved and gave value to every member of the chosen people.

In Yahweh's paternal ordering of all things, Israel found power and wisdom, benevolence and fidelity, and also God's holiness and justice, which inscribed their claims in the history of the people and manifested the moral extensions of the religious life.

Religion and the Israelite's piety were therefore clarified by the awareness of belonging to the chosen people. The sense of collectivity, of belonging to a clan, a tribe, so keen among primitive peoples, was equally manifest in the Jewish people, among whom the individual was guided in his acts by the usages and the law of the people.[2] In his social and religious life the Israelite acted and prayed as a member of a community. The Covenant had only deepened and spiritualized this consciousness of constituting an entity, a block, a bastion of God in the midst of the pagan world. This did not prevent personal religion from developing, as seen in even the earliest traditions of God's people.[3]

The awareness of belonging to God's people was the foundation of the Jew's trust in his prayer; one placed the other in its true dimension. Even in his personal distress the Jew ran into the collective problem; or, more exactly, the trial enabled him to transcend the framework of an ethnic community, particularly during the post-exilic period and to discover the spiritual community. The case of God and of his people was at stake. The impious sneered and blasphemed: Where is their God? The *ana-*

wim rose above their suffering and humiliation because they knew they were the remnant, the bearers of the Promise.

The God of history

The Israelite did not address his prayer to an unknown God, but to the personal God who proclaimed himself the God of Israel and who made Israel his people, "the God of Abraham, the God of Isaac and the God of Jacob" (Ex. 3, 6; cf. Gn. 31, 42, 53; 32, 10; 48, 15). The story of the chosen people, which the Psalter is constantly retelling, was of major importance for their religious consciousness. It was the action of the faithful and good God, the holy and just God; it was the foundation of trust. The pious Israelite needed the experience of other petitioners, just as his own helped all the others. This explains the overlapping of individual piety with collective piety which, far from opposing or succeeding each other during the course of history, supported and enriched each other. The wealth of individual prayer is distinctive and without parallel among the other religions of the East.[4]

Attempting to set collective piety against individual piety would mean taking insufficient account of the fact that the Jewish religion, from its beginning, showed evidence of a strong awareness of the individual, for example, in matters pertaining to marriage;[5] the Law had a very individualistic structure. Individual prayer was old. Throughout Jewish history we meet with strong, praying personalities, such as Moses, David, Elijah.

This history is an endless rebounding. Faith, revived by the prophets, waited and hoped for the salvation promised to Israel. The failures, humiliation, the ruin of hope and temporal alliances interiorized this waiting among believers. The psalmists called for this salvation with a vehemence that misfortunes and suffering only made all the more pathetic; meanwhile, the true Israel discovered her full dimension.

The God of the world

Faith in Israel's God grew with the centuries. Yahweh was

not only the God of Israel, he was the one and only God, Creator and preserver of the universe; the God of the universe was the God of Israel. The work of God in creation, together with the story of salvation, is one of the essential themes of the biblical hymns.[6] This faith developed, particularly with Elijah, the defender of God's transcendence. The prophets made the people realize that God's imprint on them gave them a mission among the other nations.

This discovery enriched Jewish prayer in a very particular way from the time of the Exile. In an idolatrous country, which Amos had labeled an "unclean soil" (7, 17), the Israelites continued to organize their daily life and to pray in the midst of the pagans. In the letter he sent to the exiles in Babylonia, Jeremiah exhorted them to pray to Yahweh on behalf of the Gentiles (Jr. 29, 7). This was a selfish prayer, since their prosperity depended on that of Babylonia, but one which greatly helped them to rise above rancor and revenge, and to create a new community with the pagans in and through prayer. The God of Israel was the God of the nations who wished to be adored by them.

The new Israel was prepared in the crucible of the Exile. Under the inspiration of second Isaiah, post-exilic prayer became universalist. The reign of Yahweh extended to the whole earth, Sion became the religious capital of the world. The pagans would have their place in the city of God, where Egypt and Babylonia meet (Ps. 87; cf. Ps. 117). The psalms of the Kingdom develop more especially the royalty of God on earth (Pss. 135, 6; 8, 2). Eschatology corresponds to protology.[7] Yahweh will reign (Ps. 98) but through the mediation of a Davidic delegate (Pss. 110; 89; 72).

A Personal God

God is truly Someone, a living Being, to the praying Israelite. He was not an idea, an abstraction, but a Person who not only had unchanging perfection, but who knew anger and love, who listened and who helped. Beneath the anthropomorphisms which

Characteristics of Jewish Prayer

shock our Cartesian minds, we must know how to discern our encounter with the living God. Jacob's wrestling, his hand-to-hand tussle with God, illustrates the realism of the Jewish faith.

When the petitioner challenges God with such familiarity as: "Wake up, Lord! Why are you asleep?" (Ps. 44, 23), he manifests the impetuosity of a prayer which wrestles with the living God and wishes to take his citadel by assault. Behind these attitudes, Jewish prayer, now vehement, now enthusiastic, espoused the rapid movement of the oriental soul in dialogue with its God. It is made complete in the most intimate profession of faith; the impious may triumph, but the just man takes refuge in the joy of the divine presence and the fervor of Yahweh's friendship. If he dared not yet call him Father, he had fewer doubts concerning his fatherly good will than about his own filial legitimacy.[8]

Israel fused the revelation of God's nearness and his transcendence into a single prayer. The revelation of the first was made to the patriarchs, the second during the Mosaic and prophetic period. God appeared in the paradox of his greatness, goodness, holiness, and love, immanent in history and dominating it by his transcendence. The Jew dreaded being consumed by contact with fire, yet sought that fire. His prayer coupled the adoration of Isaiah with the effusion of Jeremiah.[9]

The authenticity of this prayer of man to his God gives it a universal dimension, one beyond time, and enables the Church and each believer to make it his own. It expresses the drama which underlies the whole history of salvation from the Old to the New Israel; man in the fervor of his prayer answers God who calls him. God himself inspires man's reply.

The themes of prayer

Prayer placed the Israelite in his true relationship with God, where the history of the past and of the present appeared to him as the favor of God's benevolence. Consequently, descriptive or narrative praise, when it is not central, occupied an important place in Jewish prayer. Even if it only served to introduce his petition, praise corresponded to the state of the man who knew he was only a sharecropper on God's earth, a debtor to a sovereign who had graciously made a covenant with him. The Covenant was at the heart of this prayer, as it is at the heart of revelation.

In praise as in petition, material and temporal gifts predominate; health and life play an important part in the Psalms (Gn. 27, 28; Pss. 49; 25). Jewish thought knew nothing of Greek dichotomy. Man is body and soul or, more correctly, an incarnate soul; corporal and spiritual goods are intimately bound together, the more so since the absence of a theology of the hereafter restricted the drama to the framework of terrestrial life. Even in Jeremiah material gifts were sacraments of God's munificence.[10]

After the Exile spiritual goods took precedence over earthly riches. Wisdom was in the category of another value. The prophets had learned to ask for "the knowledge of Yahweh," which henceforth appeared as the Lord's supreme gift. Under the action of God's patient education, the Israelite discovered the meaning of gratuitousness; goods faded before the sovereign Good. In transcending the nothingness of riches, the Jew ended by begging happiness from God and communion of life with him.[11]

More often he asked for deliverance from his enemies than from his sins. Pardon for transgressions is found only rarely in the Bible and in the Psalter. It is true that Psalms of confession are particularly intense in the avowal of sin (Pss. 32; 51; 103; 130). A few others may have been revised along these lines (Pss. 31, 39; 69). In post-exilic times compunction of heart, so often preached by the prophets, became, like humility, characteristic of Jewish piety. The groundwork for "metanoia" of the heart was laid by the Psalms.

The Psalms of supplication give a surprising amount of space to enemies, against whom they hurled terrible curses (Pss. 35, 4-8, 26; 58, 7-10; 109, 2-20), which violently shock the Christian reader.

The pious Israelites, particularly the "anawim," daily confronted the wicked whose contagion they avoided, even while feeling the bite of flattering lips (Pss. 12; 52; 64; 120; 140). Behind this conflict the eternal drama of the two cities was being played, whose frontiers passed through Israel. The open defiance of these two powers is the dialectic of history, from Paradise to the Apocalypse. St. Augustine drew his theology of the two Cities from the Psalter.

Behind the scene of this struggle, the stake was not personal satisfaction (at least not openly) but God's cause. The struggle against the invading paganism, encouraged by the great and the mighty, transcended the sufferings of the "anawim"; it was a matter of safeguarding God's design. With a rigor that knew nothing of the tempering of Christian charity, the prayer of the righteous was not content with asking for deliverance; it implored the condemnation and even the extermination of the adversary.[12]

This attitude is explained by the incompleteness of Jewish revelation. So long as the theology of the hereafter was not developed — and it was to be developed only very late — the righteous expected an almost immediate punishment of the guilty and the wicked, failing which God's holiness and justice would suffer an irreparable defeat.[13]

However, the prosperity of the wicked, a scandal to the pious Israelite who expected earthly rewards, obliged him to refine his understanding of God. The book of Job and the prayer of the Psalms invited him to disregard the comfort of his own justice, to humiliate himself in silence before him who alone is just, whose benevolent love is the only good and the only reward that finally counts.

Prayer and cult

Biblical prayer was intimately bound up with cult. The Hebrew word *'atar,* borrowed from the language of the cult, means to pray.[14] The expression "to seek God" can also signify cult (Ho. 5, 6). The Psalter has preserved some prayers for us that accompanied cultual acts: the prayer of the king leaving for war (Ps. 20), prayers accompanying vows (Pss. 61; 65) of sacrifices of thanksgiving (Pss. 21; 66; 100; 116; Jon. 2; Jr. 33, 11), priest blessings over the people (Ps. 134), Psalms for religious feasts (Ps. 29), the feast of Tabernacles (Ps. 30) or of the Dedication. There are several Psalms that may have been recited during cultual offerings (Pss. 69; 100). We find traces of primitive cults in Jewish prayer; cries and appeals may have been synonymous with prayer.[15] The gesture of open arms may originally have come from magical rites (Ex. 17, 11).[16]

The bond which linked cult and prayer may also be found in the blessings and maledictions that are efficacious and irreversible,[17] unless their effects have been neutralized (2 S. 16, 12; 21). Yahweh remained the master of benediction and of malediction. He may effect them or cause them to cease (Dt. 30, 7; 2 S. 16, 12). We know that Jeremiah along with the psalmist called upon God to execute vengeance (Jr. 11, 20; 12, 3; Ps. 137). Intercession in the course of worship had likewise a particular efficacy, which depended on the observance of the divine will (Dt. 28; Lv. 26; Ex. 32, 33).[18]

Cult and prayer have forged the soul of Israel; they have given their distinctive stamp to Jewish religion to such an extent that it is sometimes difficult to discern whether a particular prayer is collective or individual.

Places of prayer

In a cultual religion prayer remained intimately bound up with the place of worship. Isaiah mentions prayer in connection with sacrifices, feasts, and solemnities (Is. 1, 15). Since Abraham the invocation of Yahweh was bound up with his altar (Gn. 12, 8). The places of worship brought the Israelites nearer to God and enabled them to perceive his presence better. Hannah and Elkanah made a pilgrimage to present their supplication to God (1 S. 1, 3).

The Temple of Jerusalem occupied a central place in Jewish religion. God chose it as his dwelling (Dt. 12, 11); it was "a house of prayer for all the peoples."[19] The Jews stretched their

Characteristics of Jewish Prayer

hands toward the Temple when they prayed.[20] When they raised them to the sky, as Jesus was to do in his turn, they strove to reunite themselves to God, present there as in Sion.[21]

Prayer was not restricted to Jerusalem and the Temple; the Jew could pray anywhere. The sons of Abraham prayed to the God of their fathers in the land of the Aramaeans (Gn. 24, 42-44), Isaac in his house (Gn. 25, 21). Abraham himself prayed in the land of the Philistines (Gn. 21, 33), Moses in Egypt (Ex. 8, 8; 9, 33; 10, 18); the same can be said of Samson (Jg. 16, 28), of Elijah in Phoenicia (1 K. 17, 20). Isaac prayed at home (Gn. 25, 21), as did King Hezekiah (2 K. 20, 2), and later Ezra (Ezr. 9, 5). After the Exile a private room facing Jerusalem was consecrated to prayer. Sarah prayed in an upper chamber (Tb. 3, 10-11; cf. Jdt. 9, 1ff; Dn. 6, 11). Jeremiah raised his voice against the illusory confidence of the Jews regarding the indestructibility of the Temple (Jr. 7, 4-7).

Exile and separation from Jerusalem made the chosen people understand the value and the limitations of the Temple's sacramental grace, token of the presence of an omnipresent God. The Psalms show how much ground had been covered and how little prayer was tied to locations and to cultual celebrations. The synagogues were to tip the scales on the side of prayer rather than on that of sacrifice.[22]

Sacrifice occupied an important place in the Jewish religion. Nevertheless, it was a permanent stumbling-block to religion "in spirit and truth"; the people's earth-bound concepts were easily contented with a material, legalistic observance, in which the offering was not seconded by a movement of the soul and did not express a gift of the heart. The prophets never ceased scolding this attitude. To attribute to them an absolute opposition between prayer and sacrifice would be to betray their sometimes paradoxical thought, which is reflected in the Psalms.[23]

How were sacrifice and prayer to be united? Altars and sacrifices existed from the time of the Pentateuch (Gn. 12, 8; Dt. 26, 6ff); there was no question of prayer in Leviticus nor in Deuteronomy (cf. I S. 6). The Psalms attest, on the contrary, that prayer accompanied or preceded the sacrifice of thanksgiving.[24] Nehemiah joined the two (Ne. 12). Most of the Psalms have sprung from private piety, which outstripped ritual sacrifice.

The organic union of Temple, sacrifice, and prayer was to be achieved only by the Messiah: "Destroy this sanctuary, and in three days I will raise it up" (Jn. 2, 19). Prophet and priest, Servant of Yahweh and messianic King, gatherer of the nations and Savior of the world through his oblation, he was already foreseen in the Old Testament (Is. 53; Ps. 22). Only the souls of the "anawim" were open to perceive this.

In its slow elaboration and in its completion, Jewish prayer was the expression of the faith of God's unique people. It remained fundamental for the Old as for the New Testament. Without Jewish prayer, Christian prayer resembles a temple without foundations. The Old Testament served it as a loamy soil into which it plunges fertile roots.

The believer, like God's people, must follow the journey of long preparation, be dissatisfied with what is incomplete, and hope for ultimate fulfillment. Prayer implies this rooting in the Bible which permits progressive enrichment; it resembles a symphony which, starting from a theme, continually spins out new harmonies.

Chapter III

1. What characterizes the prayer of the Old Testament is that, first of all, it is addressed exclusively to Yahweh, "the jealous God." P. Van Imschoot. *Theology of the Old Testament* Vol. I: God, trans. Kathryn Sullivan, R.S.C.J. (New York, 1965).

2. This point has been raised particularly by W. Eichrodt, *Theology of the Old Testament*, trans. J. A. Baker (Philadelphia: Westminster Press, 1967), Vol. II, p. 231-233.

3. See the remarkable demonstration of this in J. de Fraine, "Individu et société dans la religion de l'A.T.," *Biblica* (1952), pp. 324-355; 445-475. Cf. G. Von Rad, "Der Lobpreis Israels," *Antwort* (1956). pp. 677-678.

4. Remark made by W. Eichrodt, *Theology of the Old Testament, op. cit.,* Vol. I., p. 175. The same view is held by F. Heiler, *Prayer,* pp. 274ff.

5. W. Eichrodt, *op. cit.,* Vol. II, p. 234. See particularly J. de Fraine, in article cited.

7. The term *protology* refers to the account of creation in Genesis.

8. We shall have occasion to return to the subject of God's paternity in the

Characteristics of Jewish Prayer

Old Testament, which has only a metaphorical value according to Father Lagrange, *Revue biblique*, V (1908), 481. "The image of the Father is not born out of piety," says J. Hempel, *Gott und Mensch im A.T.* (Stuttgart, 1936), p. 173. The relationship of paternity is a descending, not an ascending one. The comparison comes about, according to Hempel, not from any idea of generation, but from that of creation and dominion.

9. A. Greiff, *Das Gebet im A.T.*, pp. 95-98.
10. *Ibid.*, pp. 109-110.
11. E.g., Pss. 4, 8; 16, 11; 17, 15; 23; 27, 4; 36, 10; 63, 2-7; 73, 25-26; 131.
12. Particularly Pss. 137, 7-9; 149; 109; 139.
13. A. Gelin, *The Key Concepts of the Old Testament*, p. 70. See also p. 75ff.
14. W. Eichrodt, *Theology of the Old Testament*, I, 172.
15. Cf. Gn. 4, 26; 12, 8; 1 K. 8, 43; Jr. 11, 14; Jg. 3, 9, 15; 6, 6; 1 S. 7, 8.
16. A. Greiff, *Das Gebet im A.T.*, pp. 38, 52-54.
17. Gn. 3, 14, 17; 4, 11-12; 27, 36-37.
18. Cf. P. Van Imschoot, *Théologie de l'A.T.*, II, 169.
19. Is. 56, 7; 1 K. 8, 27; Ps. 102, 15; cf. Mk. 11, 17.
20. Is. 1, 15; Pss. 28, 2; 134, 2.
21. Ex. 9, 29; 17, 11; 1 K. 8, 22, 54; Is. 1, 15; Ezr. 9, 5; 2 Ch. 6, 12. Cf. A. Greiff, *Das Gebet im A.T.*, pp. 37-38.
22. A. Greiff, *Das Gebet im A.T.*, p. 29.
23. Pss. 50, 14-15, 23; 69, 31-32. Cf. Pss. 40, 7-8; 51, 18-19.
24. Pss. 22, 26; 54, 8; 61, 9; 116, 18; Jon. 2, 10.

PART II

Prayer in the Synoptic Gospels

It is impossible to disassociate the prayer of Jesus from the apostolic community. All we know about Jesus' prayer has come to us through this community. The redaction of the first gospels was the work of Christians who wrote down Jesus' words and actions in an orderly way. These writings were transmitted orally for years. We shall not begin our study of prayer with this period nor shall we use the writings of the apostolic community. Were we to proceed in this way we would give the impression of contrasting the Christ of the community with the Jesus of history. We would even be giving the impression that we concur with those authors who go so far as to claim that Jesus Christ was the creation of apostolic fervor.

Even if Jesus' prayer is known to us only through the primitive community, it is possible to discern its originality. Christian prayer was patterned after that of Jesus, while respecting the originality of the Lord's personal prayer. When studying Christ's interior life in the Synoptic gospels, it is important to take cognizance of the time separating the redaction of the gospels from the events themselves, and to take into account the editing activity of the evangelists.

Chapter I

JESUS AND THE PRAYER OF ISRAEL

"Not to abolish, . . . but to complete"; these words apply to Jesus' prayer. However personal it may be, like his human life, it was deeply rooted in the people of Israel. In Christ this prayerful people found its ancestral prayer completed.

Continuity and completion — these, from the very first are the essential notes that characterize Jesus' prayer. In order to place ourselves in the perspective of history, we must remember that the testimonies regarding Christ come to us through the evangelists, who gathered his *logia* together.

The Temple of Jerusalem[1]

The Temple of Jerusalem, under the Roman rule, remained Israel's spiritual center. Not only Palestine but the Jewish communities of the Dispersion, turned towards it as the high place of their faith and their hope.

One of the first, most absorbing cares after the Exile was to rebuild the national sanctuary and restore its cult. The Temple Jesus frequented was that of Herod the Great, the third to be built. Herod had begun it in the eighteenth year of his reign, i.e., during the years 20-19 B.C. Its construction required prodigious labor; the priests studied architecture in order that they themselves might build the interior portions, access to which were forbidden to the laity. Nine and a half years after the enterprise had been begun, the king celebrated the dedication of the rebuilt Temple on the anniversary of his accession to the throne. But the work of finishing it lasted for years longer, even into the time of Christ (Jn. 2, 20), and was only completed under the proconsul Albinus (A.D. 62-64).

The sanctuary of Herod's Temple was similar to that of Solomon's. The side buildings were greatly enlarged. Three porticoes, or *atria,* each higher than the other, led the way toward the inner sanctuary: the atrium, or court, of the Gentiles; the woman's court for Jewish women, and finally that of the Israelites' court, accessible only to men.

The court of the Gentiles was flanked on the east and on the south by two wonderfully constructed porticoes. That of the east, called Solomon's Porch, is known to us through the New Testament (Jn. 10, 23; Acts 3, 11; 5, 12). It dominated the Kedron valley. It was here that the Tempter took Jesus (Lk. 4, 9).

In this atrium which served as a forum, Gentiles and Jews met to discuss business and exchange news. The doctors of the Law, surrounded by their disciples, taught and argued there. On the occasion of great religious feasts, this atrium became a veritable public market, where sellers and money changers offered their services to foreign pilgrims.[2]

St. Luke's Gospel begins and ends in the Temple of Jerusalem (Lk. 1, 8-9; 24, 53). There Simeon proclaimed the mission of Jesus: "the salvation . . . prepared for all the nations to see" (Lk. 2, 31-32). There, too, Jesus addressed to his mother his first recorded words: "Did you not know that I must be busy with my Father's affairs?" (Lk. 2, 49) In the Temple Jesus found himself at the heart of his mission. There he asserted his messianic office, according to the prophecies, by openly proclaiming the Good News, as he himself stated during his trial,[3] and by performing miracles, proofs that he was the Messiah (Mt. 21, 14).

The expulsion of the sellers from the Temple, related by the four evangelists, takes on an even more solemn significance. The Synoptics, confined to the framework of a single journey to Jerusalem, place the episode before Christ's Passion. It is by no means impossible that John attempted to establish the chronological order by placing the event at the beginning of Jesus' public life. It was at the time of the Jewish pasch, which made Jesus think of his own Pasch; the allusion is hidden. The disciples did not understand the allusion until after the Resurrection.

Jesus may have witnessed similar scenes of religious marketing about the Temple on other occasions. Now his mission must be accomplished in broad daylight, and he cleared the sacred enclosure of its dealers with a scourge of cords: "My house will be called a house of prayer for all the peoples (Is. 56, 7), but you have turned it into *a robber's den*" (Mk. 11, 17; cf. Jr. 7, 11).

The citation from the last part of Isaiah, after the Exile, quotes an oracle which sees the Temple as the gatherings center of all nations, grouped in a common cult and prayer. Ezekiel had foretold a "new Temple" for the latter times (40-48). Henoch, too, had prophesied that a house, larger and taller than the first Temple, would be built in messianic times.[4]

This inaugurated Jesus' messianic mission. What manifests itself here is the secret of his divine power.[5] The expulsion of the sellers showed where Jesus stood in relation to the Old Testament: the Messiah recognized the sanctity of the Temple and its cult. At the same time he proclaimed the break with the past, which his presence made null and void, and the irruption of a new era and a new cult. The Synoptics only suggest this (Mk. 13, 2; 14, 58; Mt. 12, 6); St. John explicitly teaches it (Jn. 2, 17-22; 4, 21-24). Jesus' prayer was no longer bound to the Temple. The gospels state that he prayed outside its precincts; nowhere do they mention that he ever prayed in the holy place, still less that he offered sacrifice there.

In the light of the Resurrection the disciples understood Jesus' words: "Destroy this sanctuary, and in three days I will raise it up." This prediction, quoted by the Synoptics, distorted by false witnesses during the trial, is given by John in its original form (Jn. 2, 19). From now on, Christ's person replaces the cult of the Temple. The Shekinah of God is no longer attached to a definite place but to a Person, in whom the divine glory is visible. It manifests itself in the mystery of Jesus' death and Resurrection. It was the sign Jesus gave to the scribes and Pharisees (Mt. 12, 38-45).

The death of Christ put an end to the provisional economy of the Temple, at the moment when the symbol became reality in the Messiah. The Jewish cult gave way, in the Christian order, to a new cult centered on the mystery of the glorified body of the risen Savior.[6] The break was to become effective under the pressure of events, when the Jews became conscious of Christian emancipation.

The Synagogue[7]

Far from taking the place of the Temple, the synagogue only reinforced the unique significance of the Temple in the cult of Israel. There were synagogues even in the precincts of the Temple and in the humblest villages. These "houses of prayer" were used for meetings at which Jews prayed and listened to the reading of the Bible.[8]

In synagogue meetings first place was given to instruction intended to make the Torah enter into the very flesh and blood of those in attendance (Pss. 19, 8-12; 119). The Law was translated into Aramaic and commented on in that language every sabbath and feast day. The congregation was entirely passive during the service.

Gradually prayer was added, composed of extracts from the Torah and edifying texts. These texts were repeated by the congregation as a confession of faith. The Shema originated in this way (Dt. 6, 4-8; 11, 13-21; Nb. 15, 37-41). Josephus considered this institution very ancient.[9] The Shema remains the framework of Jewish prayer; it has been lengthened by other formulas which are original compositions.

Possibly about this same period a totally independent prayer, the Tephillah, appeared. It has been described as the prayer par

Jesus and the Prayer of Israel

excellence. It enjoyed a glorious destiny in the religious history of Israel. The Jews called it, in its later form, *Shemone Esre,* or *Eighteen Blessings.*

These are the eighteen benedictions which every Israelite had to recite three times a day. It was both a communal and private prayer, recited by one person only in the synagogue in the name of all, but which everyone was bound to say in private. The translation which follows is based on the Palestinian version, which is manifestly older than the Babylonian one, especially in the form that has won wide acceptance.[10]

God, open my lips, and my mouth shall pronounce Thy praise.

1. Blessed be Thou, O God, the God of our fathers, the God of Abraham, Isaac and Jacob, the great God, strong and terrible, most exalted One, Creator of heaven and earth, our shield and the shield of our Father, our trust in every generation. Blessed be Thou, O God, the shield of Abraham.

2. Thou art strong, humiliating those who exalt themselves and pronouncing judgment against the oppressors, Thou livest forever, bringing the dead back to life. Thou causest the wind to blow and the dew to fall, Thou supportest the living and revivest the dead, and on a sudden Thou wilt bring us salvation. Blessed be Thou, O God, Who bringeth the dead back to life.

3. Thou art holy, and Thy name is awe-inspiring. There is no God besides Thee. Blessed be Thou, O God, the Holy God.

4. Favor us with the knowledge which comes from Thee, and with the intelligence and understanding which comes from Thy Torah. Blessed be Thou, O God, Who favorest us with knowledge.

5. Cause us to return unto Thee, O God, and we shall return. Renew our days as before. Blessed be Thou, O God, who delightest in our conversion.

6. Forgive us, O Father, for we have sinned against Thee, wipe out and remove our iniquities from before Thine eyes, for great is Thy mercy. Blessed be Thou, O God, Who forgivest abundantly.

7. Look upon our distress and fight for us, redeem us because

of Thy name. Blessed be Thou, O God, Redeemer of Israel.

8. Cure us, O God, of the wounds of our hearts, of sorrow and longing. Remove them from us and heal our sicknesses. Blessed be Thou, Who healest the sicknesses of Thy people Israel.

9. Bless this year, O our God, in our behalf, so that it shall be good for all kinds of harvests, and let us see soon the time of our redemption. Send dew and rain to the earth, and feed the earth with the treasures of Thy goodness and blessings. Blessed be Thou, O God, Who blessest the years.

10. Sound the great trumpet for our freedom, and raise the standard for the calling together of our exiles. Blessed be Thou, O God, Who gatherest in the scattered members of Thy people Israel.

11. Restore our judges and our counselors as at the beginning. And be Thou alone Ruler over us. Blessed be Thou, O God, who lovest justice.

12. Let there be no hope for renegades, and wipe out the kingdom of pride speedily in our days, and may all Nazarenes and heretics perish instantly, may their names be erased from the Book of Life and not be inscribed with those of the righteous. Blessed be Thou, O God, Who humblest the proud.

13. Mayest Thou have mercy on those who are converted to justice, and give us ample reward together with those who do Thy will. Blessed be Thou, O God, the trust of the righteous.

14. Have mercy on Thy people Israel, on Thy city Jerusalem, on Zion the dwelling place of Thy glory, on Thy Temple, and on the kingship of the House of David, Thy truly anointed one. Blessed be Thou, O God, the God of David, Who buildest Jerusalem.

15. Hear, O God, the voice of our prayer and have pity on us, because Thou art a God full of grace and mercy. Blessed be Thou, O God, Who hearest prayer.

16. Be gracious unto us and dwell in Zion, and may Thy servants serve Thee in Jerusalem. Blessed be Thou, O God, Whom we serve with reverence.

17. We Thank Thee, our God and God of our fathers, for all Thy kindnesses, for Thy love and mercy which Thou hast bestowed upon us and upon our fathers. When we stumble, Thy love supporteth us. Blessed be Thou, O God, Who lovest to be gracious.

18. Send Thy peace to Thy people Israel and to Thy city and Thy portion, and bless us all together. Blessed be Thou, O God, Who makest peace.

This prayer type is a benediction. It is made rhythmical, strophe by strophe, with the refrain "Blessed are you . . . ," which repeats the essential idea. The first three strophes are a praise of God, the God of the fathers who, in the course of history, has been a shield to his people, the living God who has given life even to the dead; this can be taken to mean both individuals and the entire nation.

Next come the petitions: understanding and knowledge of the Law; the return to God and forgiveness, salvation and healing of the people's sufferings; the goods of this earth and the gathering together of the dispersed; a return to the days of the Judges. The prayer next asks for the punishment of apostates and the reward of proselytes, before imploring the effusion of God's mercy on Jerusalem and the house of David. It ends with a prayer of praise and implores peace for Israel, for the city, and for Yahweh's heritage.

The *Shemone Esre,* like the *Our Father,* is an eminently collective prayer. It seems to have been influenced by Si. 51, 12, and by the piety of the "anawim."[11] It was the prayer of the Jewish congregation. In the time of Christ it was recited two or three times daily by all Israelites.[12] We find probable allusion to it in the Gospel of Luke (10, 26-27).

The synagogue service, while drawing its inspiration from the Temple, had its own proper character. It was composed of the recitation of the Shema,[13] the reading of the Torah and the prophets, translated and explained, and the priest's blessing, to which the congregation replied, "Amen." Emphasis was placed on preaching and instruction; the cultual portion was secondary.

A new cult here comes to light, an unadorned, spiritual cult, accessible to the few, in which prayer replaced sacrifice.[14] The liturgy was more democratic, more independent of the priesthood and the laity played an important part in it. The synagogue plunged Jewish life deep in prayer. Its influence was noticeable in the formulas used in private devotion.[15]

In addition to the services of the synagogue the Israelite prayed three times daily (Dn. 6, 11). In this way prayer beat in rhythm with Israel's life. One of these three recitations coincided with the evening sacrifice in the Temple (Nb. 28, 4). According to Temple custom (Lk. 1, 10), the people were allowed to assist at the sacrifice, although we are not told whether it was the morning or evening one. It seems more likely that St. Luke had the morning sacrifice in mind.

In the time of Christ the three prayers were firmly established at the hours of the morning and evening sacrifices, 9:00 A.M. and 3:00 P.M., with the third at a later hour. This evening prayer, once optional, became customary, then obligatory, about 100 A.D.

The origin of this threefold prayer is explained differently. Some look to Dn. 6, 11 and Ps. 55, 18; others see in it an institution of the three patriarchs. R. Shemuel b. Nachman finds the three great moments of the day in it. The same rhythm is found in the community of Qumran and from the second century (*Didache*, 8, 3). This threefold prayer was recited wherever the Israelite found himself at the given time, in his house, in the street, or in the fields.[16] Many Jews linked the morning and evening prayers with the daily recitation of the Shema, followed, in the morning, by the Eighteen Blessings.

Meal prayers were obligatory even for women and slaves. It is referred to in Dt. 8, 11-14. The blessing raised the meal to the dignity of a religious act in which the guests took part. The master of the house broke bread with a prayer of blessing. If there were any wine, he blessed it, saying: "Praise be to you, O Lord our

Jesus and the Prayer of Israel

God, King of the world, who created the fruit of the vine." Those present answered, "Amen." Then the householder broke the bread and distributed it. He was the first to eat some of it. The same blessing was given over the oil. The Israelite neither ate nor drank anything without a blessing.[17] The doctrinal reason underlying this custom was that the earth belonged to God (Ps. 24, 1). He who returned no thanks was a thief. The rabbis based this practice on Lv. 19, 24 and Dt. 8, 10. All these blessings began with the words: "Blessed are you, Yahweh, our God, King of the universe."

The householder asked the most worthy guest to say the final prayers. The latter took the chalice of benediction (*to poterion tez eulogias*), looked at it, and recited the prayer composed of four benedictions.[18] In this manner the whole meal became for the believer an "eulogia."[19]

On feast days and the sabbath table prayer was more solemn. On the day of the passover, Psalms 113-118 were recited. The preliminary course was introduced by the festal benediction and the blessing of the chalice. The meal proper began with the prayer over the unleavened bread and its breaking. After the eating of the paschal lamb, the cup which passed the third time round was called the cup of benediction, and over it the prayer of thanksgiving was recited.[20]

We find Jewish influence in the benedictions of the New Testament, in the twofold sense of God's blessing which descends on man, and of man's blessing which recognizes God's goodness. This was the theme of Zechariah's prayer of thanksgiving (Lk. 1, 64). Simeon blessed Jesus' parents (Lk. 2, 34). The mother of the Messiah was assured by the angel of God's blessing (Lk. 1, 28, 42). The crowd entering Jerusalem acclaimed the Messiah with the greeting: "Blessings on him who comes in the name of the Lord" (Mk. 11, 9; Mt. 21, 9; Lk. 19, 38; Jn. 12, 13); in this way they acknowledged him as the faithful envoy of the Father and expressed their submission to him.[21]

It is difficult to give more details regarding the usual formulas of Jewish prayer. The Kaddish, which contains some resemblances to the *Our Father*,[22] may go back to the first century A.D. The same may be said of the Avinu malkênu.[23] We cannot date with any certainty the prayers of the Musaph and of the Havdala.[24] Alongside stereotyped forms, Judaism engaged in spontaneous and personal prayer. When the *Shemone Esre* was being drawn up, the question was asked whether the insertion of personal prayer was permissible. The answer was yes.[25]

The parable of the Pharisee and the publican (Lk. 18, 10), both of whom went to the Temple for personal prayer, sketches in a vivid manner a scene from daily life. The rather rigid ordering of official prayer inspired and developed the sense of personal prayer.

The stumbling block of over-stereotyped prayers was their encouragement of a certain formalism which was expressed in the casuistry of the rabbis.[26] The prescriptions concerning phylacteries opened the way to abuses and to a conceiving of prayer as a kind of magic.[27] When Christ warned them against such deviations, he tore the mask from hypocritical prayers which do not express an impulse of the heart (Lk. 18, 10; Mt. 6, 5; Mk. 12, 40). Nevertheless Jesus found an intense life of prayer in Israel,[28] which, through its Judeo-Christian origins, was to leave an indelible mark on the Church.

Jewish prayers

The piety of Jesus was one with this Jewish piety. He participated in the cultual life of the synagogue, where he sanctified the sabbath and spoke frequently.[29] It is in the synagogue of Nazareth that Luke places the scene where Jesus applied Isaiah's prophecy to himself, which appears as an inaugural vision. There Christ affirmed that under the very eyes of the congregation the messianic promises were being fulfilled. Jesus' miracles confirm this same irruption of the new era (Mt. 12, 6; Mk. 1, 25).

Jesus' teaching contrasted with that of the scribes: "His teaching made a deep impression on them because, unlike the scribes, he taught them with authority" (Mk. 1, 22). The Jews at first were astonished that Jesus should teach without having attended the rabbinical schools. More than that, Jesus interpreted and explained Scripture with a depth never before attained; he was not a commentator but a prophet; he read Scripture more in its spirit than it its letter; he perceived in it the voice of God, the design of the Father, who assigned him his messianic mission.

His actions, like his person, were an integral part of Scripture: "You study the scriptures, believing that in them you have eternal life; now these same scriptures testify to me" (Jn. 5, 39). Therein lies the originality of Jesus' teaching. He showed how God's word was accomplished and found its fullness in him (Mt. 5, 17; Lk. 24, 27). He opened the way for the preaching of the Apostles, which would ceaselessly show that Jesus fulfilled the Scriptures. The Christian cult integrated that of the synagogue while transforming it.[30]

Like the Israelites, Jesus recited the Shema. In multiplying the loaves he behaved like the head of a household; he prayed over the bread (Mt. 6, 11); he gave thanks at table over both the bread and the wine (Mk. 6, 41; 8, 6; Jn. 6, 11: Mk. 14, 22). He blessed the fishes before offering them to the crowd (Mk. 6, 41; 8, 7). While respecting the ancient rites, Jesus gave them such a personal fervor and intensity that the disciples of Emmaus immediately recognized him by the way in which he blessed and broke bread (Lk. 24, 30).

We find the same fidelity to Jewish traditions at the Last Supper, where he instituted the new rite within the context of the old pasch.[31]

Jesus wore a fringed garment (Mt. 9, 20; Mk. 6, 56). He prayed in Aramaic (Mk. 14, 36; 15, 34), standing (Mk. 11, 25), hands open to welcome God's gifts, more often than not with his eyes raised to heaven (Mk. 7, 34; 6, 41; Jn. 11, 41). At Gethsemane Jesus fell on his knees (Mt. 26, 39; cf. Ep. 3, 14).[32]

This conformity should not mislead us about the revolutionary upset Christ wrought in the accepted traditions. He asserted his rightful independence by breathing a new spirit into these traditions, and he openly criticized the ostentatious forms of prayer in the synagogue (Mt. 6, 5), because this prayer had lost its original meaning of dialogue with God.

The Psalter

The Psalter occupied a favored place in Jewish piety. It inspired the eighteen blessings. In the days of Jesus, Judaism's piety was nurtured on it. Quotations from the Psalms adorn the *Magnificat* and the *Benedictus*.

Jesus explicitly referred to the book of Psalms (Lk. 20, 42; 24, 44). It was the book of his mission and of his religion. To the Tempter as to the Jews he replied with quotations from the Psalter (Mt. 4, 6; Jn. 10, 34; Mt. 21, 42).[33] The paschal mystery of the Old and of the New Covenant is enshrined in the song of the Psalms and ends with the Hallel which Jesus sang with his own.[34] The prayer of Gethsemane alludes to the psalmist (Mk. 14, 34; Ps. 42, 6, 12). Psalms 22 and 69 appear in filigree in the account of the crucifixion and death (Jn. 19, 24). Two evangelists relate that Jesus recited Psalm 22 on the cross (Mt. 27, 46; Mk. 15, 34). St. Luke puts the prayer of surrender of Psalm 31 on the dying lips of Jesus: "Into your hands I commit my spirit" (Lk. 23, 46).[35]

Most post-exilic rabbis had already imputed a messianic and eschatological signification to Psalm 22, without applying it to the person of the Messiah. Other rabbis applied it to David, to Israel, or to Esther. The *Pesiqta* was the first to apply it to the Messiah.[36]

By using the prayer of his people Jesus expressed his solidarity with them; he was in all things completely like his brothers (cf. Heb. 7, 26; 2, 17-18); he was, however, without sin. The drama of Christ came from the fact that he fulfilled, as the suffering Just One, the prophecies of Isaiah.[37] The reproaches directed at him during his passion were a homage to his mission as Son of God, King of Israel, and Savior of mankind. Even his enemies admitted that he placed his trust in God and that he had boasted that he would rebuild the Temple in three days.

Psalm 22 is, as it were, the liturgy of this paschal drama; it was the high priest's prayer at the evening offering. In Matthew's account Psalms 22 and 69 are continually cropping up.[38] No better way could be found to express the way in which Christ gave his fullness and his fulfillment to the history and the prophecies of Israel. Psalm 22 especially sums up Jesus' life and prayer; it expresses the suffering and the dereliction of him who, together with the *anawim,* became the object of universal scorn,[39] from the Jews, pagans, and evildoers. But dereliction and trial do not have the last word. The same Psalm concludes with the description of the triumph of the oppressed and with the coming of God's kingdom, hastened by the suffering of the innocent and faithful Servant. Beyond the drama, the Crucified unveils a universal gratitude and gathering together.

Though the evangelists give us only the first verse of the Psalm, the certainty of triumph is clearly developed in the different gospel accounts: the power of the Crucified (Mk. 15, 26); the freedom of a life clearly offered (Mt. 27, 50; Lk. 23, 46); Jesus' refusal to use his power for personal ends (Mk. 15, 31); cosmic signs which mark the mourning of the earth that recognized its sovereign;[40] the descent into the underworld and the resurrection of the dead, which were signs of the messianic fulfillment.[41] And completing these signs, the confession of the pagan centurion (Mk. 15, 39) expressed the theme of the entire Gospel: "In truth this man was the son of God."[42]

This fusion of the humiliation and exaltation of Jesus is characteristic of Matthew's Gospel (4, 3, 11; 16, 16-23; 11, 27); we find it developed in the Gospel of St. John.

The rending of the veil hiding the Holy of Holies symbolized the abolition of the old cult, superseded by the institution of the new.[43] The Jewish Temple made way for the living Temple (Mt. 27, 40). It was the ninth hour, the hour of the evening sacrifice when the Israelites recollected themselves in prayer; to St. John it was the hour when the Jews sacrificed the paschal lamb. From then on the Temple became empty and without purpose. Christ on the cross united sacrifice and prayer. In taking up the formulas which expressed the faith of the fathers, in meditating on the meaning of their history, Jesus conferred fullness and efficacy on them through his bloody oblation.

The prayer of the Psalter on the lips of the sacrificing Christ became action in essence by merging itself with the offering of the new and definitive Covenant, a unique act, *ephapax*, which from now on established the *actio* of the Eucharist. It expressed the drama of the people, the struggle against the powers of darkness in a victorious perspective. In this way the Psalms are, as it were, consecrated, and the Church of the Risen Christ will repeat them until the final assembly of all.

"The evening sacrifice," offered on the cross, concluded with a psalm of trust and abandonment into the hands of the Father. This was the psalm which served as the evening prayer of Jesus' contemporaries. The work entrusted to Jesus by the Father was completed.

The community of Qumran

The discovery of the Qumran manuscripts, following that of the Damascus Document, has singularly enriched our knowledge of the religious milieux in the days of Christ.[44] It would be rash, however, to draw any hasty conclusion at a time when these documents have not yet all been published, or to overvalue their importance to the detriment of the inspired books.

The members of the monastic community of "the new Covenant," which must have come to birth in the pietistic milieu centered around the Temple,[45] had fled a perverse world to prepare themselves in solitude for the arrival of the two Messiahs, that of Aaron and that of Israel.[46] They led a community life, eating, praying and meeting in common: "Let them eat together, recite the blessings together, and confer together."[47] The members of

Jesus and the Prayer of Israel

the community had no private possessions but shared their goods in common.

The regulations in the Rule concerning religious meals may be reduced to the following: "When the table is prepared for the meal or the grape juice for drinking, let the priest be the first to stretch forth his hand to bless the first-fruits of the bread and of the grape juice."[48] Any mention of wine was avoided, and only grape juice (*tiros*) was specified.

Prayer in common must have taken place at sunrise and at sunset.[49] To this was added an evening vigil of the "Seniors" for a third of the night all the year round; this consisted of the reading of the Book, the study of the Law, and the recitation of the blessings in common.[50] One man in every ten was specially charged with the study of the Torah, day and night, for the edification of all.[51]

In the Rule of the Community, the calendar enumerates the religious feasts: the beginning of the four seasons of the year, the time of the new moons, the holydays appointed at the beginning of every month, New Year's day, the sabbatical year, the jubilee year.[52] The enumeration ended with a final hymn which seemingly attempts to burst through the framework of the calendar and asks that God be blessed at all times, in all places, and in every circumstance.[53] "Whether I come or go, I shall bless his name; whether I sit down, stand up, or lie down, I shall sing to him. I shall bless him with the offering which comes forth from my lips for the sake of all which he has given to men, and I shall do this before I lift up my hands to partake of the delicious fruits of the earth . . . Whether I experience terror or fear, I shall bless him in the place of anguish and desolation; I shall thank him for his marvelous works, and I shall praise him for his power. Every day I shall lean on his mercies, and I shall confess that the justification of all the living lies in his hands, and that all his works are truth. When anguish begins, I shall praise him, and I shall sing to him also for his deliverance."

For the members of the community the true sanctuary where

"the saints" are gathered together was no longer Jerusalem, but the community itself.[54] In this sanctuary sins were no longer expiated by holocausts and sacrifices but by prayer — the offering of the lips — and by perfect behavior which will be "the gift of a pleasing offering."[55] This was a religious movement which stressed the spiritualization of prayer and of cult.

The documents thus far published furnish us with a whole collection of blessings,[56] of which one, the blessing of the prince of the community, seemingly the Messiah of Israel, is akin to the Benedictus.[57] These blessings do not seem to have been used in the assemblies; they give the impression of being bookish compositions.[58] What strikes us at first sight in the benedictions and hymns is their biblical inspiration. The imitation is startling: the parallelism of the verses, and the resemblance of the metaphors and ideas.

Upon close examination we are surprised not to find any allusion to God's salvific acts as related in the Old Testament.[59] The Qumran chants upset even the biblical framework and the literary styles.[60] They are prayers which ask for almost nothing, now individual lamentations about dangers incurred from treacherous and cruel enemies, now psalms of praise in which man sings the goodness of the sovereign God, to whom he owes grace and salvation.[61]

Does the "I" of these psalms express an individual or a collective prayer? H. Bardtke remarks that it is used in contrast to the community, which would incline us to opt for an individual interpretation.[62] The same author adds that the biblical resemblance is more external than real. These psalms were intended primarily to teach and to edify; according to him, they served to inculcate the sect's doctrine. We would then be in the presence of a veritable catechism, composed by a methodical-minded author skilled in the direction of souls.[63]

It is certain that the chants furnish us with valuable information on the theology of the monastic groups of Qumran. The psalmist was a member of a community which he called "the alliance, the council of saints, the assembly of the sons of God." Its members were penitents, disciples of the Master of justice, in the service of God in order to praise his name and proclaim his wonders.[64]

The sons of light are at grips with the sons of darkness, the followers of Belial. Summoned by a personal vocation, the disciples of the alliance received the spirit of sanctity, which purified them from sin by grace, sanctified them by isolating them from abomination, by giving them wisdom, justice, and holiness in the community of the sons of truth.[65]

The perspective of the Qumran community is distinctly eschatological and messianic.[66] Its members interpreted the impiety that encircled them and the convulsions of history as harbingers of the final events. They applied the prophecy of Isaiah to themselves (Is. 40, 3).[67] The disciples awaited the messianic era, when the poor will be God's favorites, who will snatch them from the hands of the mighty. The Messiah will renew the Covenant, will restore the kingdom forever, and will judge the poor in justice and the humble in equity.[68] The liturgical texts describe the new Jerusalem, the times to come,[69] in which heavenly happiness is seen as a paradise, an "eternal garden," irrigated by living waters,[70] enjoyed in the company of the saints and angels.

The hymns of the monastic societies of the Judean desert thus enlighten us concerning the piety and the religious fervor of a select group in the Hasmonaean period. Waiting in the desert, the sons of light were a ferment in a world besieged by the sons of darkness, and were preparing themselves for the imminent coming of the Lord.[71]

PART II

Chapter I

1. In the period of post-exilic Judaism, when the holy nation had become a church, interiorized piety was concentrated around the Temple. Cf. E. Lohmeyer, *Kultus und Evangelium* (Göttingen, 1942), pp. 15-25. The same applies to that which settled into a ritual formalism; hence the drama which sets Jesus in opposition to the observers of the Law and the rites. J. Nielen, *Gebet u. Gottesdienst* (Freiburg im br., 1937), pp. 44-49.

2. Cf. Mt. 26, 55; Lk. 21, 37, 38; Mk. 11, 27; cf. also Mt. 21, 12, 14, 23; Jn. 7, 14; 8, 2, 20; 18, 20.

80   *Prayer — The New Testament*

3. For the cult of the Temple, cf. E. Schürer, *History of the Jewish People in the Time of Jesus Christ,* trans. Sophia Taylor and Rev. Peter Christie (New York, no date), Vol. I, Second Division, pp. 207-306. An abridgement of the First Division of this work by Schürer appeared in one volume (New York, 1961) entitled *History of the Jewish People in the Time of Jesus.*

4. *Book of Henoch* 90, 28-29.

5. Cf. also Mk. 1, 27; 2, 10; 11, 28.

6. O. Cullman, *Les sacrements dans l'Evangile johannique* (Paris, 1951), pp. 41-44. J. Horst, *Proskynein* (Gütersloh, 1932), p. 183.

7. The synagogue appears as an institution of the diaspora, which ended by being accepted in Palestine. The first synagogues of which we have any traces are found in Egypt, dating from 230. Cf. W. Bousset - H. Gressman, *Die Religionen des Judentums im späthellenistischen Zeitalter* (Tübingen, 1926), p. 172.

8. Philo, *De Septenario,* VI; Josephus, *Antiq.,* IV, 212-213.

9. *Antiq. jud.,* IV, 213. Cf. also Strack-Billerbeck, *Kommentar zum N.T. aus Talmud und Midrasch* (Munich, 1928), I, pp. 189-207. SB will stand for the reference to this work hereafter.

10. M. J. Lagrange, *Le Judaïsme avant Jésus-Christ* (Paris, 1931), pp. 466-468. Concerning the *Shemone Esre,* cf. SB IV, I, 208-249, which gives a translation of it and a long study.

11. The first and last three blessings form the oldest part. Blessings 12 and 13 come from Gamaliel II, blessing 14 is even more recent, 10 and 11 may antedate the year 70; 6 and 7 were composed for a day of fast and later were recited daily. Cf. I. Elbogen, *Der jüdische Gottesdienst* (Frankfurt, 1924), pp. 27-41

12. Custom requires the use of a shorter version. L. Blau believes that the thrice-daily usage comes from the Persian religion, where it was known. However, contrary to the Persian usage, Judaism affirms the transcendency of its God. Cf. "Liturgy," Jewish Ency.

13. To measure the influence of the Shema in the time of Jesus, we have but to compare Jewish prayer with that of the gospels: Dt. 6, 4 and Mt. 11, 15; Dt. 6, 11; 11, 21 and Mt. 5, 5; Dt. 6, 10 and Mt. 8, 11; Dt. 11, 17 and Lk. 4, 25. Cf. Jeremias, "Das Gebetleben Jesu," *ZNTW,* XXV (1926), 123.

14. G. Harder, *Paulus und das Gebet* (Gütersloh, 1936), p. 35, n. 4.

15. Should there be no priest, a member of the community could give the blessing in a deprecatory form. Cf. Schürer, *Geschichte,* II, p. 535. Bousset-Gressmann, *Die Religionen des Judentums,* p. 175.

16. SBI, 397. For the times set aside for Jewish prayer, cf. SB II, 696-702.

17. We must not forget that *eulogein* and *eucharistein* translate the same Hebrew word. Cf. *eulogein, TWNT,* II, 760. To be more exact, *eucharistein* has no Hebrew equivalent.

18. SB IV, 627. For a more detailed account, see E. Von der Goltz, "Tischgebete und Abendmahlgebete," *Texte und Untersuchungen* (1905).

19. For the inscription on a Jewish tomb, cf. H. W. Beyer, art. *eulogeo, TWNT,* II, 758, n. 25.

20. J. Jeremias, *ZNTW,* XXXIII (1934), 203. Cf. also SB IV, 54; J. Jeremias, *The Eucharistic Words of Jesus* (New York, 1966), pp. 40ff.

21. The blessing is taken from Ps. 117, 20 which is applied to messianic salvation. In Mt. 23, 59 and Lk. 13, 35, Jesus applies this blessing to his *parousia.*

22. The resemblances have been greatly exaggerated by Elbogen, *Der jüdische*

Gottesdienst, p. 93. For the contrary view, cf. H. Greeven, *Gebet und Eschatologie im N.T.* (Gütersloh, 1931), p. 82.

23. SB I, 408.
24. I. Elbogen, *Der jüdische Gottesdienst*, pp. 46, 122. SB IV, 192, 236.
25. SB IV, 233.
26. *Ibid.*, IV, 230-231.
27. *Ibid.*, IV, 250, 277.
28. The story of Akiba who, even in martyrdom recited the Shema at the specified times, is characteristic. To his disciples who wanted to prevent him from doing so, he retorted: "During my entire life time, I was preoccupied with the verse "with all your soul" (Dt. 6, 5). I kept asking myself when I would be able to accomplish this. Now that the opportunity has been given to me, you wish to stop me!" G. Kittel, *Problème des p. Spätjudentums* (Stuttgart, 1926), p. 93.
29. Mt. 4, 23; 9, 35; 13, 54; Jn. 18, 20.
30. J. Nielen, *Gebet und Gottesdienst*, pp. 49-53.
31. J. Jeremias, *Die Abendmahlsworte Jesu*, pp. 47-49.
32. Accepted Jewish postures at prayer were bowing during the blessings, and four kinds of prostrations which Bar Kappara enumerates: prostration made face to earth (Gn. 37, 10); standing or kneeling, and the petitioner stretching forth his hands. Joining the hands together expressed unconditional surrender into the hands of God. SB II, 259-262.
33. The quotation from Ps. 118, 22-23 on the cornerstone was first applied by the rabbis to Abraham, then to David, and finally to the Messiah. SB I, 875-876.
34. Jn. 13, 18 relates the allusion of Jesus to Ps. 41, 10.
35. This Psalm served as an evening prayer. SB II, 269.
36. SB II, 574.
37. Matthew's Gospel depicts Christ as the suffering Just One from his birth, especially:

Mt.	Is.
2, 2	55, 1
3, 3	40, 3
5, 11	51, 7
6, 16	58, 5-9
8, 11	59, 19
8, 17	53, 4
12, 18-21	42, 1-4; 41, 9
14, 25	43, 16
20, 28	53, 10
21, 13	56, 7
24, 38	54, 9
25, 35	58, 7
26, 67	50, 6
27, 12	53, 7
27, 30	50, 6
27, 38	53, 12
27, 60	53, 9

38. Table for the use of Psalms 22 and 68:

Psalm	Mt.	Mk.	Lk.	Jn.
22, 2	27, 46	15, 34	23,	19,
8	39	29	35	

Prayer — The New Testament

9	43			
22, 16	35	24	34	24
19				
68, 22	34, 48	23, 36	36	29

39. This theme is frequent in the Psalms and is expressed by the cry: "Eli, Eli." The text of the Psalm is quoted in the Hebrew, not the Aramaic. Jesus had recourse to the sacred form. The quotation has caused much discussion; the codices present variants. But "Eli" is generally accepted. The allusion to Elijah is an additional proof of this (Mt. 27, 47). Cf. L. de Grandmaison, *Jesus Christ, His Person - His Message - His Credentials* trans. Basil Whelan, O.S.B., and Ada Lane (London: Sheed and Ward, 1932), p. 202.

40. Cf. Mt. 27, 46, 51; 24, 29; Mk. 13, 24.
41. Cf. Mt. 27, 52; cf. 1 Pt. 3, 19; 4, 6; Mt. 27, 47-49; 16, 14; 9, 25.
42. Cf. Mk. 1, 11; 9, 7! -12, 6; 13, 32; 14, 61.
43. Mt. 27, 51; cf. Mt., 21, 12; 13; 24, 1-2; Heb. 9, 13-28; 10, 19.
44. It is impossible to draw up an exhaustive bibliography. For the texts we had recourse to D. Barthélemy - J. T. Milik, *Qumran Cave I* (Oxford, 1955); G. Vermès, *Discovery in the Judean Desert* (New York, 1956); A. Vincent, *Les manuscrits hébreux du désert de Juda* (Paris, 1955), particularly the Hebrew edition of the *Megillôt Genuzôt*, I and II (Jerusalem, 1948 and 1950), edited by E. L. Sukénik.

We gathered much information from M. Baillet, "Deux cantiques d'action de grâces du désert de Juda," *Bulletin de littérature ecclésiastique* (1956), pp. 129-141; H. Bardtke, "Considérations sur les cantiques de Qumrân," *Revue biblique*, LXIII (1956), 220-223; J. Baumgarten - M. Mansoor, "Studies in the New Hodayot (Thanksgiving Hymns)," *Journal of Biblical Literature*, LXXIV (1955), 115-124, 178-195; LXXV (1956), 107-113; A. Dupont-Sommer, *Aperçus préliminaires sur les manuscrits de la Mer Morte* (Paris, 1950); G. Lambert, "Un psaume découvert dans le désert de Juda," *Nouvelle revue théologique*, LXXI (1949), 621-637; "Traduction de quelques 'psaumes' de Qumrân et du 'pêsher' d'Habacuc," *ibid.*, (1952), pp. 284-297; J. T. Milik, "Duo cantica ex volumine Hymnorum nuper invento ad Mare Mortum," *Verbum Domini*, XXX (1950), 362-371; R. Tournay, "Les anciens manuscrits hébreux récemment découverts," *Revue biblique*, LVI (1949), 218-227; *ibid.*, LVII (1950), 621-626; G. Vermés, "La secte juive de la Nouvelle Alliance d'après ses hymnes récemment découverts," *Cahiers sioniens* (1950), pp. 178-202; M. Wallenstein, *Hymns from the Judean Scrolls* (Manchester, 1950).

It is also important to take into account the radical thesis of H. E. Del Medico, *L'énigme des manuscrits de la Mer Morte* (Paris, 1957).

45. D. Barthélemy, *Revue biblique*, LX (1953), 422.
46. *Rule of the Community*, IX, 11. Cf. J. T. Milik, "Manuale disciplinae," *Verbum Domini*, XXXI (1951), 152; M. Burrows, "The Messiahs of Aaron and Israel," *Anglican Theol. Rev.* (1952), pp. 203-206.
47. *Rule of the Community*, VI, 2-3.
48. *Ibid.*, VI, 4-5.
49. *Ibid.*, X, 1-3.
50. *Ibid.*, VI, 7-8.
51. *Ibid.*, VI, 6-7.
52. *Ibid.*, X, 1-8.
53. *Ibid.*, X, 9-17. We are partly following the translation of G. Vermès, *Discovery in the Judean Desert*, p. 153.
54. *Rule of the Community*, VIII, 5-6.

55. *Ibid.*, IX, 4-5.
56. "The Benedictions," *Qumran Cave I*, pp. 118-129.
57. *Ibid.*, p. 128.
58. At least this is the opinion of the two editors, D. Barthélemy and J. T. Milik, *ibid.*, p. 120.
59. The remark came from H. Bardtke, "Considérations sur les cantiques de Qumran," *Revue biblique*, LXIII (1956), 223-224.
60. This is a reflection of M. Baillet, "Deux cantiques d'action de grâces du désert de Juda," *Bulletin de littérature ecclésiastique* (1956), 13.
61. *Ibid.*
62. "Considérations sur les cantiques de Qumrân," *Revue biblique*, LXIII (1956), 227-228.
63. *Ibid.*, pp. 229-231.
64. Cf. G. Vermès, "La secte juive de la Nouvelle Alliance d'après ses hymnes récemment découverts," *Cahiers sioniens* (1950), pp. 178-202.
65. *Rule of the Community*, XI, 7-9.
66. *Ibid.*, IX, 6-11.
67. *Ibid.*, VIII, 12-16.
68. "Megillôt Genuzôt," I, Plate XII, *Revue biblique* (1950), p. 617. Cf. also *Document de Damas*, XIX, 10-11.
69. "Description of the New Jerusalem," *Qumran Cave I*, pp. 134-135.
70. *Ibid.*, "Canticles of Thanksgiving," p. 137.
71. A final remark is necessary on the subject of the Qumran hymns. There are a certain number which begin with "Odeka 'Adônai," whence the name of Hodayot, which Sukénik gave them. How are we to translate this? In the Psalms, the Septuagint translated the Hebrew verb by *exemologeisthai*, which means to confess, to praise. *Eucharistein* is never used. H. Bardtke likewise translates "I praise thee," and not I give thee thanks," as many translators do. Would it not be better to avoid ascribing to the religious of Qumran a sentiment which is not biblical, and which we know belongs specifically to the New Testament? Cf. the very clear stand of C. Westermann, *Das Loben Gottes in den Psalmen*, pp. 17-18.

Chapter II

THE PERSONAL PRAYER OF JESUS

Studying Jesus' prayer in the light of that of his people must not mislead us as to its originality and novelty. We must analyze it through the brief indications left by the evangelists and the various texts, in addition to the *Our Father*, which have preserved these prayers for us.

The gospels mention the prayer of Jesus fifteen times; Matthew mentions it three times, Mark and John four times, and Luke eleven. Among the evangelists Luke is the one who most persistently depicts Jesus' human appearance and most especially mentions his prayer.

Brief indications

The first mention of Jesus' prayer is found at his baptism. Luke is the only one to correlate Christ's prayer with the descent of the Holy Spirit. In Luke it corresponds to the role prayer plays in obtaining the descent of the Holy Spirit in baptism (Acts 8, 15, 16). Is this sufficient reason to see in Luke's precise statement only a simple "literary ornamentation"?[1]

It is significant that the solemn proclamation of Christ's messianic mission appears as heaven's visible reply to his silent prayer.

The account of Jesus' temptation does not explicitly speak of prayer but does presuppose it. Why else would Jesus have sought solitude?[2] The desert was the place of testing (Dt. 8, 2-6); Jesus was led there by the Spirit of God (Mk. 1, 12) to undergo the trial. He faced it with prayer and fasting. A twofold parallelism is evident in the account. Moses[3] and Elijah has sought the solitude of Sinai to encounter God; the new Moses sought a dialogue with his Father. The confrontation with the Tempter especially calls to mind the first temptation in Eden. Jesus here shows himself as subject to the lot of mankind, as one "who has been tempted in every way that we are (Heb. 4, 15)."

Satan's suggestions recall those of the serpent: the use of signs and miracles and the power of the Son of God for his own personal profit. Jesus' reply, daily repeated by every Israelite in the Shema, parts company with that of the first man tempted in the garden of Eden, breaks with sin. Jesus had no other care than the glory and the will of God. The messianic power the Father had granted him must serve only to manifest the divine sovereignty. This victorious reply of Christ is the *leit-motif,* as it were, of his whole existence[4]; it expressed the attitude from which he was never to deviate.[5] The same temptation was to be repeated; it was to be shattered by the same submission,[6] even to the acceptance of the Cross.[7] Jesus' piety manifested the real Adam, he who joins heaven and earth together through a mystical exchange and reopens paradise (Mk. 1, 13; Jn. 1, 51).[8]

Mark's Gospel gives us an episode from Peter's catechesis, rich in personal memories. Jesus had just healed Peter's mother-in-law and had cured the sick and the possessed of Capernaum. "In the morning, long before dawn, he got up and left the house, and went off to a lonely place and prayed there" (Mk. 1, 35).[9]

Jesus refused to yield to the temporal dreams of the crowd, enraptured by his miracles. His mission, in the technical sense of the term,[10] was not to work prodigies, misunderstood by the crowd as he well knew, but to proclaim the sovereignty of God (*keruxo,* Mk. 1, 38). This consciousness of his mission, his total submission to the Father were deepened in solitary prayer, in the silence of nature. Luke explicitly mentions (5, 16) Christ's habit of seeking solitude to commune with God.

Before choosing the Twelve who were to guide the "New Israel," Jesus, conscious of the gravity of his decision, had recourse to prayer on the mountain, the high place of divine communications, and devoted the entire night to prayer. He felt the need to submit his work, the organization and the future of his Church, to the will of his Father (Jn. 5, 19-20; 8, 28-29). This total dependence is expressed by Luke in both Jesus' first and last words (2, 49; 23, 46).

The three Synoptics report the confession at Caesarea. St. Luke alone specifies that only after praying[11] did Jesus ask: "Who do the crowds say I am?" (9, 18) The situation was no less solemn than the choosing of the Apostles. In contrast to the defection of many disciples, the confession at Caesarea marked a summit of his public life for Christ, his disciples, and for the future of the Church. Jesus' prayer was efficacious since his Father revealed the secret of his Person and his messianic dignity to Peter.

Exactly six days later (Mt. 17, 1; Mk. 9, 2) the Transfiguration took place. The precision of the evangelists shows how clearly they remembered what they recorded and the relationship between the confession at Caesarea and the confirmation given by Heaven. The scene is a continuation of Jesus' baptism. At the same time it enables us to judge the road already covered. Heaven's reply confirms the mission of Yahweh's Servant (Is. 42, 1) and his dignity as Son (Ps. 2, 7). Moses, who was present, bore witness to the Son who must be "heard,"[12] as prophesied in Deuteronomy. Here, as in biblical tradition, the mountain that Jesus seeks out for prayer is the place where God manifested himself. The three Apostles who witnessed the transfiguring prayer are the same ones who were present at Gethsemane. Peter, deeply moved by the scene, was able to recall the event which Mark so picturesquely relates.[13]

Luke — and perhaps Mark, if we are to believe Origen[14] — speaks of the prayer of Jesus twice (Lk. 9, 28-29). The Transfiguration is brought about, as it were, by prayer: "As he prayed, the aspect of his face was changed" (Lk. 9, 29). God's presence was visibly manifested that night by the brilliance of light. The disciples were able to perceive the true character of their Master and, in some way, the reflection of the incommunicable intimacy which united Father and Son in prayer.

Another saying, of unquestionable authenticity, which Luke alone reports, enables us to state what precisely was the object of Jesus' prayer: "But I have prayed for you, Simon, that your faith may not fail" (Lk. 22, 32). The Master does not dissociate his mission from that of his disciples. Bound together by the faith confessed at Caesarea, Peter and the others must proclaim to the brethren and to the world the message which will be none other than the Good News of the kingdom. Their strength can find support in the prayer and the assistance of their Master.

Several times the gospel narratives show us Christ at prayer "looking up to heaven" (Mk. 7, 34; Mt. 14, 19; Mk. 6, 41; Lk. 9, 16), a custom not common at this period;[15] the Israelite simply turned toward the Temple. Did Jesus wish to signify the abolition of the Temple, to teach that the Father to whom he prayed was in heaven? In any case, this attitude expressed the very personal relationship which unites him to his Father. Jesus' prayer shows what power he makes use of, what service he is bound to, and what mission his miracles must make resplendent.

Surviving prayers

If we omit the *Our Father,* which is our prayer more than that of Jesus, the Synoptics give us only three personal prayers of Christ: his thanksgiving upon the return of the disciples, and the supplications at Gethsemane and on the cross. The Gospel of St. John enriches our documentation (Jn. 11, 41; 12, 27; 17).

One point common to all the prayers quoted by the Synoptics and St. John is the invoking of God as Father: *Abba.* Calling God Father was not unknown even to pagan religions. Heiler even states that "the relation of the praying man to God as a filial relation is a primitive religious phenomenon. In this address to God, Pygmies and Australians, Bantu-peoples and

Indians, clasp hands with Greeks, Romans, Assyrians, and Hindus."[16] It matters little whether this invocation is addressed to the one god of the tribe or designates the mysterious divinity who orders the universe and the scattered tribes that inhabit it. Lactantius sees in this divine paternity an implicit recognition of monotheism.[17]

Clement of Alexandria,[18] who found this appellation in Homer, warns against forming any hasty conclusions. Could it not be a matter of simple verbal resemblances?

In antiquity the idea of fatherhood is associated with that of lordship. One limits the other. Fatherhood is more a metaphor and a title than a reality. "Father Zeus, thou rulest over gods and men," says Homer.[19] Aristotle is more explicit: "Authority over children should be that of a king; the power of a father over his child is based on the fact that he has begotten him, that he rules him with love; this is a species of government.[20]

Father and lord are therefore synonyms to express the necessary and reciprocal relationships between sovereign will on the one hand and absolute submission on the other. The divine generation which forges these bonds expressed, first, the fact that God is the owner and, as such, must provide subsistence for all mankind and for each of its members.

This concept does not seem to have gone beyond the schools of Greek philosophy, since it appears neither in plays nor in papyri. It was found in Stoic circles where Cleanthes' "Hymn to Zeus" has particularly exalted it. This Greek idea influenced Jewish thought only in Josephus and Philo. In the same sense the Romans gave to Jupiter, Janus, Mars, Neptune, Quirinus and Saturn the titles of *pater, parens,* and *genitor.*[21]

The Semitic religions which use the appellation of Father for their gods also express by this word the idea of possession, and in their Lamentations they associate with it the idea of the commiseration of the "merciful Father."[22] Both of these notions are found in the hymn to the god Sin.[23]

The Israelite people rested their faith in the Father on a positive fact, their divine election. The father-son relationship was conceived more in the descending than in the ascending line of son-father. The first evidence dates back to the Exodus from Egypt when God himself stated: "Israel is my first-born son" (Ex. 4, 22).

Israel owes its existence to God: "Is not this your father, who gave you being, who made you, by whom you subsist?" (Dt. 32, 6) [24] This concept of paternity expressed, first, God's sovereignty and the reciprocal relationship of authority and submission.

The idea that God is Father is manifested even in Israel's personal names. Abiram signified "My father is exalted" (cf. Nb. 16, 1), Abiezer, "My father is help" (Jos. 17, 2), Abijah, "My father is Yahweh" (1 Ch. 7, 8), Abitub, "My father is goodness" (1 Ch. 8, 11).[25]

We find this affirmation of paternity as sovereignty throughout the Bible. Malachi still writes after returning from the Exile: "The son honors his father, the slave respects his master. If I am indeed father, where is my honor?" (Ml. 1, 6). This concept is found even in Christ himself (Mt. 11, 27).

The biblical notion of paternity surpasses the concepts found in the history of ancient religions. It expresses the singular birth of a people chosen for its supernatural mission. Prophetism (Is. 1, 2), especially postexilic prophetism (Is. 43, 6; 45, 11; 64, 7), repeats it. Because of his own personal experience the metaphor in Hosea expressed the deepest tenderness:

> "When Israel was a child I loved him, and I called my son out of Egypt" (Ho. 11, 1).

The idea of fatherhood expressed the love of God, who looks after the work of his hands;[26] he chastises in order to instruct;[27] he is merciful.[28] This paternal love is manifested in his unalterable fidelity toward his people; man, even when untrue, even when unfaithful to the Covenant which demands his submission, is sure that God will grant him pardon and salvation.[29] The king, as representative of God's people, and marked in a particular way as the chosen one, is called son of God in Davidic prophecy (cf. 2 S. 7, 14; Pss. 2, 7; 89, 27).

The Exile developed personal religion in Israel, and God appears there as the Father of the individual, of the righteous man who, like the people, is *pais Kuriou uios theou*. The Israelite called on God saying: "Lord, father and master of my life."[30] This invocation passes into postexilic literature:

> Their soul will keep all my commandments and will act according to these precepts, and I will be their Father and they will be my children. And they will all be called the children of the living God, and all the angels and all the spirits will know them and realize that they are my children, that I am their Father in truth and in justice, and that I love them" (Book of Jubilees I, 24).[31]

Rabbinical literature is even more specific and speaks of "the Father who is in heaven." In Jewish prayer the title of Father remains rare. We find it in the eighteen blessings: "Grant us, Father, the knowledge . . ."[32]

On the lips of Jesus the title of Father is in continuity with the Old Testament. It is the God of Israel's history who reveals himself today, transcendent and immanent in the elected people, with the same moral claims (Mt. 6, 4); but the accent is on his boundless goodness and tenderness, open to all, good and evil without exception. The parable of the prodigal son enables us to gauge, through the attitude of the elder son, the distance separating Jesus' teaching from Jewish concepts.

The use of Father as a name for God ran no risks of shocking the audience. When Jesus spoke of the Father, he carefully avoided any ambiguity, always bringing into sharp relief the difference between his filiation and that of the disciples. *The Father,* without any qualification or explanation, was used only by Christ to indicate God.[33] The vocative *Father* is found in Jesus' prayer, never in that of the disciples, except in Luke's version of the *Our Father,* where it springs from the usage of the primitive community.[34]

My Father is used only by Christ when speaking of God.[35] He uses it in contrast to *your* Father when speaking to his disciples.[36]

Only once in the New Testament does man say *our Father*. The apostolic writings usually say more specifically *God, our Father*; rarely do they speak of the Father; the evangelists never qualify this title of the Father, because in itself it is a name of God.

The correlative term son, *uios*, used in the singular and in the absolute sense of *the* Son, or Son of God, is employed exclusively by Christ. The expression *Son of the Father* never appears; it would be tautology, since the name of Father need not be specified.[37]

Christ's use of the word Father acquires a new meaning, because it actually fulfills the eschatological promise made by Yahweh to his people. The Son of the Father has been sent to carry out the work of salvation. "My people will therefore know my name; that day they will understand that it is I who say, 'I am here'" (Is. 52, 6). Along this line of thought it may be said that the name Father completes the revelation of the tetragram (YHWH-Yahweh) made to Moses. Christ fulfilled the prophecy. God is Father, therefore, because he has sent him who carries out God's eschatological work (Mt. 11, 13). Knowing the Son means recognizing God's paternity; Jesus is the one and only Son (Mt. 11, 27; Mk. 13, 32).

When Jesus called God "Father" in his prayer he drew mankind into the mystery of his personal relationship with God; this mystery establishes his nature and his mission. Jesus' personal prayer extends the revelation of the Father to the baptism and the Transfiguration. It is the Son's reply to the Father's word, sharing in the same mystery and in the same work of salvation.

Jesus' confession (Mt. 11, 25-26; Lk. 10, 21)[38]

We have two accounts of Jesus' prayer of thanksgiving, both perhaps going back to the same source. St. Luke explicitly states that Jesus was "filled with joy by the Holy Spirit,"[39] which is an explanation of the rabbinical terminology "Jesus spoke and said"; Matthew uses the latter to express the idea that someone

The Personal Prayer of Jesus

is speaking in the Spirit, in ecstasy, with prophetic inspiration,[40] as did the inspired ones of the Old Testament.

Matthew	Luke
At that time Jesus exclaimed, "I bless you, Father, Lord of heaven and of earth, for hiding these things from the learned and the clever and revealing them to mere children. Yes, Father, for that is what it pleased you to do."	It was then that, filled with joy by the Holy Spirit, he said, "I bless you, Father, Lord of heaven and of earth, for hiding these things from the learned and the clever and revealing them to mere children. Yes, Father, for that is what it pleased you to do."

In Matthew, chapter 11 is dominated by John the Baptist's message and Jesus' answer, which culminates in the verse, "the Good News is proclaimed to the poor" (Mt. 11, 5); this contrasts with the announcement "Happy is the man who does not lose faith in me" (Mt. 11, 6).

Luke places this prayer at the time the seventy-two return from their mission. Jesus warns them against any lust for power and against the danger of attributing God's work to themselves. Their personal rejoicing must consist in the fact that their names are written in heaven (Lk. 10, 20).[41]

The authenticity of the pericope in Matthew is confirmed by the threefold progression which Cullmann[42] sees as bearing a close resemblance to Mt. 16, 17-20, because of the Semitic phrasing of the prayer (Mt. 11, 25-26, 27-28, 30): the phrase "I bless you" is frequently found in the Bible and in Jewish prayer; the term "wise men" is one the rabbis applied to themselves; the phrase "for that is what it pleased you to do" is doubly Jewish because of the passive voice and because of the words "in your sight" which a literal translation would call for.[43]

The prayer properly so called is common to Luke and Matthew. Matthew's ternary account is a progressive explanation of verses 25-26, in which the statements interweave and complete each other. The text of the prayer itself is clear. "I bless you,"[44] expresses the thanks which gushed forth in recognition of God's works from creation to salvation. Christ's praise rests on God's paradoxical behavior, which is in harmony with his sovereign design, revealing to "mere children" what he hides from "the learned and the clever."

Some exegetes have questioned the meaning of the form *tauta*. It is explained in the following verse: God reveals the reciprocal relationships between Father and Son.

Jesus' prayer first extols the transcendence of God, "Lord of heaven and of earth," a formula which sums up the revelation of the Old Testament. It gives thanks because the Father has transmitted the fullness of his power (cf. Mt. 28, 18), to him who is the Son, through an exchange of nature and love; and the Son communicates it to the disciples chosen from among the "mere children" of the earth.

By God's choice the revelation of the Father is made in the Son through the contradiction which reaches its climax on the cross. In the presence of this scandal[45] "the learned and the clever," who expect nothing from anyone or anything, who impose burdens on the *anawim* without giving them the means to bear them, fail to discover through lack of humility "the wisdom of God" (I Cor. 1, 24).

It is the mere children, "those who are nothing," who discern "the Chosen One," revealed by the Father at the Transfiguration (Lk. 9, 35; 23, 35), known only to God, unrecognized by men.[46] In Jesus they find their Savior (Mt. 11, 28-29), who shares and relieves their fate.

Jesus overthrows the world's values, those of the learned, and sets up new and real ones. Why this paradox? Only those who are waiting in expectation, only the poor in spirit (Mt. 5, 3), can find their own condition in the poor, suffering, scorned Servant who mingles with sinners.[47]

Jesus' prayer unveils for us the reciprocal relationship between the Son and the Father, the duality of Jesus' human and divine experience, at the same time revealing the mystery of God and of man's drama in the Messiah. His thanksgiving is inspired by the joy of seeing his messianic mission fulfilled according to the disposition and the good will of God.[48]

The prayer at Gethsemane

The events of Gethsemane, which the three Synoptics relate (Mt. 26, 39-44; Mk. 14, 35, 36, 39; Lk. 22, 41), enable us to follow the continuity and the progression of Jesus' prayer.

Once more Christ retires into solitude,[49] at night, on the eve of the most bewildering and the most decisive happening of his life, which Luke calls "the hour." As in the desert, it is the hour of open encounter with the prince of darkness, of temptation, of the "appointed time" (Lk. 4, 13). The victory over the angel of chaos is consecrated by the assistance rendered by the angels of comfort (Mk. 1, 13; Lk. 22, 43).

Jesus had wished his three favorite apostles to be witnesses of his transfiguring prayer (Mt. 17, 1) and of his Father's glory which invested his whole being. At Gethsemane, too, they were chosen to know Christ in the torments of his humanity (Mt. 26, 37; Mk. 14, 33).

The prayer of thanksgiving had extolled the Father with joyousness, in recognition of the wisdom of his ordering of all things (Mt. 11, 26). The prayer of the Garden of Olives bows before that same will, which almost makes Jesus' flesh fail (Mt. 26, 39, 42, 44).

Matthew	Mark	Luke
(26, 39, 42, 44) And going on a little further he fell on his face and prayed. "My Father," he said "if it is possible, let this cup pass me by. Nevertheless, let it be as you, not I, would have it." Again, a second time, he went away and prayed: "My Father,"	(14, 35-36) And going on a little further he threw himself on the ground and prayed that, if it were possible, this hour might pass him by. "Abba (Father)!" he said "Everything is possible for you. Take this cup away from me. But let it be as you, not I,	(22, 41-42) Then he withdrew from them, about a stone's throw away, and knelt down and prayed. "Father," he said "if you are willing, take this cup away from me. Nevertheless, let your will be done, not mine."

he said "if this cup cannot pass by without my drinking it, your will be done."

Leaving them there, he went away again and prayed for the third time, repeating the same words.

would have it."

The historicity of this episode has been called into question by the very arguments that corroborate it. John's silence is in accordance with his familiar procedure of giving in advance the meaning of events which are already well-known (Jn. 12, 24-27), and to which he does not return. He alludes to them during the Passion (Jn. 18, 11).

The divergences between the Synoptics do not affect the prayer itself. Matthew alone relates very specifically that Christ prayed *three times*. Matthew and Luke quote this prayer in the conditional: *ei dunaton estin,* Mark unconditionally: *parenegke*. It must be borne in mind, however, that the latter gives a sterner, harder character to the whole episode. He uses the verbal form while Matthew and Luke prefer the noun *telema,* as in the *Our Father,* which underlies the prayer of Gethsemane. The Epistle to the Hebrews undoubtedly alludes to the events of the Garden of Olives when it says that Jesus "offered up prayer and entreaty, aloud and in silent tears" (Heb. 5, 7; cf. 2, 18).

The text of this prayer of Jesus demands some explanation. It is introduced by the declaration: "My soul is sorrowful to the point of death." This reminds us of the sufferings of the psalmist, whose text appears throughout in filigree (Ps. 42, 6, 12; Jon. 4, 9). The psalmist sets the tone of the prayer Jesus addresses to his Father.

All three Synoptics indicate to whom the prayer is addressed: the Father. Mark gives us the Aramaic form: *Abba*. Jesus turns toward his Father at the moment when the earth is sinking beneath his feet, in a movement of faith and trust in divine omnipotence. Mark's text emphasizes Jesus' boundless trust (Mt. 19, 26; Mk. 9, 23); "everything is possible" to God. We are certainly dealing with a trial of power.[50] God's power, manifested in creation, likewise appears in the history of the world which it governs for the salvation of men. Once again Jesus acknowledges the wisdom of God's design.

The chalice,[51] a metaphor that had already been used in the intervention of the mother of the sons of Zebedee (Mt. 20, 22),[52] signifies the existence of struggle and temptation, with all that it implies of joy and trial, with death to follow. Jesus' human condition does not spare him the trial of temptation which expresses fidelity in all situations. This trial is found throughout biblical history[53] and in the *Our Father* (Mt. 6, 13).

The Father's will and the Son's will seem opposed to each other. But finally the will of Jesus submits to that of the Father, not only to bring salvation to men but to do so by the means he finds necessary (reply to Peter, Mt. 26, 53). As it happens, we are dealing with the road to death, along which Jesus experiences the meaning and the gravity of sin.

The Synoptics give us only fragments of Jesus' prayer, which lasted for several hours of the night. The details they relate emphasize the human character of this supplication: *epesen epi prosopon* (Mt. 26, 39); *epipten epi tes ges* (Mk. 14, 35); *theis ta gonata proseucheto* (Lk. 22, 41). The prayer and the interior struggle which rack him between his Father and men aim at his free acceptance of being delivered "into the hands of sinners" (cf. Is. 53, 9). His human nature, "his flesh," to use Jesus' own expression, balks before this drama in mortal agony. "Jesus speaks in this prayer as if he were a man to whom the divine will were imperfectly known and who had not the strength to support the crisis of death."[54]

Prayer appears here in its dynamism; Jesus' soul suffers and appeals; crushed, it turns toward *Abba, Pater*. The granting of the prayer does not consist in turning the divine will from its plan, but in clearly submitting, flesh and spirit, even unto death, while drawing from the "bloody" prayer, strength, peace, light and joy.

On the Cross

Among the sayings of Jesus on the Cross, two are reported by Luke alone; one is common to Matthew and to Mark.

Matthew (27, 46)	Luke (23, 34, 46)
At about the ninth hour, Jesus cried out in a loud voice, "Eli, Eli, lama sabachthani?" that is, "My God, my God why have you deserted me?"	Jesus said, "Father, forgive them; they do not know what they are doing." And when Jesus had cried out in a loud voice, he said, "Father, into your hands I commit my spirit."

Both of Luke's quotations begin with the word *Father*. The first is, "Father, forgive them; they do not know what they are doing" (Lk. 23, 34).[55] This prayer is authentic despite its lacking several witnesses. It is too singular to have been invented.

Whom is Jesus talking about? Of the executioners, it would so seem at first sight; but they are only the hirelings of an operation that goes far beyond them. The Jews mainly are meant, and the people who demanded the crucifixion.

This prayer of Jesus expresses more than the greatness of forgiveness, it reveals a merciful love, the leit-motif of all Luke's Gospel. Faith in the God of mercy and faith in man meet here. Jesus here affirms his unshakable trust in humanity and in its salvation beyond any possible forfeiture. "He sealed the divine forgiveness he had come to bring by his own act of pardoning, offering his Father as expiation for humanity's sin, his own acceptance of the injustice heaped upon him," writes Guardini.[56]

By jumping over the wall raised by sin, the prayer enables Jesus to contemplate his Father's dispositions for forgiveness and salvation. In the prayer the two wills agree and express an existential attitude: the prayer enables us to understand the redemptive work of Jesus, who obtains through his expiation the forgiveness he asks of his Father.

Christ brings Christian life into a new perspective: in forgiving the trespasses of our neighbor we are only adopting God's attitude toward us, as the *Our Father* teaches. This is the road that was to be followed by Stephen (Acts 7, 60), Ignatius of Antioch,[57] and many martyrs.

The magnanimity of forgiveness contrasts with the prayer of dereliction which Matthew and Mark report and which echoes that of Gethsemane. Jesus bears the load of sin to such a degree as to identify himself with it.

Luke supplies us with Jesus' last prayer on the Cross: "Father, into your hands I commit my spirit" (Lk. 23, 46). Jesus imparts to the psalm his own personal stamp; he gives it its fullness. His last words are a final act of filial trust in the Father whose will he has accomplished to the very last detail in order that salvation may be brought about. His last prayer, recited "in a loud voice," is not the exhausted end of a dying man, but a clear, free, and total offering by the High Priest "even to accepting death, death on a cross." Prayer and oblation are expressed in one and the same sacrifice.

PART II
Chapter II

1. E. Von der Goltz, *Das Gebet in der ältesten Christenheit* (Leipzig, 1901), p. 3.
2. Mk. 1, 35; Lk. 5, 16; Mt. 14, 23; Mk. 6, 46.
3. All the scriptural quotations used there by Jesus come from the Pentateuch. Dt. 8, 3; 6, 16; 6, 13.
4. Compare the first temptation with Jn. 6, 15, and the proof of a sign requested in Jn. 6, 30; compare the second with Mt. 12, 38 and 16, 1; compare the third with Mt. 16, 22-23.
5. Cf. Mk. 1, 43; 7, 34; Jn. 2, 4; 7, 6; 11, 41-42.
6. Cf. Mt. 12, 28; Lk. 10, 18; 11, 20.
7. E.g., Jn. 12, 31; 14, 30; 16, 11; Mt. 27, 39.
8. The ideal of paradise is signified by the presence of peaceable animals, according to a prophetic image (Is. 11, 6; 65, 25), and by the service of angels assured to the children of the Father (Mk. 1, 13). Cf. Ps. 91, 13; cf. also Lk. 22, 43.
9. H. Greenven (*Gebet und Eschatologie im N.T.* Gütersloh, 1931, p. 13,) who follows Bultmann, concedes with him that the theme of a praying Christ became a literary cliché only because the disciples kept this memory of him.

10. Cf. the parallel Lk. 4, 43: *oti epi touto apestalen*.
11. Note, however, a hesitation in the text which is missing in *D, it syc*.
12. Cf. Dt. 18, 15, 18-19; Acts 3, 22; 7, 37.
13. Are we to attribute to this Petrine tradition the allusion in 2 P. 1, 17, attributed to the same Apostle?
14. Origen (*Hexapla*, III, 559) and several minor manuscripts also read in Mark: *en to proseuchesthai auton*.
15. SB I, 685. At table, he who prayed lowered his eyes.
16. F. Heiler, *op. cit.*, p. 59.
17. *Div. inst.*, IV, 3.
18. *Stromata*, VI, 17, par. 151, 4.
19. *Odyssey* XX, 112; cf. *Odyssey* XIII, 128; cf. also *Iliad*, IV, 235; V, 33; XIII, 631.
20. *Politics*, I, 12.
21. Cf. G. Appel, *De Romanorum precationibus* (Giessen, 1909), p. 103.
22. St. Lagdon, *Sumerian and Babylonian Psalms* (Oxford, 1909), p. 103; J. Hehn, *Hymnen und Gebete an Marduk* (Leipzig, 1903), No. 21, p. 365; No. 14, p. 352.
23. *In Altorientalische Texte und Bilder zum alten Testament*, edited by H. Gressmenn (Tübingen, 1909), p. 241.
24. Cf. also Nb. 11, 12; Is. 63, 16; 64, 7; Ml. 2, 10.
25. Following A. Gelin, *The Key Concepts of the Old Testament*, p. 32.
26. E.g., Jb. 10, 8-12; 14,15.
27. Cf. Dt. 8, 5; Ps. 118, 18; Jb. 5, 17.
28. Cf. Dt. 1, 31; Ps. 103, 13; Is. 49, 5.
29. Cf. Dt. 8, 3-6; Pr. 3, 12; Jr. 3, 19; 31, 20.
30. E.g.Si. 23, 1, 4; Cf. Tb. 13, 4; Ws. 2, 16; 14, 3; 3 Mc. 5, 7; 6, 3, 8.
31. Cf. also *Book of Jubilees*, XIX, 29; *Test. XII*, Jud., 24.
32. SB I, 393.
33. Mt. 11, 27; 24, 36. More frequently in John: seventy-five times in his Gospel, nearly always in the discourse of Jesus; twelve times in his first epistle.
An excellent study on the subject has been made by W. Twisselmann *Die Gotteskindschaft der Christen nach dem N.T.* (Gütersloh, 1939).
34. Apart from this particular case, Lk. 11, 1, we find the vocative five times in Lk., twice in Mt., and three times with "my" which amounts to the same thing, since the Aramaic original had no personal pronoun.
Along the same lines, see L. Williams, in *Journal of Theological Studies*, XXXI (1929), 42.
35. In Lk. four times; in Mt. fourteen times, in six of which it is used with "heavenly" (both having the same Aramaic substratum); twenty times in Jn.; never in Mk.; never in the Sermon on the Mount.
36. Only once in Jn.; in the epilogue of the Gospel (Jn. 20, 17); three times in Lk.; twelve times in Mt., who adds "heavenly" or "in heaven," except in four cases.
In the Sermon on the Mount we find *your* Father three times, *his* or *their* Father once.
37. *Son* in Mt. 11, 27, and Mk. 13, 32.. *Son of God* twelve times in John's Gospel, ten times in his first epistle. *Sons* in the plural is found only once, and then in the future (Mt. 5, 9), while *children of* God, never used by the Synoptics, is found three times in John's Gospel and four times in his first epistle.
38. According to certain exegetes,, we are dealing with source Q.
39. The same verb is used by Mary in the *Magnificat*, with which our prayer has common traits.

40. SB I 606.
A certain number of exegetes had sought the *Sitz im Leben* (life-situation) of the prayer recorded by Matthew in Greek literature. E. Norden (*Agnostos Theos*, Leipzig, 1923, pp. 280-308) considers it to be derived from a propaganda theme; T. Arvedson (*Das Mysterium Christi, Eine Studie zu Matt.*, XI, 25-30, Leipzig, 1937, p. 7) from a coronation rite.

Msgr. Cerfaux has made a careful analysis of the sources of the text. He believes that Jesus' prayer proceeds from apocalyptic and wisdom literature. He compares Matthew's text more especially with the book of Daniel, from which Christ borrows the expression "Son of Man" (cf. particularly Dn. 2, 23; Mt. 11, 25); Christ borrows likewise from the poetic compositions of the Servant of Yahweh of Isaiah (cf. Is. 51; Mt. 25, 26). Cf. L. Cerfaux, "Les sources scripturaires de Mt.," XI, 25-30, *Ephemerides Theologicae lovanienses*, XXX (1954), 740-746; XXXI (1955), 331-342.

41. "Written in the Book." The Jews pictured God as holding the register of those destined for life (Dn. 12, 1; Ex. 32, 32; Is. 4, 3 Ps. 69, 29); this concept was current in the time of Jesus. SB II, 169.

42. O. Cullmann, *Peter, Disciple, Apostle, Martyr*, trans. Floyd V. Filson (Philadelphia: Westminster Press, 1962), pp. 184-186, 193.

43. J. Bonsirven, *Les enseignements de Jésus*, (Paris, 1946), p. 426; G. Dalman, *Die Worte Jesu* (Leipzig, 1898), pp. 142, 173.

44. Found in the Bible, Ps. 18, 50; Si., 51, 1.

45. Cf. Mt. 11, 6; 1 Cor. 1, 28.

45. Is. 42, 1; 52, 14; 53, 2-3.

47. The very plausible thesis of Msgr. Cerfaux, who compares Jesus' prayer with Daniel's apocalyptic language (Dn. 2, 23) and the poems of the Servant of Yahweh (particularly Is. 51), induces us to seek in the soil of the Old Testament the inspired formulas that express the relationship between the Father and the Son, whose mysteries he has come to reveal. Cf. "Les sources scriptuaires," *Eph. Theol. lov.*, XXXI (1955), 333.

48. This was clearly seen by J. Nielen, *Gebet und Gottesdienst im N.T.*, pp. 6-7.

49. Cf. Mk. 1, 35; Lk. 5, 16; 6, 12.

50. As in the desert (Mt. 3, 9); cf. Mt. 19, 26.

51. For the meaning of "chalice" see W. Lotz, "Das Sinnbild des Bechers," *Neue Kirchliche Zeitschrift*, XXVIII (1917), 396-407.

52. For the sons of Zebedee cf. E. Schwartz, "Über den Tod der Söhne Zebedai," *Abhandlungen der könig. Gesellschaft der Wis. Göttingen*, VII, 5 (1904). Schwartz's position is criticized by F. Spitta, in *ZNTW*, II (1910), 39-58, 89-104.

53. Cf. Gn. 22, 1; Ex. 20, 20; Dt. 8, 2, 16; 13, 4.

54. Maldonatus, quoted in J. Lebreton, *The Life & Teaching of Jesus Christ Our Lord*, trans. Francis Day (New York: Macmillan Co., 1950), II, 314.

55. This verse raises a problem of textual criticsm. It is omitted by several uncials: B D* WH, 38, 435, the Sahadic version, the best mss. of the Bohairic, syr. sin. Tischendorf, Von Soden. Souter, Vogels retain it as does Sinaiticus, with A C L and other uncials. Westcott and Hort, who omit it, consider it was inserted through a borrowing from an authentic tradition.

56. R. Guardini, *The Lord*, trans. E. C. Briefs (Chicago: H. Regnery, 1954), p. 303.

57. *Letter to the Ephesians*, 10.

Chapter III

THE LORD'S PRAYER[1]

Among the prayers of Christ, the *Our Father* occupies a privileged place. It has been called "the Lord's Prayer," not in the sense of a prayer used by him, but one he himself gave as a model for all Christian prayer. Tradition has seen in it a treatise on prayer in action. Tertullian even calls it: *breviarium totius Evangelii*. No other gospel text has been so often commented on.[2]

Context

The gospels give us two versions of the *Our Father,* the longer in Matthew (Mt. 6, 9-13), the more compact in Luke (Lk. 11, 2-4), each in a different context.

In Matthew the *Our Father* is inserted in the Sermon on the Mount. The precepts given by Christ on almsgiving, prayer, and fasting constitute a grouping whose three parts are of approximately the same length and structure (Mt. 6, 1-4, 5-6, 16-18). Three times Jesus sets the new practices in opposition to those of the Pharisees, who "have had their reward" (Mt. 6, 5, 16), and demands that good works be performed in secret (Mt. 6, 4, 6, 18).

In this context, Matthew gives a group of verses relating to prayer in which Jesus opposes the Jews. These verses have no parallels in the texts on almsgiving and on fasting and have no real connection with what precedes or what follows them. In this preamble to the *Our Father,* Matthew passes from the singular to the plural. Moreover, the words "your Father knows what you need before you ask him" (Mt. 6, 8) do not seem the proper introduction to a text of prayer and of communal prayer. Matthew's context, therefore, does not seem to be the original one.

In Luke the text of the *Our Father* is found in the Peraean section which seems to be drawn from an independent collection. "Now once he was in a certain place praying, and when he had finished one of his disciples said, 'Lord, teach us to pray, just as John taught his disciples.' He said to them, 'Say this when you pray: Father, . . . '" (Lk. 11, 1-2).

While Matthew juxtaposes the *logia* to provide a complete teaching on prayer, Luke is more interested in the historic localization of the *Our Father.* The mention of John the Baptist emphasizes that he is dealing with historic facts. A certain disciple, speaking for the others, asks for a prayer since the disciples of the Precursor already had one (Lk. 5, 33); this would forge a common bond between Jesus and themselves.

We are reduced to conjectures regarding the site of the events related by Luke.[3]

The two versions

The existence of two versions poses new problems for exegetes. Some see two instructions given in two different sets of circumstances. This solution does not satisfy the majority of commentators, who prefer a single instruction.

It seems that the two evangelists did not make use of the same source for the *Our Father.* Which version, then, gives us the original form?[4] The exegetes who think this question can be answered opt for Matthew's text. It is closer to the Jewish milieu and the formulas of prayer known to us; its composition is too well balanced to admit later additions. Besides, it is always easier to omit than to insert something. As such, the *Our Father* gives us, particularly in its first section, a perfect résumé of Jesus' teaching.

Tradition, besides, has preferred Matthew's version, which we find, with a few slight variations, in the *Didache*. The manuscripts attest that Matthew's text has often garnished that of Luke. Lastly, the allusions to the *Our Father* in canonical and extra-canonical literature lean more frequently on Matthew's version.[5]

Luke has a habit of condensing what previous evangelists had said and of giving only the essentials. This procedure of Luke enables us to measure the latitude allowed the evangelists in their editing.[6]

The Jewish roots of the Our Father

Jesus' prayer, as it appears in the New Testament, is faithful to Jewish formulas. Numerous Jewish texts allow us to establish a comparison with the *Our Father*. The difficulty arises from the uncertainty of their date. Which of them antedate Christ?[7] And, even if they do predate Christ, what assurance have we that they were not influenced later or in an indirect way by Christian literature? Besides, it is difficult to form an exact idea of the latitude the East permitted even for official and liturgical texts.

For this reason, doubtless, J. Hermann[8] advises going back to biblical and Jewish prayer to uncover the sources of the *Our Father*. A simple synoptic table shows the resemblances which exist between the *Our Father* and the *Shemone Esre* (vv. 3, 6, 7), and between the *Our Father* in its first three supplications and the Kaddish, insofar as the latter's present form precedes the Lord's Prayer.[9]

Lord's Prayer	*Bible*	*Shemone Esre*	*Kaddish*	*The Rabbis*
1	1	1	1	1
Our Father in heaven.			May the heavenly Father receive the prayer of all the house of Israel.	

Prayer — The New Testament

2 May your name be held holy.	2 I mean to display the holiness of my great name (Ez. 36, 23; cf. Ps. 111, 9).	2 You are holy and your name is wonderful (3).	2 May your great name be exalted and sanctified.	2 Our Father who art in heaven, may your name be praised through all the eternities (Seder Elij. SB. I, 410).
3 Your kingdom come.	3	3	3 May his reign rule our lives.	3 Then his kingdom will be manifested to every creature (Assumption of Moses, 10, 1).
4 Your will be done on earth as in heaven.	4 God is in heaven, you on earth (Qo. 5, 1; I M. 3, 60).	4	4	4 Do your will in heaven, on high, and grant a calm courage to those who fear you on earth (R. Eliézer, SB. I, 419-420).
5 Give us today our daily bread.	5 Give me neither poverty nor riches, grant me only my share of bread to eat (Pr. 30, 8; cf. Ex. 16, 4; Ps. 147, 9).	5 Bless Yahweh our God, this year (9).	5	5 May God be blessed every day for the daily bread he gives us (SB. I, 421).
6 And forgive	6 Forgive your	6 Forgive us,	6	6 Our Father,

The Lord's Prayer

us our debts as we have forgiven those who are in debt to us.	neighbor the hurt he does you, and when you pray, your sins will be forgiven (Si. 28, 2).	our Father, for we have sinned against you; wipe away our iniquities; remove them from your sight (6).		our King, pardon and remit all our faults, remove and wipe away our sins from before your eyes (Avînu malkênu, SB. I, 421)
7 And do not put us to the test.	**7**	**7**	**7**	**7** Do not lead us into the power of sin, nor into the power of error, nor into the power of temptation, nor into the power of betrayal. May I be ruled by the power of good, and not by the power of evil (SB. I, 422).
8 But save us from the evil one.	**8**	**8** See our need and fight our combat, and deliver us for the sake of your name (7).	**8**	**8** Save us from the impudent and from impudence, from the evil man, from evil encounters, from the strength of evil, from evil companions, from evil neighbors, from Satan

				the corruptor, from your strict judgment, from a bad adversary at the tribunal (Berakhot, SB., I, 422).
9 (Doxology) For yours is the kingdom and the power and the glory forever. Amen.	9 Yours Yahweh, is the greatness, the power, splendor, length of days, glory... Yours is the sovereignty, Yahweh (I Ch. 29, 11).	9	9	9

Like the *Our Father,* the eighteen blessings are drawn up in the plural, a strong rabbinical tendency which even bordered on superstition.[10] But what good is served by pursuing this work of Mosaic experts and seeking verbal resemblances? Rabbinical prayer drew upon the same sources as Jesus' prayer, the Bible. But the waters which the rabbis hoarded in cisterns Christ holds in plentitude, even to the extent of overflowing (Jn. 7, 37).

To familiar, fixed formulas Jesus gives a new life; he breathes life and soul into this body. He builds Christian prayer with Jewish stones. Mankind's reply to Yahweh's revelation finds its full meaning on the lips of Christ. When he gave us a prayer, Jesus did not intend to utter things different from what the stammerings of the Israelites have expressed; Christ's prayer expressed the plenitude of the one and only Master concisely and clearly. That is what gives the Lord's Prayer its new compactness.

Structure

To convince ourselves of this, all we need do is analyze the structure of the *Our Father.* The prayer is divided into two parts.

The first part has God for its subject, the second mankind. The three supplications concerning God give us, in abbreviated form, the revelation of the Old Testament, at the same time revering the rhythm of its progression.[11]

May your name be held holy recapitulates the first revelation made to Moses of God's transcendence (Ex. 19, 20-25). God chooses for himself a people to bear witness of him before the other nations of the earth.

Your kingdom come. Of these scattered Hebrews, Yahweh first makes a nation, then a kingdom. King David, a figure of Christ, signifies the first approach of the kingdom of God which Christ comes to perfect on earth.

Your will be done. The kingdom of Israel is precarious because of prevarication. Disaster, the Exile, suffering, and humiliation prepared the way for the understanding necessary to read the Law from within, to find therein the Father's benevolent will, and to respond to it, by an inward conversion, in an exchange of love.

These progressive revelations, which are like so many beacons in Israel's history, attain their goal in Christ, who sums them up and is their essence. He brings them their fullness by manifesting the ever-operative agape of his Father. The supplications that he puts on our lips are none other than those which inspired action and prayer in him. The *Israel of God* in the Lord's Prayer beseeches that the sacred history of its election should also attain the plenitude of Christ.

The structure of the second part of the *Our Father* is more difficult to discover. Parallel texts in biblical and rabbinical literature are far less explicit and convincing. Jesus seems to be following here a more empirical, steadily rising road, the very road followed by God's own teaching. The last three supplications are in harmony with the newness of the gospel.

Give us today our daily bread. To his people God gave manna, then the fertile land of Canaan. To the crowd Jesus gave needed bread before speaking of spiritual food.

Forgive us our debts . . . takes into consideration man's spiritual condition; he is a sinner. Therefore, prayer can only be an appeal, one already uttered by the psalmist, and the expression of a need which Christ reveals to men. But this appeal makes demands of man, whose situation before God is identical with the situation between men.

Do not put us to the test. The Christian condition implies a necessary confrontation with temptation and the Tempter, as Christ's example shows; his victory is the basis of our confidence in our prayer.

Is it foolhardy to find a parallelism between these last three supplications and the first three? God cares for the people to whom he reveals himself. Sin is a debt incurred toward God, and he alone can remit it. Finally, temptation lays bare the opposition between man's will and God's will.

If this is the meaning of the three parallel supplications formulated in the Lord's Prayer, then we can gauge the fullness that Jesus brings to the history of God's people. He is the fulfillment needed by the men who constitute the new Israel.

The doctrine of the Our Father

It is not the purpose of this book to make an exhaustive commentary on the *Our Father,* but to clarify its main ideas. The Lord's Prayer is not a stereotyped formula; it seeks to express the existentialist attitude of the believer before God.

Our Father in heaven[12]

Christ always took the greatest care to observe the distance that separates our status from his in regard to the Father. God is our Father because he is our Lord; such is the teaching of the Old Testament. The gospel deduces the moral demands of God's paternal sovereignty from the Old Testament.[13] Jesus adds shades of meaning to this power of goodwill and forethought which form the bases of our confidence that he will hear our prayer. The Father proves his goodness to us by sending his Son in the messianic era in order to bring salvation to all, with a preference for the poor and the persecuted. Its newness does not lie in a new name but in a new usage. To Jesus the affirmation of the divine paternity is equivalent to teaching that the prophecies have been fulfilled.

Matthew and Luke do not explicitly deduce our supernatural filiation from this paternity of God which opens the kingdom of heaven. Matthew speaks of us as God's children only in the future (Mt. 5, 9, 45). The apostolic community, John, and Paul were to deduce explicitly from it the filiation of those who call God their Father, in whom the Spirit prays: *Abba,* Father.[15] For this reason John and Paul are silent on the teaching of the kingdom and concentrate on the doctrine of divine filiation which deepens the doctrine of the kingdom. They explain the message of the *Our Father* by finding in it the relationship of sons which, through grace, introduces mankind into the community of life with the Father. The name *Father,* therefore, expresses a completely new revelation, mysterious but true, which the gospel brings to us.

The Lord's Prayer passes from the vertical plane of the Father-Son relationship to the horizontal plane. Mankind says *our* Father. It is, therefore, the prayer of the community, of the elect, who enter into a new relationship, abolishing all previous ties of blood or race.[16] The *us* who need our daily bread are those to whom God has revealed himself, the humble and the poor (Mt. 11, 25).

In the perspective of the gospels, man is not an isolated being; he is a member of the messianic community and of the kingdom. The presence of the Father's agape can only be experienced in the fraternal communion of the brotherhood. Founded on faith and hope the present community anticipates the eschatological community.

The complement *in heaven*[17] was already familiar to rabbinical thought, which considered heaven as the impenetrable abode of God. Yahweh is both close and distant, immanent and transcendent. He is not restricted to Sion, to the Temple, nor to a mountain; he is supremely independent. Heaven signifies more a divine presence than a divine localization; it can be compared to the parallel expression *the kingdom of heaven.* God is found wherever he manifests himself. He who prays is at the gates of the kingdom of heaven, which Jesus came to open for him.

From its very beginning Christian prayer appears as a recognition of its object, faith, and faith no longer presents itself as a doctrine but as a presence. Prayer places us face to face with Someone and in a personal relationship with Someone.

May your name be held holy[18]

The question has been asked: are we dealing here with a petition or a blessing? The parallelism with the prayer of the Kaddish and the two petitions that follow prove that we are speaking of a petition. The use of the passive, which is also found in Jewish prayers, is a form of respect.

Before we determine the meaning of this petition, it is absolutely necessary for us to grasp the meaning of the words. *Name* is a specifically biblical term which is found throughout the Old Testament. When the evangelists or St. Paul use it, they are referring to biblical quotations: "Blessings on him who comes in the name of the Lord" (Mk. 11, 9).

St. John, on the other hand, speaks more often of the *name of the Father.* "I have come in the name of my Father" (Jn. 5, 43); this means: I have come by the authority and with the mission received from my Father. Jesus works "in my Father's name" (Jn. 10, 25).[19] The name of God is most often coupled with the verb *hallow* in the Apocalypse, which is steeped in Old Testament terminology. There the name of God is feared (Re. 14, 7) and praised (Re. 15, 4); the elect write it on their foreheads (Re. 3, 12; 14, 1; 22, 4).[20]

God revealed himself to Moses by disclosing his name (Ex. 3, 14): "I am who I am." Yahweh did not wish to communicate his metaphysical entity; the accent is not on being but on existence and action.[21] God is an active presence. Whether he intervenes to punish or to sustain, in every circumstance God manifests his all-powerful entrance into history. Second Isaiah specifies that this God of history is the first and the last, transcending time and therefore eternal.[22] Since he is one, he gives history its unity (Ze. 14, 9). He guides the universe and unifies it (Jb. 1, 21). The revelation of the God who gave Moses his name and directed the history of the Jewish people is completed in the revelation of his paternity; his name is Father.

The fundamental idea common to all religions expressed by the verb *hallow, to make holy*, which is close in meaning to sacredness and purity, is to separate, to set aside for the cult.[23] Everything is hallowed which belongs to divine worship: men and things, places and times (Mt. 23, 17, 19). God himself is holy because he is the object of worship.

However frequently expressed and however ancient this idea may be in the Bible,[24] it is nevertheless not fundamental. It links sanctity with the name of God, i.e. with his nature. Yahweh is *holy* by reason of the transcendence of his nature, which contrasts with everything created.

God's holiness is manifested in his action; being and act in him are one.[25] The work of God has only one goal, to sanctify what is not sanctified by nature but is capable of being sanctified by grace. In the road to be covered, man measures the distance which separates him from God, just as he finds the gift which unites him to God.

Even while it separates him from his creation, sanctity unites God with earth and its history. Sanctity expresses the mystery which makes Yahweh dwell in "inaccessible light"; it unveils his unfathomable being and reveals itself to whomever it pleases. The action of divine sanctity which manifests itself is called God's *glory* in both the Old and the New Testaments, as the chant of the Seraphim proclaims (Is. 6, 3). To sanctify, therefore, means to manifest God's glory. The creation of the world, from its beginning to its end, in its entirety and in each individual, has but one goal, God's glory.

In the history of his people, God manifests his holiness by choosing them to proclaim the divine glory before all nations. This mission demands fidelity and the proper dispositions of heart. God's holiness is a judgment; it judges and condemns all that does not conform to its demands. Before sending Isaiah to his people, God purified him. The same light which reveals God's holiness to the prophet shows him that his lips are unclean, that he is a sinner, dwelling among a sinful people (Is. 6, 3-5). Sin "profanes" the holy name of God;[26] for this reason the prophets never ceased decrying it.[27] It is the obstacle to God's sanctifying action. Yahweh saves the world by cleansing it of its sin. Sanctifying the world[28] means giving to man the duty of revealing God's sanctity. The end of history is to make God's glory known.[29] God's *wonders* have no other goal than the manifestation of the glory of the divine name.

With the help of these preliminary ideas it is easy to discern the significance of the petition *may your name be made holy*. The aorist tense used, as in the two following petitions, is the narrative tense. It deals with a unique event which fulfills the promises of the prophets: "I am not doing this for your sake, House of Israel, but for the sake of my holy name, which you have profaned among the nations where you have gone. I mean to display the holiness of my great name, which has been profaned among the nations, which you have profaned among them" (Ezk. 36, 22-23).

The prophecies are fulfilled in Christ. He is holy in his origin (Lk. 1, 35); he is marked by the Spirit, who is holiness and power. The demons discern "the Holy One of God" in him (Lk. 4, 34; Mk. 1, 24). Peter makes the same confession (Jn. 6, 69). Christ is holy because his life and his works manifest and glorify the Father.[30] The work of the Father, accomplished by Jesus, sealed in the unique offering of the Cross, *sanctifies* the faithful; it is manifested in the works of the faithful in so far as they are the works of God and incite the world to glorify "the Father in heaven," infinitely close and infinitely exacting.

In the sanctification of God's name all initiative comes from the Father. But this initiative acts on free agents; his action tends to incite man's action, man renewed by water and the Spirit. The divine action will be complete only when, under the influence of the Spirit, it attains total utilization of the gift received by men.

The first petition of the *Our Father* is linked with and fulfills the first two commandments of the Decalogue. It expresses the deep meaning, the principle and the end of creation. It is the duty of the "holy," chosen people to reveal God to the world. The countenance of the sons reveals the invisible countenance of the Father. The Church is "holy" because it was chosen to be the salt of the earth.

This first petition not only has a universal bearing, its significance is also eschatological. The aorist tense suggests that we are dealing with a single historical fact, but one which affects all history. The world of sanctification, undertaken by Christ, will be completed only on the day when all who worship, praise, and glorify the Father will be united in the house of God. Doubtless it is for this reason that the Apocalypse associates the theme of sanctity with the evocation of "the elect and the saints" who celebrate the celestial liturgy.

Some commentators, not without reason, consider the first petition a doxology,[31] in the style of Jewish and Christian prayer and in the sense of a *Praise to God's glory.* The Israel of God anticipates and prepares in prayer the new people and the new earth, singing the name of the holy God, the principle of all holiness.

Your kingdom come[32]

The prayers of Christ's time, such as the Kaddish, already joined the sanctification of God's name to the coming of his kingdom. The progression is the same as that of revelation. The first petition addresses God in the holiness of his nature, which is bound up neither with time nor with history and is always the same; the second introduces us to earthly time, being addressed to the Lord who guides the universe and draws it to himself.

The Messiah, according to the formula already employed by rabbinism, is the *erchomenos* (Mt. 11, 3; Lk. 7, 19; cf. Hab. 2, 3), he who opens the era of salvation. The verb expresses the meaning and the nature of his coming. Numerous are the texts both in St. John and in the Synoptics where Jesus uses the word in the first person.[33] The Johannine writings state clearly that he is coming "into the world" (Jn. 6, 14; 11, 27), "in the flesh" (I Jn. 4, 2). The crowd acclaims him as he "who comes in the name of the Lord."[34] Just as he came, Christ will return in his messianic glory (Mt. 10, 23; 16, 27; 25, 31), with his kingdom (Mt. 16, 28). The parousia is described in Jewish apocalyptic terms.

Like the Old Testament, the New uses *erchesthai* when speaking of times and events. The verb *erchomai* is applied first of all to Christ as Messiah, to express the meaning and the nature of his coming. The texts in which Jesus uses the word in the first person are characteristic: they affirm his consciousness of his messianic mission.

Erchesthai also qualifies the time when important events take place (Mt. 9, 15), the coming of decisive days, introduced by the formula *eleusontai emerai* (Lk. 17, 22; 21, 6; 23, 29). The gospel uses the present or the future,[35] *the days will come*.[36] John utilizes the formula *the hour is coming*.[37]

Finally, the verb characterizes situations and dispositions which will come to pass.[38] The point here is God's intervention, which manifests to the world his presence, his works, as the reason for and the end of creation.[39]

Jewish prayer in the time of Christ was nurtured on the expectation of a new eon and God's universal victory. The Kaddish petitions: "May your kingdom be affirmed in our lives." The Jewish concept of a kingdom of heaven in which Yahweh exercises, in an eschatological future, his royal functions, ever present but still hidden, is found again in the "world to come" of the New Testament. It is linked with two other ideas, we might say, two spheres of thought.

The kingdom first appears as a stable reality comparable to a house or a city; its inhabitants "enter" it (Mt. 5, 20; 7, 21; 18, 3), "take their place at the feast" (Mt. 8, 11), "eat and drink" at its table (Lk. 22, 30), or are "turned out" (Mt. 8, 12); and leaders govern it (Mt. 16, 19). It is the place of gathering. The parables speak of a King and his guests (Mt. 22, 1-14), of a father and his sons (Mt. 21, 28-31), of a place where "the subjects of the kingdom" are gathered together (Mt. 8, 12).

This idea widens into a clear representation of the world to come, where all the peoples of the world will meet (Mt. 8, 11). The kingdom is coming; it can be seen (Mk. 9, 1) and possessed (Mt. 25, 34). It has many rooms (Jn. 14, 2). It may be sought and found (Mt. 13, 44-48). It is a power which manifests God's invading action. Its frontiers remain vague and indiscernible; its coming lacks precision both in time and in shape; it is and it is coming; it is here and it is elsewhere; it is bound to time and place, and it is supremely independent of them.

In this context the petition "your kingdom come" becomes clear. Certain commentators have interpreted it as the present reign, in which God's kingdom is developed by missionary efforts, *the reign of grace*. Others have seen in it the reign to come at the end of the world, *the reign of glory*. At times each point of view has permitted the inference of two advents, one in time, one at the end of time. None of these conclusions takes sufficient account of the aorist, the tense which relates a historical event, particularly since God is the subject of the action. God is not divided into grace and glory. We are dealing with a single and definitive coming, in which the paternal action of the divine agape realizes its plan of salvation.

A certain tension surrounds this petition because of the opposition which exists between the reign of God and its adverse forces, Satan, sin, and death. This opposition, in which man is caught as in the meshes of a net, is greater than he is; he is the prisoner of superior forces. The kingdom is a city yet to come, opening today on to future realities and fulfillments which draw man forward toward a completion which does not yet exist.

The assembly of God's people is a spiritual, not a political reality. It is a community in love, justice, adoration, and purity. Where praise and thanksgiving begin, there begins the reign of God. But from the beginning to the completion, the course of the whole history of salvation remains to be run. This tension between expectation and realization, between the present and the future of the kingdom, is found again in the gospels, particularly in the parables. There are even secrets hidden from the Son of Man.

Is Jesus proclaiming the kingdom or inaugurating it? For pedagogical reasons Christ at first says that the kingdom is imminent. He tries to free his audience from overly temporal concepts in order to prepare them for the reception of the Good News in all its purity.

The coming of Christ is decisive for the kingdom of God. It is the pivotal event of salvation history, the fulfillment of all the prophecies of the past, which become clear in him, and of the prophecies of the future, which are yet to come. This advent of God's power is not only manifested in him but is made present by his coming. His entry into glory through death and his victory over hostile forces proclaim that Jesus efficaciously carried out his work. The central point of history is, therefore, no longer situated in the future but in the past. The Resurrection inaugurates the new eon. Christ's reign has begun, but his work is not completed. It will be completed only with the end of the present world, that is, when the kingdom has come.

From the advent of the King to the advent of the kingdom the tension remains. With the coming of Christ, "the last days" have begun, but they continue until their culmination. Christian eschatology does not follow Christ's coming; it begins with it: in him the end is already present with the eternal goods to come. The term of the Church on earth, the time of the missionary era, allows Christ's reign to take possession of time and the earth until the plenitude of the Spirit and the resurrection of the body.

The Church is born for, and in the expectation of, this perfect fulfillment. This is what gives magnitude and fervor to Christ's prayer: "May the Father's kingdom come." The same faith and the same hope were to be expressed in the prayer of the apostolic community: the *Marana tha.* It asks for the assembling of all men in the unity of Christ, the transfiguration of mankind and the universe by the resurrection, God's final judgment on all things.

Your will be done

The third petition is not found in Luke. Matthew's text presents several variants.[40] *Heaven*[41] is in the singular, as is usual, whenever it is joined with *earth* to signify creation. Between heaven and earth Scripture sometimes sees an opposition, at other times an exchange. The plural *heavens* is used when the word is taken in an absolute sense as God's dwelling.[42]

Antiquity was preoccupied with harmonizing man's will and the divine will. Socrates[43] said to Crito: "May it be as the gods please." Jewish thought does not aim at harmony but at submission, not so much at desiring what God wants, but at doing it. This is commanded by the Torah. Jewish thought does not ascend from man's will to God's but descends from God to daily life. The words *thelo* and *thelema,* when referring to God, express the will which commands, while supremely and efficaciously guiding creation and history. (I Mc. 3, 60). The stress is not laid on the faculty of willing, but on the object of the will. A suggestion of love is found there, spiritualized, affirming benevolent complaisance, akin to *eudokia.*[44]

This benevolence is manifested more particularly in the Son's mission and in the fulfillment of the plan of salvation.[45] St. Paul links it with the mystery. St. John expresses it by *ergon,* the Father's work.[46] Matthew usually links the *thelema* to the name of the Father and to the concept of *mikroi.* This paternal disposition is exercised most clearly in his goodwill for the poor and the humble.[47] With *eudokia* (Mt. 11, 26), the notion of will receives its proper shade of meaning from the divine paternity, which places man in a dependence of love.

In man, will is not a mutilation, a renunciation, but a consenting to God's plan. It is not a refusal but an acceptance, not a destruction but a committment. It expresses a stand taken by the person praying. Corresponding to God's gift there are requirements and demands.

The third petition of the *Our Father* is dominated by God's salvific plan, which is fulfilled within the kingdom. The divine goodwill is manifested in everyday cares and happenings. God's will lit up the path of Jewish history by accomplishing what the Jews asked. Thanks to this paternal goodwill, God replies with patience to man's desception and infidelity (Rom. 3, 26).

The plan of salvation includes man and assigns him his proper place. God's work is accomplished in him and with him (Heb. 13, 21; Ep. 1, 9). The events of Gethsemane illustrate this encounter between God and man. The conflict does not arise from the opposition of two wills but from the encounter between the Father's eschatological plan and the part demanded of Christ. It is not man who trembles and refuses, but the Son of Man recognizing the immensity of the task. Christ's reply is not a surrender but a decision and a committment in the face of the work of salvation.

On what will does God call? The Latins have seen here the moral will which guides man and brings about the reign of God within him. But the Lord's Prayer aims at the community before the individual. St. John Chrysostom finds in it the eschatological will, which disposes men, even now, to carry out the will of the future city.[48] The supplication presupposes the tension existing between God's already expressed will and the dimension of time, of history, and therefore of mankind, in whom and with whom the consummation of the divine work is realized. This eschatological tension exists within both community and individual to the extent that any part of either the community or the individual rejects God's will.

The gift of the Father implies a filial committment; it is both demand and a call. The filial relationship requires the entry of the whole being and of all humanity into God's sphere in order that the plan of salvation may be carried out. God's will takes possession of us and draws us into its own movement. It permeates, it provokes to action. "Man's worth is the worth of his acts," said St. Francis.

To obey means to enter into God's action; this presupposes a poverty of spirit that welcomes God's gift and makes it fruitful; at the same time we are mindful of the distance which separates us from God and his gratuitousness. We pray to enter more deeply into the mystery of salvation. Such is our life's quest and the drama of the world; by submitting to this, each person takes an active part in the establishment of the kingdom.

The phrase *on earth as in heaven* does not apply to the third petition only but to the first three, as Origen remarked.[49] What does it mean? The biblical text closest to that phrase is found in the book of Machabees: "Whatever be the will of heaven, he will perform it" (I Mc. 3, 60). In the Psalter, the same assertion is found in the form of affirmation but not of prayer: "In the heavens, on the earth, in the ocean, in the depths, Yahweh's will is sovereign" (Ps. 135, 6).

The phrase may signify that the divine will is being fulfilled on earth as it is already being carried out in heaven, its indisputable domain, where the only concern of the angels is to serve God's will. Other authors consider the phrase a petition that God avert all hostile forces, all the powers of darkness which oppose him.[50]

If *on earth as in heaven* actually has reference to the first three petitions, it is more sensible to read an eschatological determination into it. A certain number of commentators explain that earth must imitate heaven's actual obedience. This means finding in the three petitions an actor other than God. Moreover, the correlation *os . . . kai*[51] indicates a perfect resemblance, which implies identity in time in order for any correspondence to exist.

We cannot, therefore, translate: *may* your will be *done* on earth as it is *already being done* in heaven. We would be slipping from the present into the future.

God is the principle of unity in all creation, earth and heaven (Gn. 1, 1); he is Lord of heaven and earth (Mt. 11, 25). His work consists in bringing about unity in the entire universe. To this effect he gave his power to Christ "in heaven and on earth (Mt. 28, 18).[52] Corresponding to protology (see n. 93, Intro.) there is an eschatology. We are hastening the day of the latter by our prayer.[53]

Give us today our daily bread

The contrast between the first three petitions and the last three is great. The former are placed on God's plane; the latter deal with man's needs.[54]

In the Old Testament *to give bread* means to nourish, to provide for someone's needs. The prophetic and poetic books praise God for giving bread, and from this divine example imply the duty of sharing one's bread with the hungry. Every gift, and particularly the bread of mealtime, comes from God. This thought is also found in the Jewish meal prayer and in the eighteen blessings. The Israelites prayed for bread when they were in need, because they knew that God cares for the poor.[55]

In the New Testament the same verb is found in the context of the multiplication of the loaves (Mt. 14, 19; 15, 36; Jn. 6, 31, 34-35) and of the Last Supper (Mt. 26, 26). Its phrasing takes on a religious significance.

Bread represents the meal of the poor, and the meaning here is less broad than in the Aramaic, where it signifies food.[56] It is the bread we must have, without which we die of hunger. The necessity of bread is further emphasized by the *semeron*. This today contrasts with Jewish prayers, which petition for a whole lifetime or without any indication of time.[57] The Jews habitually baked only one day's supply of bread. The Lord's Prayer must be related to the instruction given to the disciples to go forth without provisions (Mk. 6, 8); this instruction corresponds to the attitude of the man who is not solicitous for the morrow (Mt. 6, 34).

The word *epiousios,* almost unknown in ancient literature, presents a real problem to exegetes. A whole library may be said to have been dedicated to the study of this word. It is found only once on a papyrus in a list of expenses[58] where it signifies a day's costs. Even Origen was aware of the difficulty raised by this word, for which he knew no parallel. He devoted a quite modern semantic study to it.[59]

Various translations are given for it. The Syriacs translate *panis continuus, panis necessitatis,* or *panis abundantiae.* We find the same version in the Armenians. Much importance has been given to the Gospel according to the Hebrews which, according to St. Jerome, translated it as *tomorrow's bread.* This version has rallied much contemporary support. The Latins translate Matthew's text as *cotidianus,* Luke's as *supersubstantialis,* which denotes inconsistency at least. The translations we have before us are therefore "tomorrow's bread," or "daily bread," "the bread to come" or "the necessary bread."

How are we to understand the petition?

In the Old Testament God is the Providence of his people. He sent them manna in the desert for their daily food.[60] The prophets reiterated the care that Yahweh took for the nourishment of his people (Ho. 2, 6-7, 10-15). To Hosea the stay in the desert appeared as the time of love and betrothal, when God watched with a bridegroom's care over those who lived only through him (Ezk. 16, 19). The notion of love implied in the verb "to give" here found a singular prominence.

Marks of divine preference were assured to the poor and to travellers (Dt. 10, 18; Ps. 132, 15); God's goodness came to the aid of the hungry (Ps. 107, 9). Thus Jewish prayer praised the Lord for satiating men with his gifts (Ps. 104, 27-28). Trustingly the author of Proverbs asks God: "Give me neither poverty nor riches, grant me only my share of bread to eat" (Pr. 30, 8).[61]

The parallelism between the *Our Father* and this verse from Proverbs enables us to orient the meaning of *epiousios* toward what is necessary.

The gospels reflect the same biblical usage. There we find the same idea of power, associated with the concept of God feeding creation (Mt. 6, 26). This is a sporadic case; the gospels go even further. Christ took care of the needs of his audience, he healed and fed the body, he was concerned about satisfying the crowd's hunger. Even after his Resurrection he prepared a meal for his disciples and broke bread with the two pilgrims of Emmaus. The poor and the hungry play a central role in his teaching. Again we find the pedagogy of the Old Testament, in which God bestowed temporal good, manna, the land of Canaan, before promising messianic goods.

Christ is not content with satisfying hunger; he deepens the meaning of hunger and necessity. These physical needs, whose legitimacy he recognizes, have a significance, a prophetic value. God speaks through the senses.[62] Earthly food enables us to understand higher appeals.

The multiplication of the loaves, related by the four evangelists, illustrates the fourth petition of the *Our Father*. The verbal resemblances justify the comparison. On that occasion Jesus behaves as the head of a family; he gives the bread (with the same verb "to give," as in the *Our Father*) of thanksgiving and of expectation. St. John's Gospel elevates the incident to the heights of a prophecy to signify the eschatological repast. The crowd saw in it merely a kindly service of One who gives bread to those who lacked everything. "You are not looking for me because you have seen the signs but because you had all the bread you wanted to eat" (Jn. 6, 26). There is no reproach here, only the assertion of an elementary truth: man's first need is his daily bread.

But Jesus goes much further; he deepens the meaning of this hunger — "man does not live on bread alone" — uncovering a more fundamental need to which he brings the answer: "I am the bread of life. He who comes to me will never be hungry; he who believes in me will never thirst" (Jn. 6, 35).

Beyond satisfying the crowd's hunger Jesus has developed, by miracles, signs of the divine irruption, his program which is to give a deeper meaning to hunger: "Happy you who are hungry now: you shall be satisfied" (Lk. 6, 21). He bases the obligation to "break bread" with the hungry on the goodness of his Father, who gives to everyone. He comes to invite all, sinners and publicans, the poor and the crippled, pagans and Jews, to the eschatological repast (Lk. 14, 13). Though the Jews saw a law inscribed in creation itself in the fact that God gives to all their necessary food, Jesus reverses the point of view; he illuminates the present with an eschatological light. A Christian on earth must anticipate the life of eternity by welcoming Christ in the hungry (Mk. 10, 42-45; Mt. 25, 36). On the day of judgment those who have their full now shall go hungry (cf. Lk. 6, 25; Mt. 25, 42; Lk. 16, 19ff).

From now on the final assembling of mankind governs the attitude of Christians. "Man is a beggar at the gates of God." Material poverty is, as it were, the sacrament of our situation before him. It is a touchstone of God's kingdom; the poor are the object of a divine preference.

Man's first petition, therefore, concerns the bread needed for subsistence. It is the only petition which has material things for its object. By this fact it contrasts with the unlimited dimensions of the preceding petitions. Prayer for bread is limited in time as well as in its object; it halts at the boundaries of each day, basing its trust in the Father; "each day has enough trouble of its own" (Mt. 6, 34); it is content with what is indispensable: bread (Qo. 9, 7). The point does not lie in any passive surrender to Providence but in the *charity* and the sharing that are manifestations of it.

The twice-repeated plural explains the meaning of the eschatological community to the disciples. The *us* does not represent any sealed-off community. The God of the Old Testament feeds all creation (Ps. 145, 16; the eighteen blessings). The Father of Christ and our Father does not will "that one of these little ones should be lost" (Mt. 18, 14). His love must dwell in his own and must assert itself in charity. "Who is my neighbor?" He who is in need (Lk. 10, 29-37). This conclusion has a bearing on our attitude toward those who are hungry (Mt. 25, 35, 44-46). Our sharing today in necessity and hunger is already an eschatological attitude which will be revealed tomorrow.

For this reason the Christians of the first generations thought it inconceivable that one should belong to the Body of Christ without shouldering the needs of the poor and the needy.[63] Of those in the community of Corinth who ate to excess, living alongside those who were poor, St. Paul says that they were eating their condemnation, that which anticipates the final judgment (cf. I Cor. 11, 29). To grant a figurative value to daily bread in order to find an anticipation in it, as it were, of the eschatological repast, is to discover the same symbolism in it as in the Eucharist.

The phrase *daily bread* and the Johannine accounts have this in common, that their spiritual value presupposes but does not abolish their historicity. Restricting the petition for bread to merely material bread, or spiritualizing it purely and simply, would mean mutilating it.

The fourth petition places us in the concrete conditions of human life, in the very core of the world's drama; but it raises the struggle to the level of God who came and comes under the guise of the poor and hungry.

Forgive us our debts as we have forgiven those who are in debt to us

In the fifth petition of the *Our Father* the text presents more variants than we have had thus far, whether we compare Matthew with Luke or with the *Didache*.[64]

The Septuagint used the word *opheilema* with the commercial and juridical meaning of *loan* and *tax*.[65] Matthew uses the word in the same sense (Mt. 18, 32). But he also uses it, as does the

Aramaic substratum, in a religious sense.[66] He is the only one to do so; the word does not appear again in ancient Christian literature.

The verb *aphiemi*, on the other hand, is used in classical Greek in a juridical, and never in a religious sense, to signify *remit, dissolve, dismiss*. We find this meaning in the Septuagint (Dt. 15, 2; Nb. 14, 19), where it has a religious sense. The biblical substratum *nasa, salah,* designates a legal impurity. The comparison *aphiemi-opheilema* places man before God in a juridical relationship. God is Judge. He may abandon his *rights* by grace. The noun *aphesis*, remission, pertains to eschatological times and to the task of the Messiah (Is. 58, 6; 61, 1). The New Testament sometimes retains the juridical sense.[67] More often the word is used with *amartia* in the religious sense (Mk. 2, 5; Lk. 7, 47); *amartemate* (Mk. 3, 28); *paraptomata* (Mt. 6, 14). The verb expresses the restoration, by *grace*, of a relationship broken by sin.

The remission of sins plays a central role in the Old and New Testaments. It underlies the teaching and prophetic hope from Isaiah to Ezekiel.[68] In Jeremiah, in the prophecy which represents the summit of his book (Jr. 31, 31-34), the remission of sins is a characteristic trait of the new Covenant. Its novelty revolves around the interiorizing of religion, individuality, and the divine initiative of forgiveness. In this progression the last element appears as the most significant. The Servant of Yahweh, at the intersection of the sacrificial line and the line of intercession, takes on himself the sins of all (Is. 53, 6-7). The post-exilic Psalms (32; 51; 130; 143), which express the spiritual experience of the anawim, analyze the gravity of severing friendship with God and fathom the hope of remission of sins and the expectation of Israel.

The preaching of John the Baptist sums up and concentrates this expectation on the "baptism of repentance (*metanoia*) for the forgiveness of sins" (Mk. 1, 4).

Christ's mission is already expressed in his name: he "is to save his people from their sins" (Mt. 1, 21). Mt. is here re-echoing a biblical quotation (Ps. 130, 8). Christ systematically seeks the company of sinners to the point of being called "a friend of tax collectors and sinners" (Mt. 11, 19). The sacrifice of the Cross is found at the intersection of the two biblical movements of sacrifice and prayer, of justice and mercy; this sacrifice accomplished "the remission of sins."

St. Luke, particularly, develops the theme of forgiveness in the parables which are proper to him (Lk. 15) and in the teachings of his Gospel and the Acts.[69]

We are therefore in the presence of an essential theme of the gospels. The remission of sins, in conformity with the prophecies, characterizes the new order which governs the relations between God and man; it inaugurates the new righteousness and affirms the coming of God's reign. Forgiveness is the sign of this transformation and the advent, as it were, of a new creation. Less common is the setting up of a relationship between God's forgiveness and the forgiveness of one neighbor (Si. 28, 2). Such texts are more numerous in rabbinical writings, however.[70]

What bread is to the body, forgiveness is to the soul; it answers man's aspiration to become a son of God. The prayer of the prodigal son sums up the prayer of the whole Old Testament.

The metaphor of debtor and creditor implies the economy of a positive alliance between God and man; it expresses God's love and pledges the fidelity of mankind. In view of this anticipatory and gratuitous goodwill of Yahweh, man is always a debtor. He is essentially a debtor.

Because of this, Matthew's expression, which speaks of *debts*, a vaguer and less specific word than *sins*, which is used by Luke, better expresses the biblical idea. A certain asymmetry will always characterize the relationship between God and men, shattering the narrow framework of the juridical imagery. This aspect of the human condition of the chosen people is reinforced, as it were, and laid bare by sin, which widens the gap and sharpens the contrast.

Though God is goodwill, he is also justice; he is both Father

The Lord's Prayer

and Judge. His intransigence is another form of his love. His forgiveness is not simply an idea emanating from the concept of God, it is an act of God, a movement of his grace manifested in the history of salvation.

The work of Christ, the *ephapax* of his sacrifice, forms the new humanity, transforms man in the very deepest core of his being, and extends to mankind in its widest compass. Such is the meaning of "this is my blood, the blood of the Covenant which is to be poured out for the many for the forgiveness of sins" (Mt. 26, 28; Mk. 14, 24; cf. Lk. 22, 20).

Man, in the face of God's salvific work, appears as an eminently insolvent debtor. Never will he be able to give any adequate reply to God's anticipatory goodness. The very consciousness of his sin, the first stage of his return, is the first fruit of grace. It is the awareness of his status as a child of God, the meaning of the word *image,* which even sin could not totally efface. The parable of the prodigal son compares this awareness to homesickness.

The tragedy of sin in the inmost recesses of man consists not only in separation from God but also in isolating him from other men. Sin necessarily has a social or, more properly, a horizontal dimension, not simply a vertical one. The twofold aspect of the one mystery which makes Christ ask on the cross for the forgiveness of his executioners and of sinners enables us to understand that the grace of God-agape, revealed on that cross, must necessarily flow back to the rest of mankind without discrimination or restriction. The unworthiness and the sin of his neighbor are an additional reason why the Christian should turn to God.

As we scrutinize this text more carefully, which we have translated as: "Forgive us our trespasses *as we have forgiven* those who trespass against us,"[71] the experience of the wrongs of others enlightens us as to our debts toward God by emphasizing the disparity between the two. There is no proportion between the debts of others toward us and the debts we have contracted toward God, just as there is no proportion between the forgiveness we extend and that which God extends (Lk. 17, 10). Our forgiveness of others is not a cause but a condition of God's pardoning us, — a pardon which, nevertheless, remains free (Mt. 6, 14; 18, 21-35).

It is by establishing the community through forgiveness that men guarantee the acting presence of God who forgives. The plural, four times repeated, underscores all the more emphatically the fundamental solidarity of mankind. Whether personal or collective, sin is an obstacle to the establishment of the community. As the First Epistle of St. John emphasizes, the Christian is mediator between God and the world. The grace of salvation is manifested by the establishment of the eschatological community.

The fifth petition enables us to measure to what depths the gift of God constitutes a demand on mankind and a summons for man to enter with his whole being into the economy of the new Covenant which constitutes the family of the children of God.

And do not put us to the test, but save us from the evil one

We must not divide this petition into two, as Luther and some other commentators have done; the symmetrical construction of the sentence as well as the complementary meaning of the two parts necessitate our considering it as one petition only.[72]

We find this form of the petition in the *Our Father* both in the East and in the West. Chromatius, bishop of Aquileia, testifies to it in his commentary on the Sermon on the Mount: *"Quod ipsum in alio libro evangelii evidenter ostensum est: sic enim scriptum est: et ne nos inferas in temptationem quam suffere non possumus."*[73] St. Jerome likewise enjoins us to pray daily: *ne inducas nos in temptationem quam sufferre non possumus.*[74] All these testimonies enable us to measure the difficulties raised by this petition.

This petition has only one parallel in all Scripture, the scene of Gethsemane (Mt. 26, 41; Mk. 14, 38; Lk. 22, 40). It even seems to contradict the statement of St. James (Jm. 1, 13). The analogous prayers of contemporary Judaism never ask that man be preserved from all temptation, but that he remain invincible in the hour of trial. This only serves to emphasize further the novelty of the Lord's Prayer.[75]

The Bible is the book of temptation; it opens with the account of the first man and the first woman tempted in the Garden of Paradise; it ends with the great temptation in the Apocalypse (Re. 3, 10). The Old Testament more often uses the word *peirazo* in a religious sense to express man's ever-threatened condition, whatever may be the origin of his trial. A cursory glance enables us to discern the ambiguous character of temptation.

God himself tempted Abraham, putting his faith and his obedience to the test (Gn. 22, 1-19). He acts in the same way toward the whole people of Israel (Ex. 20, 20), "to test you and know your inmost heart — whether you would keep his commandments or not (Dt. 8, 2).

In the account of the Fall the serpent beguiles Eve. The adversary here seems bent on separating man from God. This concept develops and is found more particularly in the book of Job, where Satan strives to make the just fall. Job overcomes the temptation by vowing to God an obedience that is proof against any trial (Jb. 42, 2).

Wisdom literature often speaks of temptation (cf. Si. 2, 1; 33, 1), a condition which dons an educational character, as with the Greeks. This explains the prayer of the psalmist who asks to be tempted (Ps. 26, 2). The whole of human life is a continual temptation because God educates his own through trials.[76] This concept is also found in Philo. We find the same word in the context of the eschatological tribulations which announce and precede the judgment and the culmination (Zc. 1, 15; Hab. 3, 16). Daniel speaks of the just who will be tempted and "purged" (Dn. 12, 10). They undergo the trial in order to be saved (Bk. of Henoch 94, 5; 96, 20). Rabbinical literature recalls the example of the fidelity of Abraham who resisted ten temptations.[77] It speaks of the perverse instinct dwelling in man.[78]

The Qumran writings divide mankind into *Sons of Light* and *Sons of Darkness*. Mankind's human state is strained by the inevitable struggle which we find expressed also in the writings of the New Testament. The origin of this concept, foreign to the Old Testament and rabbinical thought, is widely discussed. It may have been influenced directly or indirectly by Parsiism.[79]

One initial point is clear: temptation pertains to the human condition. Insofar as Christ shares this state he, too, was subject to temptation, as the three Synoptics relate and the Epistle to the Hebrews affirms (Heb. 2, 18; 4, 15).[80]

Before studying the significance of temptation, we must solve the problem of the identity of the tempter, which is the key factor in the precise meaning of the sixth petition. The rest of our prayer, "save us from the evil one," puts us on the right track.

The question is therefore limited; who tempts man — God or Satan? By playing on the ambiguity of the word *temptation*, the Old Testament answered that both of them tempt us. It does not seem that we can say the same for the New Testament; God is never said to *tempt* man. St. James clearly affirms the contrary: "Never, when you have been tempted, say, 'God sent the temptation.' God cannot be tempted to do anything wrong, and he does not tempt anybody" (Jm. 1, 13). From this we can draw but one conclusion: the *temptation* in question does not mean a trial or a testing by God, but an *evil* which is the work of the adversary, Satan, or his agents,[81] who are always actively hostile to God and to man. The parallelism in the petition confirms what a reading of the texts has already enabled us to conclude.

But is our statement perhaps contradicted by the very petition itself: *do not put us to the test?* The answer is determined by the words "but save us." We could paraphrase as follows: Do not expose us to the danger of infidelity, but deliver us from the power of Satan.

Man is tempted. Temptation forms part of the Christian state (Heb. 2, 18; 4, 15; Pss. 11, 5; 66, 10). Whether temptation comes from the weakness of the flesh or from the demoniacal seductions that the tempter inspires in our enemies or carries out himself, the fact remains that the faithful man trembles in the ambiguous

The Lord's Prayer

situation of his exercise, living in this world without belonging to it, always subject to hostile forces.

The trials which appear as persecutions or tribulations form part of the eschatological era and accompany the transition from the present eon to the new eon. In this clash between satanic power and the *dynamis* of God, whatever infernal forces are unchained, man is caught up in the gigantic struggle that contends for the world. But God remains the mighty Lord who guides events and men. He can lead us to the kingdom without our falling into the meshes of the Adversary. This is the meaning of the sixth petition.[82]

The second part of the petition expresses the same thought in relief: *but save us from the evil one*.[83]

The verb *ruesthai* evokes the metaphor of being forcibly rescued from a dangerous situation while on a journey. God is essentially he who has sent his angel "who has been my saviour from all harm" (Gn. 48, 16). And so Jewish prayer continually invokes him for "rescue from all troubles" (Ps. 54, 7), "from the snares of fowlers" (Ps. 91, 3). "from the lion's mouth; and from the wild bulls' horns (Ps. 22, 21), "from persecutors" (Ps. 142, 7), "from my enemies" (Ps. 143,9). After the exile Isaiah clearly asks: "For you are our Father . . . , our Redeemer is your ancient name. Why, Yahweh, leave us to stray from your ways? (Is. 63, 16-17).

Second of Isaiah clearly alludes to the pact of the Covenant by which God pledged himself to guide his people during the course of their history, to shield them from erring ways, to save them from all evil (Gn. 28, 3) and from all hostile encounter on a road strewn with pitfalls[84] (Is. 48, 17).

The word *ponerou* has led to many discussions. Are we dealing with the neuter or the masculine? The sacerdotal prayer poses the same question. The Latin Church, since the time of Cyprian and Augustine, has read it as neuter, seeing in it either evil actions, baneful situations, or hostile powers from which we ask to be delivered.

The idea that God delivers from evil is familiar to the Old Testament; Yahweh delivers "from all harm" (Gn. 48, 16).[85] The two texts closest to our petition have the same form (2 Tm. 4, 18; *Didache* 10, 5). But each time we find the adjective *all*, which emphasizes the neuter and which we do not find in the Lord's Prayer.

Ponerou may be taken in the masculine in the sense of "the evil man," a rather frequent meaning of the world in the Old Testament,[86] but one which recurs less often in the New Testament.[87] More numerous are the texts which call the devil the *poneros*. This is the interpretation of the Greek Church, from Origen to Theodore of Mopsuestia, in its commentaries on this passage of the *Our Father*.

In Matthew's Gospel, when there is a question of evil, we find the adjective *paz* (Mt. 5, 11; cf. Mk. 7, 23; I Th. 5, 22). Elsewhere the singular always signifies the devil, as is proved by the two parables of the sower and of the darnel in the field (Mt. 13, 19). The parallels of the verse in which Matthew speaks of the *poneros* explicitly say Satan (Mk. 4, 15) or the devil (Lk. 8, 12). Matthew himself explicitly interprets *poneros* in this sense (Mt. 13, 39). The same applies to the text where John deals with the *poneros*[88] (I Jn. 2, 13; 3, 12; 5, 18, 19).

It seems that here Matthew wants to tear the mask from the fomenter of evil and call him by his proper name. He is not an abstraction but a person throughout New Testament literature, in Paul, John, and in the Synoptics. The symmetrical parallelism of the last petition only reinforces this representation of a struggle between two kingdoms. Moreover, the confronting forces in the apocalyptic drama that envelopes humanity in its eschatological phase are not personifications but angels and servants, demons and princes, the Father and the evil one.

The Old Testament knows no dualism between God and the devil; Satan is the public accuser who occupies a quasi-official post in the celestial court. He opposes the work of God, in which he remains integrated. Rabbinical and post-exilic literature develops demonology; Satan is the prince of evil, the prince of the anti-kingdom of God. He accuses man before God, disposes man to sin; he is the author of evil and misfortune, he fights against God and his plan of salvation. In the New Testament he is the prince of demons, as he is the prince of this world (Jn. 12, 31; 14, 30; 16, 11). Paul even calls him "the god of this world" (2 Cor. 4, 4). His kingdom extends from earth even to heaven (Lk. 10, 18). He is the adversary of God, of his creation, and of his kingdom.

In bringing about God's reign, Jesus comes into conflict with the prince of this world, whose tyranny he has come to conquer (Jn. 12, 31). "He watched Satan fall like lightning from heaven" (Lk. 10, 18). The expulsions of the devil signify the advent of God's kingdom, driving out that of Satan, which has been consolidated through the weakness of the old Adam (Mt. 12, 22, 28, 32). Christ's Resurrection first of all affirms Satan's defeat and the sovereignty of God for the period of time separating us from the end of the world. Vanquished, the devil, in the spasm of the final days which separate us from the fulfillment, can still work harm. The writings of the New Testament are full of warnings against "the prince of this world" in action. The parable of the darnel teaches the ambiguity which prevails until the consummation.

We are now in a better position to explain the sixth petition, its absolutely symmetrical construction expresses the same truth in a negative and in a positive form. To express its shade of meaning we could translate: Do not abandon us to temptation, but save us from the evil one.

The dualism which rends this world into darkness and light and man into flesh and spirit, does not recognize a two-fold initial principle. God is the creator and the Lord of the earth as he is of heaven. However mysterious and violent the power of the tempter may be, the whole of salvation history affirms the supremacy of God over the evil one.

Christian prayer rests on the victory of Jesus, who saved us from the devil. This victory does not mean a quiet and peaceful life during the period which separates us from the perfect fulfillment, but a demoniacal attack in the shape of instincts within and persecutions without. The Apocalypse does not hide from us the tragic side of the Christian condition.

Our collective prayer asks for the final deliverance in eschatological times which "has taken us out of the power of darkness and created a place for us in the kingdom of the Son that he loves" (Col. 1, 13). It is a more concrete formulation of the second petition; the kingdom of God is inaugurated in a violent struggle. In the end our prayer is, therefore, an act of faith in the lordship of God who will have the last word.

APPENDIX: For yours is the kingdom

A certain number of manuscripts include, after the *Our Father* a doxology which is certainly not authentic.[89] The oldest testimony comes from the *Didache* (8, 2) which closes the *Our Father* with: *Because yours is the power and the glory through the centuries.*[90] The *Amen* is not found there, although it is attested by Tatian (according to von Soden): *For yours is the kingdom, the power, and the glory for ever and ever. Amen.* The same doxology is found in the Syriac versions under the form: *For yours is the kingdom and the glory in the century of centuries.* We find it in Sinaiticus. It seems to have come from Syria or Palestine.

The text of the Our Father in Luke

Since Tatian and the recension of the Koine, Luke has Matthew's complete text. But the oldest manuscripts and the most important, H, W, attest Luke's very special form.[91] Some differences between Matthew's text and Luke's are not without importance. We have already had occasion to point them out.[92]

Some of these can be explained by a different translation of the same Aramaic substratum.[93] More important seems the variant in the petition for bread. Matthew writes *semeron* with the aorist, while Luke uses the present with *kath emeran*. Luke's turn of

The Lord's Prayer

phrase expresses an experience of life stretching over a period of time, excluding the eschatological explanation of *epiousios* and accentuating the personal nature of the need, which divine goodness fulfills according to the biblical concept (Ps. 145, 15; Pr. 30, 7-8). The present is found in the next petition *aphiomen*, which contrasts with the aorist, expressing the historical and eschatological intervention of God. The believer forgives, his whole life long, in the hope that God will forgive him in turn on the day of judgment. The *panti opheilonti* accentuates the individual aspect, as does the corresponding *autoi*, which replaces Matthew's *emeis*.

Luke abandoned the structure of six petitions, three of which concern God and the other three man, replacing this structure with two petitions relating to the things of God and three to those of the beseecher. Here the Christian community is no longer praying so much as the individual Christian who is asking to remain faithful during his mortal life.[94]

This sanctification through the invocation of God's name is realized literally at baptism, where "our sins are washed away while invoking his name" (Acts 22, 16; cf, 9, 15). The same name is invoked in the Eucharistic celebration (*Didache* 10, 2).[95] Martyrdom perfects the work of baptism and the Eucharist by inscribing God's name and the name of the heavenly city on the martyrs (Apoc. 3, 12).

The addition *eph'emas* may come from the first ecclesial community gathered for worship, which used the *Our Father* during baptism and the Eucharist, conscious as the members were that they were the heirs of the people of Israel. The *Didache* seemingly attests this usage by inserting the *Our Father* between the baptismal ceremony and the Eucharist.[96]

This application of sanctification to the faithful, however, seems unduly restrictive, as Tertullian already remarked; as a result, other commentators interpret: May his kingdom come in us. This is sufficiently in accordance with the words of the Lord when he sent forth his disciples with this message: "Whenever you go into a town . . . say, 'The kingdom of God is very near to you' " (Lk. 10, 9). In this interpretation the Church is conscious of bringing about God's kingdom on earth, which presupposes an already organized Church. Subsequently this manner of praying underwent great development in such western countries as Germany and England.

More important is the variant of Luke's second petition: May your Holy Spirit come down on us and cleanse us.[97] *Eltheto to agion pneuma sou eph'emas kai katharisato emas.*

This text goes back as far as Marcion who, according to Tertullian, even placed it before the prayer for the kingdom. It seems to be inspired by Luke 11, 13: "The heavenly Father will give the Holy Spirit to those who ask him." It may be an insertion by some prepaulinian communities of Jewish stock who found the hope of the Old Testament fulfilled in Jesus,[98] or it may come from the use of the *Our Father* during Christian initiation (Harnack), and which crept into the Lord's Prayer as early as the second century.

The two versions of the *Our Father* attest both to a twofold tradition, perhaps coming from Galilee and Jerusalem, and to the liberty allowed the communities. The text of the prayer does not seem to have been stereotyped and unchangeable.

The fact remains that both versions place the community at prayer in an eschatological perspective, in the expectation and the hope of the final fulfillment; they free the prayer of any apocalyptic coloration by formulating the object of Christian prayer in sober and clear terms of inexhaustible depth which prepare the way for the Roman liturgy.

PART II
Chapter III

1. For the exegesis of the *Our Father* we have relied heavily on the commentary of E. Lohmeyer, *Das Vater unser* (Göttingen, 1952).

2. For Christian antiquity it is sufficient to refer to F. H. Chase, *The Lord's Prayer in the Early Church* (Cambridge, Eng., 1891). We shall return to this later in the course of our study.

3. Father Lebreton in *The Life & Teaching of Jesus Christ Our Lord,* II, 61, localizes the *Our Father* in the Garden of Olives, following a tradition which dates back to the ninth century. H. Vincent and F. M. Abel, *Jérusalem*

The Lord's Prayer

(Paris, 1914), II, 375, do the same by comparing Mt. 6, 14-15 with Mk. 11, 23-26 on forgiveness, delivered while Jesus was passing by the Mount of Olives. This conjecture adds a little solemnity to the scene, if the *Our Father* is in some way a prelude to the prayer of Gethsemane.

4. We doubtless make too hieratic a representation of tradition. The early Christians show more flexibility in regard to the texts. We have but to compare the different gospels relating the same fact or the same teaching. In several passages St. Luke summarizes, where the other evangelists are more explicit. Did Christ give a fixed text of the *Our Father*?

5. The same applies to Mk. 11, 25; Jn. 12, 28; 17, 15; Acts 21, 14; 2 Tm. 4, 18. Polycarp of Smyrna asks the Philippians in his letter to them "to pray to God not to lead us into temptation" (*Ep. Pol.*, 7, 2). And the account of his martyrdom has him say: "Your will be done" (*Mart. Pol.*, 7, 1). For the inscription from Pompeii of A.D. 78 and that of Doura, cf. E. Lohmeyer, *Vaterunser,* p. 8.

6. We shall not discuss Harnack's hypothesis, which would have liked to reduce the prayer to the petition for the coming of the Holy Spirit (*Uber einige Worte Jesu,* Berlin, 1907). J. Hensler, *Das Vaterunser* (Münster, 1914), has rigorously refuted this.

7. The extreme reserve of Elbogen (*Der jüdische Gottesdienst*) in dating Jewish prayers is instructive.

8. J. Hermann, *Der alttestamentliche Urgrund des Vaterunsers* (Leipzig, 1934).

9. J. Elbogen has definitely exaggerated this dependence (*Der jüdische Gottesdienst,* p. 93).

10. SB I, 410-411.

11. Luther divided the *Our Father* into two parts, one having three, the other four petitions.

To Hillel and the school of Beth-Hillel, the septenary form seemed indispensable for all prayer. The prayer of the synagogue, the *Shemone Esre,* in the time of Christ was composed of two strophes each of seven verses. Cf. O. Holtzmann, *Berakot* (Giessen, 1912).

It is perhaps better to look for the septenary form in the address and in the six petitions which follow: cf. J. Schniewind, "Das Evangelium nach Matthäus," *NTD* (Göttingen, 1950), p. 81. The same distribution is suggested in J. Hermann, Der alttestamentliche Urgrund des Vaterunsers.

12. A short address, comparable to that of Jewish prayers such as the *Shemone Esre.*

For the concept of *Father,* cf. above, pp. 91-92.

13. E.g., Mt. 7, 21; 12, 50; 5, 48; 6, 14; 18, 35.

15. 1 Jn. 3, 1; Rom. 8, 15; Ga. 4, 6; this seemingly influenced the appellation "Father" in Luke's recension.

16. To understand the novelty of this position, compare the *Our Father* with the eighteen blessings, in which the historical situation still plays an important part.

17. Certain commentators see in the complement "in heaven" a further clarification that seeks to distinguish the heavenly Father from the earthly father, or from father Abraham. E. Lohmeyer, *Das Vaterunser,* p. 40; J. Hermann, *op. cit.;* H. Bietenhard, *Die himmlische Welt im Urchristentum und Spätjudentum* (Tübingen, 1951), pp. 77-80.

18. A petition common to Matthew and Luke.

19. The usage is even more common in the sacerdotal prayer (Jn. 17, 6, 11, 26).

20. Among the Semites the name not only designated the person. It even

expressed it and defined it in its inmost nature. We know what magical power the name of a divinity assumes in certain religions. To call someone by name is to have an advantage over him.

21. Cf. Ex. 3, 14; 33, 19; Ezk. 12, 25.
22. Is. 40, 28; 41, 4; 43, 10; 44, 6; 48, 12.
23. "To sanctify," *agiazein*, renders, both in the New Testament and in the Septuagint, the Hebrew *gâdas* with a passive and middle shade of meaning: to reveal oneself as the Holy One (when speaking of God); to make holy or recognize holiness (when speaking of man). The Old Testament applies the verb "to sanctify" to God and to men, more explicitly to the people of God, never to pagans, unless they have been called. Sanctification presupposes election: "You therefore must be holy because I am holy" (Lv. 11, 45; cf. 19, 2; 20, 7). God is therefore the principle of all holiness (Ezk. 28, 22). Men sanctify themselves in sanctifying God and his name, to the extent that God sanctifies himself in them and sanctifies them (Is. 29, 23); for he is called the Holy One (Is. 40, 25; 43, 15).

We must associate with the concept of sanctifying those of *megalunein*, "to exalt," and *doxazein*, "to glorify." In those who are close to me I show my holiness and before all the people I show my glory" (Lv. 10, 3). The same parallelism is found in Ezk. 28, 22; 38, 23. To sanctify and to glorify are synonymous in rabbinical literature. It suffices to refer to the prayer of the Kaddish or to St. John, whose Gospel has affinities with the first petition of the *Our Father*.

24. Ex. 3, 5; Jos. 5, 15.
25. Cf. Lv. 10, 3; Is. 5, 16; Ezk. 20, 41.
26. It is of little consequence whether this is a matter of idolatry (Lv. 18, 21; 20, 3), of legal transgressions (Jr. 34, 16; Ezk. 36, 20; Am. 2, 7), of legal prescriptions (Lv. 21, 6; 22, 2, 32), of Temple prostitution (Am. 2, 7), or of the doubts of the Gentiles (Ezk. 36, 20-21).
27. E.g. Is. 29, 23; 48, 11; 52, 5; Ezk. 36, 23-27; Ps. 79, 9.
28. SB I, 412-413.
29. Cf. Hab. 2, 14; Nb. 14, 21; Is. 11, 9.
30. This is the theme of the fourth Gospel (particularly chapters 5 and 17) and more especially of the sacerdotal prayer. As John remarks, God is the only cause of sanctification, a term which is rendered by the passive form of the verb. He make the holiness of his Son apparent by glorifying him.
31. In E. Lohmeyer, *Das Vaterunser*, p. 52.
32. The second petition should be translated: "Your kingdom come." This petition is found in both Matthew's account and Luke's. The *peh'umon*, inserted in the Cambridge Codex at Lk. 11, 2, has no parallel either in the first or the third petition. Despite its lack of authenticity, this addition has influenced the German translation, "*Zu uns komme Dein Reich!*" The verb *erchomai* needs some explanation. Classical Greek uses it in connection with people and events. It is especialy found in the cult. There the prayers ask the divinity to *come*, using the imperative *elthe*, followed by the name of the god or goddess with a description of him or her. The form *elthe* has something magical about it; cf. K. Preisendanz, *Papyri graecae magicae;* J. Schneider, "*erchomai*," *TWNT*, II, 663; especially regarding the Orphic hymns. The form is used by Homer, *Iliad*, XXIII, 770; Plato, *Leg.*, IV, 712b; later by Josephus, *Antiq.* IV, 46; XX, 90.

The Septuagint uses the verb *erchomai* in a cultural context: to come to the cult to worship at Jerusalem. It is used in prayer when speaking of someone who *comes* before God (Pss. 102, 1; 119, 41, 77). The word also expresses the coming of God, of his word, of his angels, of his prophets among men. More particularly it signifies the coming of the Messiah (Dn. 7, 13). He is the one "who comes in the name of the Lord" (Ps. 118, 26).

Erchesthai is also applied to events, to epochs that come and go (2 Ch. 21, 19), and more particularly to the coming of the eschatological days (the day of salvation and the day of judgment Ps. 80, 3). The verb sometimes expresses the coming of fortunate events, but more often that of catastrophes (Psalms; Job).

The Testament of the Twelve Patriarchs (As 7, 3), uses it for the eschatological coming of God. The New Testament also has recourse to the verb "to come," both concerning people and events.

33. H. Windisch, *Paulus und Christus* (Leipzig, 1934), p. 156.
34. Cf. Mt. 21, 9; 23, 39; Lk. 13, 35; 19, 38; Mk. 11, 9.
35. Cf. 1 S. 2, 31; Am. 8, 11; Lk. 23, 29.
36. Mt. 9, 15; Mk. 2, 20; Lk. 5, 35; 17, 22; 21, 6.
37. Jn. 4, 21, 23; 5, 25; 16, 25.
38. Mt. 6, 10; Lk. 11, 2; 17, 20; 22, 18.
39. *Basileia* has both the meaning of kingdom and reign. The two meanings alternate in the Old Testament. To his people God first gave a land, then a leader, then a king. The zenith of the Jewish kingdom was the reign of David. In him was completed the first movement of sacred history. In gratitude David wished to build a Temple to Yahweh. The prophet Nathan told him that it is not man who builds God's temple, but that God will build himself a Temple of living stone from the flesh of David (2 S. 7, 12, 16). Instead of closing with a temple, the story expands with a promise, a Messiah, who will restore the throne of David (Mt. 1, 1). The significance of the Davidic reign enables us to look deeper into the meaning of the kingdom. What mattered was neither country nor land, but man's status in relation to God. Israel was the people whose king was Yahweh. The lordship of God extends to all creation (Henoch 9, 4); his rule over heaven and earth was affirmed in an exemplary manner in his people (Pss. 103, 19; 145, 11). The Psalms of enthronement sing of God's victory over the enemies of his reign (cf. also Is. 52, 7; 6, 5).

Post-exilic Judaism based Yahweh's reign on the manifestation of Sinai; there Israel recognized God's lordship, called the kingdom of heaven. Sin had come to destroy this reign. But Yahweh was to intervene once more to reestablish the kingdom of Israel, by triumphing over Satan, sin, and death. Rabbinical thought never speaks of this kingdom as *coming*, but as *manifesting itself*. SB I, 418.

40. *as* is missing in D a b c k, in Tertullian, and in Cyprian.
41. The article *tes* before *ges* is found in D pm W.
42. Authors translate the *en* differently, sometimes *on* the heavens, sometimes *in* the heavens.
43. Plato, *Crito*, 43d.
44. We find the word, with the nuance of love, in Ignatius of Antioch, *Rom.*, 8, 1, 3.
45. Father Jacquemin speaks of the *decree of our salvation* in *La partée de la 3me demande du Pater* (Louvain, 1949), p. 16. However, frequent this expression may be, it is not a happy one: it is too anthropomorphic and too juridical. Into what unsound problems has not this idea of so-called decrees led theologians?
46. If the first two petitions have frequent parallels in rabbinical thought and in the Kaddish, the same is not true of the third petition. Only an echo of this prayer can be found in that of Eliezer (A.D. 90-100): "Do your will in heaven

142 *Prayer — The New Testament*

above; grant a quiet heart to those who fear you on earth and accomplish what seems good in your sight." SB I, 419-420.

47. E.g., Mt. 18, 14: 6, 10; 7, 21; 12, 50, 21, 31.
48. *Comm. in Matth.,* Hom. 19, 4; *P.G.,* LVII, 279.
49. *De oratione,* XXVI; *P.G.,* XI, 500.
50. J. Schiewind, *Das Evangelium nach Matthäus,* p. 84.
51. Which is equivalent to *os . . . autos.*
52. St. Paul develops this theme at some length: Ep. 1, 10; Col. 1, 16, 20; Ph. 2, 10; cf. also Re. 5- 13.
53. Mk. (13, 27) uses the phrase *heaven and earth* in regard to the last Judgment with the same meaning.
54. The first petition of the second series is common to both recensions of the *Our Father.* Luke slightly alters the text; the verb is in the present *didou,* whereas, Matthew uses the aorist, as in the first petition, *dos.* Instead of *semeron,* Luke writes *kath-emeran.* Nevertheless, we do find the word *semeron* in Luke in D p c i t.

The turn of the phrase is not symmetrical in relation to the first petitions; the complement, with the only epithet of the whole prayer, begins the sentence, and is in the active. Instead of *us* we have *emon* and *emin.*

The verb *didomi,* meaning "to give (bread)" is peculiar to the gospels. The root of the verb expresses the love which is manifested in the gift.

55. E.g., Gn. 28, 20; Ex. 16, 8; Is. 58, 7; Ps. 146, 7.
56. According to E. Lohmeyer, *Das Vaterunser,* p. 96, who gives sound arguments.
57. *Shemone Esre.* SB IV, 631.
58. F. Preisigke, *Sammelbuch griechischer Urkunden aus Ägypten* (Strasbourg, 1915), I, 5224.
59. *De oratione,* XXVII, 7-12.

The word *epiousios,* from *epi* and *ousia,* "necessary for subsistence" (Origen, John Chrysostom, Jerome), or from *epi ten ousan (emeran* understood), "for the present day," or from *epioussa emera,* "for the coming day." Finally, it may come from *epienai;* and if we relate it to *to epion,* the future it signifies is bread for the future (Cyril of Alexandria; Pater of Laodicea), whether it be of the immediate future or of the eschatological kingdom.

60. Cf. Ex. 16, 4, 18, 21; cf. 2 Ezr. 9, 15; Pss. 78, 24; 105, 40; Ws. 16, 20.
61. The last verse may be a gloss.
62. C. Tresmontant, *A Study of Hebrew Thought,* trans. Michael F. Gibson (New York: Desclée Co., 1960), p. 47, speaks of "poetic materialism."
63. Read "Liturgie et action sociale," *Maison-Dieu,* XXXVI (1953), 151-172.
64. Matthew uses the noun *opheilema,* which is close to *opheile,* found in the *Didache* and in the parable of the unforgiving debtor (Mt. 18, 32). Both terms are well established in the Koine, the first mainly in papyri and ostraka, the second in Greek literature. The plural is a guarantee of its authenticity. Matthew constructs his sentence in a symmetrical fashion, using the plural in both cases, *opheilemata — tois opheiletais emon;* on the other hand, Luke writes *panti opheilonti — emin,* which is better Greek, but gives an imperative turn to a sentence which should be deprecatory.

We shall have to come back to a more important variant which differentiates the two evangelists. In the first part of the petition (but not in the second) Luke replaces Matthew's colorful noun *opheilema* by the more current word *amartia,* a usage by no means uncommon to him, since in classical Greek *opheilema* never has a religious meaning. In Matthew the comparison is introduced by *os kai,* which certain manuscripts give as *katha.* Luke writes in

a looser manner *kai gar*. Cf. also Mt. 20, 28; Mk. 10, 45. Both forms translate the Aramic *kedi*.
For this petition reference may be made to F. C. Burkitt, "As we have forgiven," *Journal of Theol. Studies*, XXXIII (1932), 253-255.

65. E. g. Dt. 24, 10; 3 Ezra 3, 20; 1 Mc. 15, 8.

66. Father Joüon, in *L'Évangile de N.S.J.Ch.* (Paris, 1930), p. 35, remarks that the Aramaic, but not the Hebrew, expresses the concept of sin as a debt, and the concept of forgiveness as the remitting of the debt.

67. Cf. Mt. 18, 27, 32.

68. Cf. Is. 33, 24; Jr. 31, 34; Is. 53, 5; Ezk. 18, 31; 36, 25-27; Zc. 13, 1; Mi. 7, 18.

69. Lk. 5, 8, 10; 7, 48; 23, 43; Acts 2, 38; 5, 31; 10, 43; 13, 38; 26, 18.

70. SB I, 421.

71. This is the position of Burkitt, *Journal of Theol. Studies*, XXXIII (1932), 253-255. On the other hand, Lohmeyer, *Das Vaterunser*, pp. 112, 126, believes that the aorist does not justify us in drawing this conclusion.

72. The second part is completely missing in Luke, despite the number of manuscripts. In the first part the variants between Luke and Matthew are of little importance. We find the same text in the *Didache*, 8, 2, and in the *Epistle of Polycarp*, 7, 2. This is the more remarkable since for the first time we have the subjunctive of the aorist, instead of the imperative which is quite customary for the negative in Koine Greek. But we must not draw any conclusion from this change. In other texts the subjunctive is no less absolute than the imperative: e.g., Mt. 7, 6; 6, 34. With time the text suffered significant alterations. The Church of Africa used to say: "Ne passus fueris induci nos in temptationem," which we find in the codex Bobbiensis, and in the translation of the *Itala*. The conjunction "and" is often missing. It is quite possible that Tertullian influenced this change. In his commentary on the *Our Father* he writes: "Ne nos inducas in temptationem, id est, ne nos patiaris induci ab eo utique qui temptat" (*De oratione*, VIII; *P.L.*, I, 1165.

Tertullian was still reciting the translation according to the Greek text, but Cyprian was already saying: "et ne patiaris nos induci in temptationem" (*De oratione*, XXV; *P.L.* IV, 536). In a parallel manner the Church of Asia Minor understood the text in the same sense. Denis of Alexandria comments: "Let us not fall into temptation" *Frag.*; *P.G.*, X, 1601. A hundred years earlier Marcion wrote: "*Kai me aphes emas eisenechthenai eis peirasmon.*" Finally, the same text was influenced by two other scriptural quotations: "Non me derelinquas usquequaque nimis" (Ps. 119, 8, and St. Paul's affirmation: "You can trust God not to let you be tried beyond your strength" (1 Cor. 10, 13). St. Hilary comments on Ps. 118, 8, saying: "quod et in dominicae orationis ordine continetur, cum dicitur: Non derelinquas nos in tentatione, quam ferre non possimus" (*Tr. in Ps. 118*), *P.L.*, IX, 510.

74. *Comm. in Ez. XIV*, 48; *P.L.* XXV, 485.

75. *Tr. XIV in Matth.*, *P.L.*, XX, 362.

We find the same idea expressed in St. Augustine (*De sermone Domini*, II, 9; *P.L.* XXXIV, 1282), and in pseudo-Augustine (*Sermo 84*; *P.L.*, XXXIX, 1909). The Greek Church gives the same variant in the liturgy of Alexandria, the liturgy of St. James, in both the Greek and Syriac versions, in the Coptic liturgy; cf. C. A. Swainson, *The Greek Liturgies* (Cambridge, 1884), pp. 6, 62, 225-226, 306-307, 343.

75. The verb *eispherein* means, first of all, a local displacement. Used in a figurative sense, it retains a certain spatial nuance (Acts 17, 20; Hermas, *Sim*, VIII, 6, 5). The Septuagint always uses the verb in a material sense, never

figuratively. Here the verb is stronger than *eiserchomai* (Mt. 26, 41), which is used in the scene of Gethsemane when Jesus exhorts his disciples to pray "not to be put to the test." The petition of the Lord's Prayer asks God himself not to lead us into temptation. God is the active subject of the sentence. The matter is obvious when we consider that the Septuagint translates the same verb by *agein, eisagein*. Moreover, we find the verb in a Berlin papyrus of the sixth century containing Mt. 6, 9-13.

The noun *peirasmos* specifies the situation from which we ask to be spared. In order to limit its significance it is important to be quite precise regarding the *author* and the *object* of the temptation. Classical Greek scarcely ever uses the word *peirazein* in a religious sense. The verb signifies "to strive, to try"; or, in a hostile sense, "to test." Both verb and noun express the results of a trial, an acquired experience. The trial then takes on an educative meaning.

76. Ws. 3, 5; Si. 4, 17; 34, 10; 44, 20; 1 M. 2, 52; Jdt. 8, 25-27.
77. *Pirke Abot*, 5, 3.
78. SB IV, 470-480.
79. Cf. R. Schnackenburg, *Die sittliche Botschaft des N.T.* (Munich, 1954), p. 219, who gives some bibliographical references on this point. *Idem*, H. Seesemann, *Peirasmos, TWNT*, VI, 27.

Among the Hebrew manuscripts of the Judean desert, the roll dealing with the war between the Sons of light and the Sons of darkness has been published by E. I. Sukénik: "Megillôt Genuzôt," I, plate VIII, Qumran Cave I (Oxford, 1955), pp. 135-136: two fragments.

A Latin translation has appeared in *Verbum Domini*, XXIX (1949), 47.

80. Sometimes this same word expresses the hostile trial of adversaries, e.g., in regard to the Pharisees and Sadducees (Mk. 8, 11; 10, 2; 12, 15; Mt. 22, 35; Lk. 10, 25.

81. Cf, 1 Cor. 7, 5; 2 Cor. 2, 11; 1 Th. 3, 5; Mt. 4, 3; Lk. 8, 12-13; Re. 2, 10.
82. Cf. study of K. G. Kuhn *"Peirasmos-amartia-sarx," im N.T.," Zeitschrift für Theol. und Kirche*, XLIX (1952), 200-222.

83. It is difficult, because of the parallelism (to mention just one reason), to hold the hypothesis of C. Jaeger, "A propos de deux passages du sermon sur la montagne," *Revue d'histoire et de philosophie religieuses*, XVIII (1938), 415-416. The author understands the temptation as that of the man who tempts God.

The text, proper to Matthew, is well authenticated by the manuscripts. We find allusions to this verse in the sacerdotal prayer (Jn. 17, 15) and in St. Paul: "The Lord will rescue (*rusetai*) me from all evil attempts (*ponerou*) on me" (2 Tm. 4, 18). The same idea is found in the *Didache* (10, 5) and in rabbinical prayers.

84. The preposition *pao* places the stress on the person of the deliverer, whereas *ek* emphasizes the danger and the action of deliverance.

85. E.g., Ws. 16,8; cf. also 1 S. 19, 9; Jb. 1, 1, 8; Mt. 5, 11.
86. E.g., Dt. 17, 12; 19, 19; 21, 21.
87. Cf. Mt. 12, 35; 1 Cor. 5, 13.
88. It is odd that Paul should translate the neuter of Dt. 13, 6; 17, 7; 19, 19; 22, 24, by the masculine (1 Cor. 5, 13).

89. It is found in codex E of Basle (07 Gregory), codex L of Paris (019 Gregory). It is missing in all the old uncials, in most manuscripts of the Itala, and in the Vulgate. Early commentators, Greek or African, make no allusion to it.

90. The text and its use are a reference to the Old Testament; cf. 1 Ch. 29, 11. As for the doxology, the manuscripts show variants: *Basileia* in the Berlin papyrus, k, *Didache*; *dunamis* is missing from the Berlin papyrus sy'; Amen is not found in T³, k, *Didache*.

The Lord's Prayer

91. We find several secondary variants in the text: Lk. 11, 2: *eltheto* instead of elthato
Lk. 11, 4: *aphiemen* instead of *aphiomen*
panti opheilonti sometimes with, sometimes without the article.
Between the first and the second petitions, D introduces *eph' emas* which is found in the German translation: this is an explanation of the text (cf. Lk. 11, 20) or an insertion by Marcion.

92.

Matthew	Luke
6, 9 pater emon, o en	11, 2 pater
tois ouranois	11, 3 didou
6, 11 dos	kath'emeran
semeron	11, 4 amartias
12 opheilemata	kai gar
os	autoi aphiomen panti
emeis aphekamen tois opheiletais	opheilonti.

93. This is the case with *os kai* and *kai gar*, which translate the participle of *hôb*.

94. Codex Bezae has introduced *eph'emas* between the first and the second petitions in Luke; the Latin text links this to the first petition, Western tradition to the second, giving the reading: "Sanctificetur nomen tuum super nos." The Bible knows a sanctification, *en*, or *enopion*, but never *epi*. However, this link exists with the subject: Let us just bear your name (Is. 4, 1; cf. Jr. 14, 9; Is. 63, 16, 19; Gn. 48, 16; Dt. 14, 23; 28, 10). We find this form again in ancient Christian literature (Jm. 2, 7; *Hermas, Sim.,* VIII, 6, 4).

95. The "name dwelling in our hearts" recalls Dt. 12, 11; 14, 23; 16, 2, 6, 11; Ps. 74, 7; Ezk. 43, 7.

96. *Didache,* 8.

97. With the variant "among us," The text is attested by two minor manuscripts, No. 700 (British Museum, 2610 Egerton) and No. 162 (Cod. Vaticanus). Gregory of Nyssa mentions it three times in his homilies on the *Our Father,* stating that this text was found in Luke. Maximus the Confessor attests the same petition and gives the text of No. 162. We have two indirect attestations, one in the *Acts of Thomas* (C. 27), the other in the liturgy of Constantinople.

98. Cf. *Test. XII, Jud.,* 24, 2; in E. Lohmeyer, *Das Vaterunser,* p. 191.

Chapter IV

THE TEACHING OF JESUS ON PRAYER

The vocabulary used by the Synoptics to express prayer is of special interest.

Semantics

The most frequently used term is the root *euche*, which in classical Greek means *to pray* or *to make a vow*. The Septuagint translated the Hebrew verb by *proseuchomai*, generally using the prefix;[1] the meaning "to make a vow" is not used. In the New Testament, except in Jm. 5, 15, the prefix is always found both in the verb and in the noun. This is the usual term to designate prayer in general as a religious attitude.

Very close to *proseuchomai* are *deomai* and *deesis*, which Luke and Paul alone use, with an exception made for Mt. 9, 38. These three words express a prayer of petition in some concrete situation or need (Lk. 5, 12; 9, 38; 21, 36; 22, 32).

Erotao, which originally meant *to question, to invite*, expresses a modest and respectful request. Only John uses it to mean prayer addressed to God. The fourth evangelist uses this verb for Jesus' prayer (Jn. 14, 16; 16, 26; 17, 9, 15, 20) or for the prayer which the disciples addressed to Jesus (Jn. 4, 31; 1 Jn. 5, 16).

Aiteo, on the other hand, means to ask, to demand, in both profane and religious usage. It expresses less intimacy and more impetuosity. Jesus never used it when speaking of his prayer nor when praying (Mt. 5, 42; 7, 7; 18, 19; 21, 22; Lk. 11, 5-13).

The verb *eulogeo* has a clearly biblical stamp and signifies *to praise*; it also conveys the idea of gratitude (Lk. 1, 64; 2, 34) when God is its subject. Rather similar to this verb is *eucharisteo*, of Hellenistic origin, which expresses gratitude toward God. We find these two used interchangeably in the account of the multiplication of the loaves[2] and of the Last Supper,[3] where the two influences, Palestinian and Greek, are manifested in the editing of the narratives.[4]

If we pass from the vocabulary to the teaching of Jesus, our investigation benefits by following the several evangelists insofar as they give evidence of autonomous traditions.

Matthew 5, 44

In the Sermon on the Mount, Matthew has grouped the essential themes of the gospel together. Prayer is alluded to in the exposition of the new law which perfects "the Law and the Prophets." Love of one's neighbor must extend even to one's enemies. "Love your enemies and pray for those who persecute you" (Mt. 5, 44).[5] The assertion "hate your enemy" is nowhere to be found in Scripture; on the contrary, even the Old Testament demands love of one's enemies,[7] and gives us some examples.[8] The fact remains that the Psalms, composed in times of persecution, curse God's enemies. Evidently we are not dealing here with personal revenge but with defending the divine cause. Complete light will come only from Christ, whose work consists in saving, not in losing.

Though hatred of one's enemies was taught by some rabbis in the days of Christ, it was by no means a general rule. However, the Romans reproached the Jews for "their hatred toward men."[9] Within the Jewish community the Pharisee hated the *am haares*, who did not know the Law (Jn. 7, 49).

Contrary to this mentality, Jesus demands — and the imperative is formal — "love your enemies." We are further urged to do this by the precept to go to the lengths of praying for our persecutors, the very people who instigated the Psalms of imprecation and malediction.[10]

The Sermon on the Mount violently contrasts with Jewish concepts. The acceptance of persecution appears as a law of growth for the kingdom (Mt. 5, 11-12); those who endure it are blessed. The example of Jesus, victim of hatred, reveals to us the foundations on which the messianic community is built. Jesus prayed for his executioners as he hung on the Cross (Lk. 23, 34).[11] Such a disposition gave his sacrifice its dimension of universal reconciliation. In this he was to be imitated by Stephen (Acts 7, 60).

The fundamental reason for this is that the God we invoke is the Father of the good and the wicked, of the persecuted and the persecutors. He came to us in the day of our sins. Our prayer would be pharisaical if we did not remember that we are faithless debtors (the *Our Father*), if we did not ask for the community of all men who have been gratuitously saved. God demands more than mere *forgiveness* (Mt. 6, 12, 14-15; cf. Mk. 11, 26; Mt. 18, 23-25); he wants this forgiveness to be manifested by positive action: prayer for the persecutor. This action is proof that the agape of God who forgives dwells in us and motivates the dialogue of filial prayer.

Matthew 6, 1-6, 7-8

The Sermon on the Mount then goes on to enunciate the principles of the new law; its practice must be inspired not by men but by love for the Father in heaven. Three typical applications of this Christian practice are given: almsgiving, prayer, and fasting.[12]

As we have seen, the *Our Father* is introduced by two groups of *logia* (Mt. 6, 5-6, 7-8). In the context of the Sermon on the Mount, Matthew explains how prayer orders relations with God: "When you pray, do not imitate the hypocrites: they love to say their prayers standing up in the synagogues and at the street corners for people to see them. I tell you solemnly, they have had their reward. But when you pray, go to your private room[13] and, when you have shut your door, pray to your Father who is in that secret place, and your Father who sees all that is done in secret will reward you" (Mt. 6, 5-6).

Christ's directives are antithetic; they are the opposite of what the hypocrites practice. Therefore, the first question is the rectification of an abuse and of a given state of affairs. Despite appearances, Jesus in no way invalidates collective prayer, whose superiority he elsewhere proclaims (Mt. 18, 19-20). There do exist hypocrites who act a part even in personal prayer; all prayer finds its worth in interior dispositions, which remain God's secret.

The efficacy of prayer does not come from us but from God accomplishing his work. This is why the spirit of prayer will always seek solitude, according to the example of Jesus, giving to the dialogue with God its twofold character of reserve and intimacy.[14]

After the hypocrites come the pagans. "In your prayers do not babble as the pagans do, for they think that by using many words they will make themselves heard. Do not be like them; your Father knows what you need before you ask him" (Mt. 6, 7-8).

It is easy to see that these two verses are not linked with what precedes them (vv. 5-6). This *logion* in itself does not introduce any text of prayer; it offers an exhortation on the interior dispositions for prayer and does not attempt to give us a model. After verse 8 we do not expect an example, only silence.

Already the Old Testament had reacted against this *Battalogia*. Isaiah wrote: "You may multiply your prayers, I shall not listen" (Is. 1, 15). Elijah spoke with biting irony of the prayer of the pagan priests (1 K. 18, 27). The history of religion, as well as religious sociology, justifies this criticism, aimed at both Jews and pagans, and denounces a threat that was ever showing its head.[15]

Prayer gives God no information;[16] it does not seek to enlighten him by our words; still less does it try to exert any magical pressure to coerce the divinity, as did the priests of Baal on Mount Carmel. Christian prayer is inspired by its object, *the things that are God's,* which the petitioner knows and desires efficaciously. It tests man, not God; "your Father knows . . . " Does this mean that prayer is useless? Why pray? St. John Chrysostom replies: "You pray not to teach God something, but to favorably dispose him toward you; you pray to draw closer to God through the habit of prayer; you pray to humble yourself, to remind you of your sins."[17]

The struggle which may exist, the tension such as that manifested in the prolonged prayer of Gethsemane, wrests from God man's consent, man's own submission. At this cost victory is assured, and the kingdom of God is inaugurated. The granting of the prayer can only be the fruit of our trust and of our filial submission.

Matthew 7, 7-11

The same Sermon on the Mount, after enunciating the superhuman demands of the new law, exhorts us once more to prayer. This exhortation in Luke follows the teaching of the *Our Father.* It is difficult to say what was the original context. The only obvious fact is that, in both cases, these *logia* are related to the *Our Father.*

What connection is there in Matthew between this teaching and what precedes it? Every hypothesis which has been expressed discourages anyone from taking a firm stand and, even more, from claiming to have found a satisfactory answer to the question. It would seem far better to deal with each text by itself so as to clarify its teaching.

The text proper in Matthew, as in Luke, is composed of aphorisms, which are followed by a comparison of the Father and the Son. "Ask, and it will be given to you; search, and you will find; knock, and the door will be opened to you.[18] For the one who asks always receives; the one who searches always finds; the one who knocks will always have the door opened to him" (Mt. 7, 7-8).

The texts of Matthew and Luke have a striking identity. We are in the presence of a *logion* which has suffered no revision. The passive form is used here as in the *Our Father* to avoid using the name of God, which is the subject understood.[19]

The verb *aiteo* is accompanied by two others which are very similar. *Zeteo,* which the Greek philosophers used for the search of wisdom (cf. 1. Cor. 1, 20) designates a spiritual attitude[20] which keys up man's effort and reveals the center of his preoccupation. The verb is associated with the kingdom of God;[21] to pray is essentially *to seek God*. The verb shows that prayer is an existential attitude which engages the whole man and his whole life.[22] *Krouo* is found only three times in the Septuagint.[23] Since God is present at prayer, he owes it to himself to open himself, given that his plan is to save man.

The imperative denotes the necessity of asking for what is primarily God's affair and which surpasses human means. God owes it to himself to bring his own work to a happy ending. This conviction constitutes the faith and the trust of the petitioner. Man is certain of being heard if he asks for what Jesus in the *Our Father* taught him to ask for, subordinating every petition to the essential, God's kingdom. The intransitive form of the verbs proves that God's gift is unlimited.

Jesus' teaching here has recourse to a comparison which, in its general tenor, is found in the same context in Luke. "Is there a man among you who would hand his son a stone when he asked for bread? Or would he hand him a snake when he asked for a fish? If you, then, who are evil, know how to give your children what is good, how much more will your Father in heaven give good things to those who ask him!" (Mt. 7, 9-11)

The comparison with Luke reveals tangible differences. It would seem that the third Gospel gives a freer translation of the original which was common to it and to Matthew. Luke introduces *patera.* He abandons the double parallelism of bread-stone, fish —

The Teaching of Jesus on Prayer

snake,[24] and substitutes fish-snake, egg-scorpion, which has a gradation, (useful-useless, useful-harmful). More important is the substitution of Luke's *Pneuma agion* for Matthew's *agatha*.

The comparison clearly shows that the preceding aphorisms dealt with God. Here he is called Father in the full meaning of the word as it appears in the *Our Father*. The evangelist draws an *a fortiori* conclusion (compare with Mt. 6, 25). The comparison starts with things essential to life: bread, fish, which constitute the diet of the poor (cf. the multiplication of loaves) and makes possible a connection with the *Our Father*. God gives what is indispensable. The gift reflects the image of the giver, who alone is good. We must lift our prayer to his height to discover this goodness and we must adjust our desires, not to our native wickedness but to the goodness of God. The word *agatha* represents the blessings of salvation (cf. Heb. 9, 11; 10, 1). God gives because he is love, in virtue of his nature and his perfection, and Luke makes this clear without misleading: God gives himself, for his perfect gift is *his Spirit*.

When affirming in a parallel *logion* that everything is the object of prayer, of granting, Mark (11, 24) clearly states that this prayer must be accompanied by the faith that moves mountains: "I tell you therefore: everything you ask and pray for, believe that you have it already,[25] and it will be yours." The singular turn of phrase in the Greek "believe that you have it already" reminds us of Mt. 6, 8 and Isaiah: "Long before they call I shall answer; before they stop speaking I shall have heard" (Is. 65, 24).

Prayer does not serve God, but man, in the measure in which it expresses his faith in it. By prayer man enters into the economy of salvation. Faith, like the working of Christ, is capable of working miracles (Mt. 9, 29); in both of these we are in the presence of God's sovereignty; God puts his power at our service.

Exegetes ask if God answers every prayer, even the most unjustified. They are posing a false problem. God's promise is granted to every prayer formulated by a living faith.

Conditions of prayer

Spiritual demands, scattered throughout Matthew's Gospel, prove in an obvious manner that prayer cannot be dissociated from daily life. Jesus very severely rebukes the Pharisees "who swallow the property of widows, while making a show of lengthy prayers" (Mk. 12, 40; Lk. 20, 47).

Prayer, supported by fasting, is more efficacious. The very structure of the Sermon on the Mount had revealed the bond that exists between the two. Jesus explicitly taught this, if the verse be authentic, at the healing of the epileptic boy: "As for this kind (of devil), it is cast out only by prayer and fasting" (Add. Mt. 17, 21).[26] Fasting, for Jesus, is a sign of faith and of the *metanoia* of children towards their Father. It makes possible a more efficacious submission to the economy of salvation through an attitude of life.

More explicit is the assurance given to the prayer of the community. We find this *logion* only in Matthew (Mt. 18, 19-20): "I tell you solemnly once again, if two of you on earth agree to ask anything at all, it will be granted to you by my Father in heaven. For where two or three meet in my name, I shall be there with them."

This text has no parallel in the other Synoptics. In Matthew's Gospel, it continues the teaching of the *Our Father* and our Lord's last promise (Mt. 28, 20). According to his habit, the first evangelist accentuates the ecclesial aspect of the gospel. Moreover, the eighteenth chapter is devoted to the community. In that chapter prayer plays an essential part.

Matthew's assertions find analogies only in contemporary Judaism, which grants a special efficacy to the communal prayer of the synagogue. R. Acha b. Chanina based this belief on the midrash which commented on Job 36, 5 and Psalm 55, 19. The Jews believed in the presence of God in their midst. R. Chanina bar Teradjon had already said: "If two people are gathered together without there being question among them of the Torah, it is an assembly of mockers. But if two people are gathered together and speak of the Torah, the Shekina dwells in their midst. Why is God called Maqôm, "the place"? Because in whatever place the just are, there, too, God is found near them."[27]

The unlimited power of prayer rests, first of all, on the community, even reduced to its simplest terms. Jesus gives the reason for this; it is assured of the invisible presence of Christ, the bond of the Christian community. This presence of Jesus brings about and extends the Shekina, i.e., God's presence among his people. What conjoins in the New Covenant is neither blood nor race, but the belonging to Christ of those who, baptized in his name,[28] live the experience of faith in the community of brothers.

In the account of the events of Gethsemane, Matthew and Mark relate the saying of Jesus: "You should be awake, and praying not to be put to the test" (Mt. 26, 41; Mk. 14, 38).

This expression, of course, refers, first of all, to the struggle against sleep. But Jesus enlarges the episode to recall to mind that vigilance is a permanent disposition of the Christian, since the danger lying in wait for him is permanent. For the Apostles the account of the Passion of Jesus shows only too well to what point prayer and vigilance were necessary to resist trial. For the Christian the fury of the infernal forces constitutes, in the eschatological era, the great temptation.

In this trial, prayer recognizes God's role, vigilance that of man.

The evangelist of prayer

There is hardly an exegete who has not pointed out the importance of prayer in St. Luke's Gospel. The evangelist shows us Christ in prayer five times, whereas the parallel passages do not mention it (Lk. 9, 18; 9, 28; 11, 1; 6, 12; 3, 21).[29] To the Greek evangelist, prayer seemed to be Christ's habitual attitude and a characteristic element of Christianity. For this reason it runs like a golden thread through his Gospel and the Acts. The third Gospel begins with the prayer of expectation of the Jewish people and ends with the thanksgiving of Christians (Lk. 1, 10; 24, 53).

The birth of John the Baptist is announced to Zechariah as God's answer to his prayer. The name of the boy means "Yahweh-is-gracious" (Lk. 1, 13). Doubtless we are not dealing here with any particular prayer but with an attitude more alive to the messianic expectation (Lk. 2, 25) than to carnal descent. In the birth of John God gives a sign of the messianic fulfillment.

Luke, too, is the only one to mention the prayer of benediction, if we except the multiplication of the loaves, common to the three Synoptics. He never uses the word *eucharistein,* not even at the Last Supper, whereas the other two evangelists use *eulogein* and *eucharistein* interchangeably, both of which translate the same Hebrew word, *bêrêk.*

The Greek word *eulogia, eulogein,* mean to speak well of or to speak well of someone, but more often they mean to praise or to exalt. The concept of blessing was rather foreign to the Greek world. The meaning of *eulogein* has been greatly changed by the religious language of Israel. The Septuagint uses the word more than four hundred times to express habitually the idea of blessing.

Primitive man possessed a power, as it were, of blessing which he could transmit to his descendants.[30] This concept appears in Ecclesiasticus: "A father's blessing makes the houses of his children firm" (Si. 3, 9).

Implicitly or explicitly the author of the blessing is the Lord God. He blesses by the goodness that he shows toward a people or an individual. His blessing is a grace that accompanies the work of his hands. He blesses creation (Gn. 1, 28), mankind, animals, and institutions.

Man, first of all, is the object of God's blessing throughout the history of salvation; Adam, Noah, Abraham, and Moses were blessed by Yahweh (Gn. 17, 7-8; 26, 3-5). The blessing of Abraham affected all his descendants until the fulfillment of the promise in Jesus Christ. The efficacy of this blessing was not magical; it was bound up with the observance of the Law and purity of life.[31]

Blessing formed part of the cult; the priest pronounced it in

Yahweh's name. This was already the case with Melchizedek, who blessed Abraham (Gn. 14, 19); with Moses, who blessed the amphictyony of Israel (Dt. 33, 1-29), with Joshua (Jos. 14, 13; 22, 6-7). The high priest Heli (1 S. 2, 20) and Samuel blessed the people (1 S. 9, 13). David blessed in the name of the Lord of hosts on the occasion of the transfer of the Ark (2 S. 6, 18), and Solomon at the dedication of the Temple (1 R. 8, 14, 55).

Slowly blessing became a privilege of the priesthood, basing itself on the example of Aaron (Nb. 6, 22-27). Later the Levites were charged with pronouncing the words of benediction (Dt. 10, 8; 21, 5; 1 Ch. 23, 13): "On your people, blessing!" (Ps. 3, 8). Under the influence of the cult, blessing was either a task of God or of his representative, or that of man "blessing God," or the name of God, i.e., recognizing in him his power to bless.[32]

Blessing the name of God was the task of the Jewish community. This was done in prayer, in the cult, and at home. To bless was to put one's trust in God in faith, hope, and thanksgiving, and to glorify him. The formula of blessing the name of God introduced prayer and enumerated the works of Yahweh (Tb. 12, 6). Post-exilic Judaism developed the role of blessing that had its own ritual in the Temple, in the synagogue, and in the religious life of Israel.

The Synoptics, Luke in particular took up and developed the idea of blessing. Man blesses God by praise and thanksgiving. Zechariah's chant begins with the words Eulogetos, "Blessed be the Lord, the God of Israel" (Lk. 1, 68-79).[33] Like Tobit he enumerates the great deeds of God. The same applies to the old man Simeon (Lk. 2, 28), who blessed God in thanksgiving because he had been granted the privilege of seeing with his own eyes the salvation of Israel. In turn Simeon blessed the child's parents (Lk. 2, 34), because they found themselves in the orbit of God's benediction. Mary was blessed when the angel visited her; she was the *eulogemene* (cf. Jdt. 13, 18; Septuagint 15, 12; Dt. 28, 3-6; Jg. 5, 24). If fertility be already a sign of blessing, *a fortiori* was this true of the mother of the Messiah (Lk. 1, 28-42).

The Messiah above all others is the Blessed One. The crowd acclaimed him, chanting: "Blessings on him who comes in the name of the Lord" (Mk. 11, 9; Mt. 21, 9; Lk. 19, 38; Jn. 12, 13).[34] Mark adds: "Blessings on the coming kingdom of our father David . . . " This verse signifies two things: the Messiah was protected by God's blessing; he was greeted[35] by the crowd that submitted itself to him.

When he gave bread to the crowd, Jesus himself, like the father of every Jewish family, pronounced the blessing over the bread.[36] The three Synoptics complete the blessing with the precise detail, *anablepsas eis ton ouranon,* which unites miracle and prayer.[37] While breaking with the hereditary usages of Israel,[38] Jesus imparted to the scene a messianic significance, in union with his Father, whose work he was accomplishing.

At the Last Supper, as in the inn of Emmaus, Jesus remained faithful to the words of blessing.[39] He also blessed children (Mk. 10, 16), and the disciples at the Ascension; these answered with a eulogy to God (Lk. 24, 50-53). In the Acts, Peter sums up Jesus' activities by saying that he was sent by God to bless (Acts 3, 25-26). Those who are elected by the grace of God, who are protected by God's blessing can only bless, even those who curse them (Lk. 6, 28), by neutralizing their curses.[40] In the eschatological separation, they will be welcomed as those *blessed* by the Father (Mt. 25, 34).

Still more surprising appears Christ's exhortation when, according to Luke, he sent the seventy-two disciples on their first mission (Lk. 10, 2-3; Mt. 9, 37):[41] "The harvest is rich but the laborers are few, so ask the Lord of the harvest to send laborers to his harvest."

It was a solemn moment. The number seventy-two recalls to mind the number of the elders who assisted Moses in the government of the people (Nb. 11, 16). The rabbis of Christ's day thought that the world was composed of seventy-two peoples.[42]

The mission of the seventy-two therefore signifies the universal proclamation of God's kingdom, placing all mankind before the choice. The metaphor of the harvest expresses God's work which is becoming effective through time and despite vicissitudes[43] until the eschatological day.[44]

By insisting on the need for laborers, Jesus seems to be inciting his own to action. But paradoxically he asks them to pray. Prayer is recognition of God's primacy in the work which fulfills the plan of salvation. Jesus' words echoed the petitions of the *Our Father*. God gives the seed and the increase. Missionary work can only consist in doing the Father's work (1 Cor. 3, 9-11; Ep. 2, 10). Jesus does not minimize the task of those he sends, but he places it in its proper place in the economy of salvation. Paul of Tarsus never dissociated the apostolate and prayer, prayer being the contemplation of the Father's work, and the apostolate prayer at work. In the same account Luke gives us two parables which are connected with prayer and which he alone relates.

The parable of the importunate friend (Lk. 11, 5-8) forms part of the same sequence which the third evangelist devotes to prayer. It is preceded by the *Our Father,* and followed by aphorisms with which it has no proper connection since the subject is not the same. The parable seems to speak of the friend's importunity as a condition of success, while verses 9-13 merely exhort us to pray with a filial trust. Matthew, moreover, had separated the *logia* to insert them in the Sermon on the Mount (Mt. 7, 7-11), far from the *Our Father*.

The parable of the importunate friend must therefore be explained, not by its context, but by its interior data.[45]

> "He also said to them, 'Suppose one of you has a friend and goes to him in the middle of the night to say, "My friend, lend me three loaves, because a friend of mine on his travels has just arrived at my house and I have nothing to offer him"; and the man answers from inside the house, "Do not bother me. The door is bolted now, and my children and I are in bed; I cannot get up to give it to you." I tell you, if the man does not get up and give it him for friendship's sake, persistence will be enough to make him get up and give his friend all he wants.

> "So I say to you: Ask, and it will be given to you; search, and you will find; knock, and the door will be opened to you. For the one who asks always receives; the one who searches always finds; the one who knocks will always have the door opened to him."

Certain exegetes have sought to find in Jesus' teaching a lesson in persevering prayer that obtains what it asks for by means of insistence and importunity.[46] In fact, God, not man, is at the center of this parable of contrasts. This is an *a fortiori* argument; if, then, a friend ends by giving in to insistence in order to have a little peace, how much more does your Father hear appeals and come to our aid.

In no way is the peevish friend an image of God. On the contrary, the Father wants to give more than we want to receive, according to St. Augustine: *Plus vult ille dare quam nos accipere.*[47] With a touch of irony, Jesus animates a filial faith and "creates the atmosphere of trusting prayer."[48]

Father Buzy reduces the parable to the following comparison: "Just as a man asking a good turn from a friend, after meeting categorical refusal, obtains what he wants by means of insistence and importunity, so God will hear our prayer provided it be persevering. God first pretends not to be heeding our prayer, even though it had to go to the lengths of importunity."[49]

God wishes to be importuned; importunity is the rule of prayer, not because it tries God's patience, but because it shows man's perseverance. God allows himself to be begged in order to excite man's patience, a fruit of the theological virtues. Such was the prayer of the paralytic by the Sheep Pool, such was the prayer of the blind man of Jericho, and such was the prayer of the Canaanite woman who ended by wearying the disciples and extorting the miracle. God knows that delay sharpens desire and magnifies the gift in our eyes.

Luke is also the only one to relate the parable of the judge and the widow (Lk. 18, 2-8).

> "There was a judge in a certain town," he said, "who had neither fear of God nor respect for man. In the same town there was a widow who kept on coming to him and saying, 'I want justice from

you against my enemy!' For a long time he refused, but at last he said to himself, 'Maybe I have neither fear of God nor respect for man, but since she keeps pestering me I must give this widow her just rights, or she will persist in coming and worry me to death.'[50]

"And the Lord said, 'You notice what the unjust judge has to say? Now will not God see justice done on his chosen who cry to him day and night[51] even when he delays to help them?[52] I promise you, he will see justice done to them, and done speedily."

In Luke's way of thinking the parable must illustrate the teaching "about the need to pray continually and never lose heart" (Lk. 18, 1). The evangelist, therefore, means to shape the sense of the parable to read in it an exhortation to persevering prayer. Do Luke's editorial additions really agree with the contents of the story? Is perseverance in prayer the teaching that actually comes from the parable?

The two characters are well known in biblical literature, the unjust judge and the helpless widow. The principal role is played by the judge who holds the center of the stage, not by the widow. The whole narrative is subordinated to him, and the lesson will evolve from him. We are not in the presence of an ordinary comparison, which might seem shocking, even scandalous, but of a parable of contrasts which develops through antithesis.

The parable is fundamentally a teaching about God, infinitely good, always ready to answer without delay the appeals of his children. Though the unjust judge only yields because of repeated pleas, God on the other hand "will see justice done." Christians will have no need to multiply prayer nor to beseech at great length; they are sure of obtaining justice and mercy.

The parable contains a lesson on Christian prayer, although only in a secondary and subordinate way. Prayer will always be heard. The granting does not necessarily correspond to our petition, but to our need. God gives what he judges just and necessary. He is not an automatic dispenser but a Father who sees better and more clearly than our appeals. "His ways are not our ways, his justice goes further than ours. He always and promptly hears the prayers of his elect, but often differently and in a better way than they expected."[53]

Prayer here appears not only as an episode but as a Christian essential, since it exercises faith. Jesus presents his teaching in an ironic way to make us realize the absurdity of fears and doubt. The Christian's life resembles that of the widow. The Christian's constant preoccupation during his life must be to turn to the heavenly Father for help. Faith carries with it the granting of the prayer. God's goodness inspires trusting prayer, which remains for the Christian the essential lesson of the parable.

The parable of the Pharisee and the tax collector follows the preceding one in St. Luke (Lk. 18, 9-14).

> He spoke the following parable to some people who prided themselves on being virtuous[54] and despised everyone else. 'Two men went up to the Temple to pray, one a Pharisee, the other a tax collector. The Pharisee stood[55] there and said this prayer to himself, "I thank you, God, that I am not like this tax collector here. I fast twice a week; I pay tithes on all I get."[56] The tax collector stood some distance away, not daring[57] even to raise his eyes to heaven; but he beat his breast and said, "God, be merciful to me, a sinner." This man, I tell you, went home again at rights with God; the other did not.'[58]

The parable does not represent a parody or a caricature of the Pharisee.[59] It is easy to find prayers from the time of Jesus which reflect the same state of mind. For instance in SB we read: "I thank you, Lord God, that you have set me among those seated in this house of instruction and not among those seated at the crossroads (money changers and merchants). I rise early, and they too rise early; I rise to study the words of the law, but they out of vanity. I work, and they work; I work and am rewarded; they work and receive no reward. I run, and they run; I run toward the life of the world to come while they run toward the abyss of destruction."[60]

If the parable does not deal exclusively with prayer, it includes it. It uses the example of prayer to characterize the spiritual attitude of the Pharisee and the tax collector.[61] Both prayers express a state of soul. The Pharisee justifies himself, his prayer is self-centered and, for this reason, is inefficacious. It is not an appeal, not even a thanksgiving implying gratitude. It shows no understanding of either dependence on God or sin. The tax collector lays bare his desperate situation. His trial balance sheet is off; before God he is only a sinner. His prayer is related to Psalm 51, 13, 19. It is a cry for divine mercy, which is inspired only by the will to save; out of goodness, God justifies the sinner, who can never merit justification. Before God man is nothing; worse, he is a sinner. The humility of his prayer therefore does nothing more than express his ontological state and the lucidity of his conscience, illumined by God's light which he welcomes.

The account of Jesus' last days in Jerusalem, the eschatological discourse which preludes the Passion, ends with an exhortation to vigilance at the approach of *the Day*.

This is found in Luke alone: "Watch yourselves, or your hearts will be coarsened with debauchery and drunkenness and the cares of life, and that day will be sprung on you suddenly, like a trap. For it will come down on every living man on the face of the earth. Stay awake, praying at all times for the strength to survive all that is going to happen, and to stand with confidence before the Son of man" (Lk. 21, 34-36).[62]

Prayer and vigilance are here associated as in the exhortation which Jesus addressed to his companions at Gethsemane, reported by Matthew and Mark (Mt. 26, 41; Mk. 14, 38).[63] The *logion* widens the exhortation and makes it a general law of Christian life. Christ's recommendation enables us to fit personal drama into the general drama; vigilance is the law of the individual as it is of the community, following the example of Christ himself when his hour had come.

Vigilance tinges the meaning of prayer; both must be active. Prayer is the consciousness of inevitable struggle; it must therefore be extended by vigilance which is an alerting of all resources. Christian prayer is an armed prayer; a filial trust in the heavenly Father does not exempt from watchfulness (cf. Col. 4, 2). The Master's exhortation echoes the petitions of the *Our Father* and illustrates the eschatological significance of Christian life.

The concept of vigilance is bound up with eschatology.[64] The parables of the servants (Mt. 24, 45-51) and of the virgins (Mt. 25, 1-13) compare the parousia to a coming in the night. In the apostolic community watchfulness is an image of Christian life itself.[65] Quite naturally, it is, therefore, necessarily allied to prayer.

But vigilance is not enough; God's grace is necessary to undergo the final trial.

APPENDIX: Luke's canticles (Lk. 1, 46-55, 68-79)

St. Luke's Gospel is the only one to retain two canticles, one attributed to Mary,[66] the other to Zechariah. Both pose critical questions which the whole third Gospel raises. First of all, both canticles testify to the fusion of the traditions concerning the Baptist and the Messiah, without any antagonism and in a perfect unity. The text of each canticle is so inextricably linked with the context that it seems necessary to admit that Luke found them in the sources from which he draws his inspiration.

We find in them the impress of pre-Christian Judaism sustained by the messianic expectation. The resemblance with certain liturgical texts of Qumran is striking. The incident, in both cases, is situated within the history of salvation. The authors are steeped in biblical literature and formulate their prayer with expressions from the Old Testament which come up in every verse. As in the prayer of the Old Testament, thanksgiving gushes from the meditation of God's designs.

> My soul proclaims the greatness of the Lord
> and my spirit exults in[67] God my savior;
> because he has looked upon his lowly handmaid.
> Yes, from this day forward all generations will
>   call me blessed,
> for the Almighty has done great things[68] for me.
> Holy is his name,
> and his mercy reaches from age to age[69] for those
>   who fear him.
> He has shown the power of his arm,
> he has routed the proud of heart.
> He has pulled down princes from their thrones
>   and exalted the lowly.

The hungry he has filled with good things, the
  rich sent empty away.
He has come to the help of Israel his servant,
  mindful of his mercy
— according to the promise he made to our ancestors —
of his mercy to Abraham and to his descendants
  for ever.[70]

The *Magnificat* is based on the canticle of Hannah (1 S. 2, 1-10) but also on a number of biblical quotations, of which the prophets and the Psalms, especially the Psalms of the *anawim*, have the lion's share.[71] Yet this does not take from it the freshness of an improvisation.

The canticle is constructed like a hymn, in strophes whose distribution is difficult to make out. It glorifies the work accomplished in Mary by the Holy Spirit. Starting from the personal application, the hymn enlarges the picture and sings of the work of salvation begun in Israel. The promises made to the fathers are fulfilled in Mary. Yahweh has manifested his holiness and mercy, his might and constancy to both.

We find here a characteristic feature of the prayer and attitude of Jesus' entire submission to God's plan, the objectivity of praise where the individual application takes place within the general history. The hymn illustrates and develops the words of Mary: "I am the handmaid of the Lord" (Lk. 1, 38).

The *Magnificat* proclaims along with the advent of the Messiah the sovereignty of God whose might is expressed in paradoxical signs by the reversal of accepted values; the *anawim* take the place of potentates (cf. Mt. 5, 3), the hungry, not the rich, are filled. This serves as a prelude to the background peculiar to St. Luke's Gospel, to the parables of the prodigal son (Lk. 15, 11-32), of the lost sheep, of the rich man and Lazarus (16, 19-31), of the foolish rich man (Lk. 12, 16-21), of the tax collector and the Pharisee, and also the Sermon on the Mount (Lk. 6, 20-49).

To judge the early date of the *Magnificat* we need only note that nowhere does it allude to the person of the Messiah, to his work, or to his Passion. In its structure the hymn is eschatological;

it presents future events as accomplished facts, as is the rule in prophetic writings (cf. Is. 44, 23; Ps. 47, 5-8).

The *Benedictus* (Lk. 1, 68-79) expresses what has been said above: Zechariah "spoke and praised God" (Lk. 1, 64). It is presented as a prophetic chant (Lk. 1, 67); Zechariah was filled with the Holy Spirit. Like the *Magnificat* his canticle is woven of biblical reminiscences.[72] He begins with a blessing after the manner of Jewish prayer.

> Blessed be the Lord,[73] the God of Israel,
> for he has visited his people, he has come to their rescue[74]
> in the House of his servant David,
> even as he proclaimed,
> by the mouth of his holy prophets from ancient times,
> and from the hands of all who hate us.
> Thus he shows mercy to our ancestors,
> thus he remembers his holy covenant,
> the oath he swore
> to our father Abraham[75]
> that he would grant us, free from fear,
> to be delivered from the hands of our enemies,
> to serve him in holiness and virtue
> in his presence, all our days.[76]
> And you, little child,
> you shall be called Prophet of the Most High,
> for you will go before the Lord[77]
> to prepare the way for him.
> To give his people knowledge of salvation
> through the forgiveness of their sins;[78]
> this by the tender mercy of our God
> who from on high will bring the rising Sun[79] to visit us[80]
> to give light to those who live
> in darkness and the shadow of death,
> and to guide our feet
> into the way of peace.

It is composed of two parts. The first (vv. 68-75) bears a closer resemblance to the *Magnificat*. It presents the future as already accomplished, following the literary style of the eschatological hymns. The canticle does not rise above the limits of Israel's expectation, and develops in an Old Testament atmosphere.

Salvation is brought by the Messiah, the "horn of salvation," who comes to fulfill Nathan's prophecy to David (2 S. 7, 12). The first beneficiary is the people, yet this primary does not exclude the remainder of mankind; God visits (cf. Lk. 7, 16; 19, 44) his people by freeing them politically from the occupying power (vv. 71, 74). Exterior independence conditions a holy and just service in interior purity.

The second part (vv. 76-79) is a prophecy concerning the role of John the Baptist in the work of salvation. Prophet of the Most High, his mission put him at the service of God (Lk. 1, 16) and of his Messiah. The latter is called "the rising Sun." The word *anatole* is a translation of the word Messiah in the Septuagint (Jr. 23, 5; Zc. 3, 8; 6, 12). It had become a synonym for the synagogue.[81] Both expressions designate the Messiah. The image signifies the irruption of light and peace on a world of darkness and division (Mt. 4, 14-16). In this way the Messiah will inaugurate the kingdom of God, to which the *Benedictus*, like the *Magnificat*, is subordinated. Of the Passion and the Cross of the Messiah or of his precursor there is no more mention in the *Benedictus* than in the *Magnificat*, whereas they loom large in the third Gospel.

The *Benedictus* adopts the accents of prophetism to proclaim the approach of the Messiah. Closer to Isaiah than to surrounding rabbinism it sings of the new times. It draws less inspiration than the *Magnificat* from the Old Testament. Its composition is heavier, its syntax less Semitic. Each portion is composed of a single sentence, tangled and massive.

Both hymns are based on the promise made to Abraham, the forefather of Israel.

PART II
Chapter IV

1. The prefix appears in Alschylus; cf., Liddell-Scott, *Greek-English Lexicon*.
2. Cf. Mk. 6, 41; Jn. 6, 11; Mk. 8, 6.
3. Mk. 14, 22 *eulogesas;* Mt. 26, 26; Lk. 22, 19; for the chalice, the three accounts give *eucharistesas*.
4. Excellent remarks on this have been made by J. Delorme, "A propos de la derière Cène," *Ami du Clergé* (1955), pp. 657-660.
5. Luke writes: "who treat you badly (*epereazonton*)." This word is used only twice, here in Lk. 6, 28, and in 1 P. 3, 16; it has a more personal shade of meaning, whereas, the verb *diokein* expresses the official persecution of the

Church (Mt. 10, 23; Lk. 21, 12; Mk. 4, 17; Acts 8, 1; 13, 50). Mt. 5, 11 and Lk. 6, 22 show the same difference of viewpoint.

7. Cf. Ex. 23, 4; Lv. 19, 17-18; Pr. 24, 17, 29; 25, 21; Si. 27, 30 — 28, 7.

8. E.g., Gn. 45, 1-15; 1 S. 24; 26; 2 K. 6, 21; Jb. 31, 29; Ps. 140, 5-7.

9. T. Soiron, *Die Bergpredigt* (Freiburg im Br., 1941), p. 297.

10. Cf. Ps. 109, 6-20; cf. Jr. 18, 21-23; Pss. 17, 13-14; 28, 4; 31, 18-19; 40, 15-16; 52, 7; 137; 139, 21-22.

11. This prayer may have, through subsequent harmonization, instigated the changing of *diokonton* into *epereazonton* used in Lk. 6, 28.

12. We have already seen how the Old Testament linked prayer with fasting, which was a means of ensuring the efficacy of the prayer: Jr. 14, 12; 2 Ezr. 1, 4; 9, 1-3; Jl. 1, 14; 2, 12; 15 — 17; the same applies to the *Didache* 8, 1-2.

In post-exilic Judaism, almsgiving appears as a work of piety, e.g., Si. 7, 10; Tb. 12, 8.

13. This allusion is to a room in which Palestinian peasants stored their tools and provisions; there is a possible allusion here to Is. 26, 20.

14. E. Lohmeyer attempts to find here the "cryptical" aspect of the Christian faith which prepares for the eschatological phase; cf. *Vaterunser*, p. 13.

15. F. Heiler, *op. cit.,* pp. 58-59, 116, 361-362.

This "babbling" is aimed at the long forms of prayer which distract, and not at prolonged prayer which consists in recollection; otherwise, the teachings of Jesus (Lk. 18, 1-8) and his example (Mk. 14, 39) would clash with the Sermon on the Mount. "It is one thing to speak much, another to pray much," says St. Augustine, *Epistle, 130,* 10, 19-20; *P.L.*, XXXIII, 501-502. A multiplicity of words dulls and distracts. The prayer of the heart welcomes God's word.

16. D. specifies: "Your Father knows your needs, *before* you open your mouth."

17. *Comm. in Math., Hom.* 4. Cf. also J. Lebreton, *The Life & Teaching of Jesus Christ Our Lord,* I, pp. 176, ftnt. 1.

18. The present in B sy Wh. Luke's text hesitates between *anoigesetai* and *anoichthesetai* (D E W pm. T).

19. SB. I, 443, gives many other examples.

20. *Zetein prosopon tou Theou*; Pss. 24, 6; 27, 8; 40, 17.

21. E.g., Mt. 13, 45; 6, 33; cf. Mt. 6, 10.

22. For the meaning of the word in Jewish life, cf. SB I, 458. The rabbis used the word for one who knocks at the gate of mercy in prayer.

23. In Jg. 19, 22; Sg. 5, 2; Jdt. 14, 14.

24. The antithesis "bread-snake" is lacking in B and the old Itala codices; it appears once in Epiphanius and Origen; the manuscripts giving the antithesis in Luke must have been influenced by the parallel text in Matthew.

25. Because the reading is more difficult, we must retain *elabete* in preference to *lambanete, lempsesthe,* which seem to be mitigations. Christ's axiom is found in the same context in Mt. 21, 22, where the primitive text has been simplified and *pistenete* replaced by *pisteuontes,* which does away with the difficulty.

26. The text is not certain. It may have been inserted from Mk. 9, 29, where the complement *nesteia* is found in a number of manuscripts.

27. In SB I, 793-794.

28. Cf. Mt. 28, 19; Acts 2, 38; 8, 16; 19, 4.

29. H. Greeven, *Gebet und Eschatologie,* p. 23.

30. For Isaac and Jacob see, for example, Gn. 27, 1-04; 49, 26.

The Teaching of Jesus on Prayer

31. Cf. Dt. 27, 9-10; 11, 26; 30, 1-14; Ps. 24, 4-6.
32. Gn. 24, 48; Dt. 8, 10; Jg. 5, 2, 9; Tb. 12, 6; Pss. 16, 7; 34, 2; 68, 27.
33. The word *eulogetos*, sometimes attributed in the Old Testament to men (Gn. 12, 2; 26, 29; 43, 28), is found in the New Testament applied only to God (Mk. 14, 61; Lk. 1, 68), and forms parts of the doxologies (Rom. 1, 25; 9, 5; 2 Cor. 1, 3; 11, 31; Ep. 1, 3; 1 P. 1, 3). It must have entered rather early into Christian liturgy; cf. Liturgy of St. John Chrysostom, F. E. Brightman, *Eastern Liturgies* (Oxford, 1896), p. 353.
34. This is the only time John uses the verb *eulogein*. A comparative study of the four accounts is interesting.

Mk.	Mt.	Lk.	Jn.
Eulogemonos o erchomenos en onomati Kuriou	Eulogemonos o erchomenos en onomati Kuriou	Eulogemonos o erchomenos	Eulogemonos o erchomenos en onomati Kuriou
Eulogemene e erchomene Basileia tou ... Basileia tou ...		o Basileus en onamati Kuriou	o Basileus tou Israel.

The exclamation of the crowd is taken from Ps. 118, 26, which Judaism applied to the messianic redemption; SB I, p. 850; Midrash, P. 118, 22, Jesus himself applies this verse to the day of his *parousia* (Mt. 23, 39; (Lk. 13, 35). We have seen the eschatological meaning of the verb "to come."

35. Originally, every salutation was a blessing, so that to bless was synonymous with to greet. Cf. 1 S. 13, 10 where Saul goes to meet Samuel to bless him, i.e., to greet him.
36. First multiplication Mk. 6, 31-44; Mt. 13, 13-21; Lk. 9, 10-17; Jn. 6, 11: *eucharistesas*.
37. Mk. 7, 34. Compare Mk. 7, 34 with Jn. 11, 41 and 17, 1.
38. SB II, 246.
39. Mk. 14, 22; Mt. 26, 26 are the only ones who use *eulogein* and only for the bread; Lk. 24, 30.
40. The blasphemy *anathema Iesous* is averted by reciting the Christian blessing *Kuriou Iesous* (1 Cor. 12, 3). The blessing here is synonymous with confession, at the *parousia;* the blessed are those who have confessed Christ; they will be "confessed" by him.
41. We find the same advice in Mt. 9, 38, relative to the mission of the Twelve. Luke speaks of two missions, one (Lk. 9, 1-6) common to Mt. 9, 35 — 10, 42 (cf. Mk. 6, 6-13); the other, which he alone relates, that of the seventy-two. The latter is found in the "travelogue," Lk. 9, 51 — 19, 27), in which Luke collects materials which are peculiar to him.
42. Some of the manuscripts (B D pc lat sy) read seventy-two which seems to originate from a falling in line with the Septuagint translation which, in Gn. 10, speaks of seventy-two instead of seventy peoples.
43. Mk. 4, 1-9, 26-20; Mt. 13, 24-30, 39.
44. Is. 9, 2; Ho. 6, 11; Jn. 4, 35.
45. The text presents a variant at verse 8, where the Sixtine-Clementine Vulgate adds "et si ille perseveraverit pulsans," which is missing in the Greek and even in several manuscripts of Jerome's Vulgate.
46. E.g., D. Buzy, *Les Paraboles* (Paris, 1932), pp. 594-595.
47. *Sermon 105, P.L.*, XXXVIII, 619.
48. J. Pirot, *Paraboles et allégories évangéliques* (Paris, 1949), p. 199. The same interpretation is found in J. Jeremias, *The Parables of Jesus*, trans. S. H. Hooke (New York, 1962), pp. 159-160.

49. D. Buzy, *op. cit.*, pp. 594-595.

50. *Eis telos* indicates movement and must therefore be related to *erchomene*. Cf. the Septuagint translation of Hab. 1, 4; Ps. 103, 9; Jb. 14, 20. *Upopiaze me* signifies to strike under the eye, in the face. Commentators are divided about the translation, as to whether the meaning should be taken literally or figuratively.

51. "The elect" designates the Christian, as does the word "saint."

52. The text here is close to Si. 35, 15-24, particularly vv. 21-23. The difficulty lies in the translation of *kai makrothumei ep' autois*, the present indicative of the verb being coordinated with a future subjunctive. The Aramaic idiom translated here represents a relative proposition (cf. Mk. 2, 15b). Other authors translate: "And would he delay in their regard." It would be better to change the punctuation by placing a question mark after *nuktos*, and leave the remainder as an independent clause; cf. H. Sahlin, "Zwei Lukasstellen," *Symb. Bibl. Ups.* (1945), pp. 9-20; J. Jeremias, *The Parables of Jesus*, p. 155; J. Horst, *makrothumia, TWNT*, IV, 384, n. 56.

53. J. Pirot, *Paraboles et allégories*, p. 192.

54. *Pros tinas tous pepoithotas* means "who put their trust in themselves rather than in God" (cf. 2 Cor. 1, 9). *Oti* has a causal sense: "They draw their justice from themselves."

55. There is no reason to regard this as a gloomy caricature; it is a portrait to which the Pharisees themselves seem to consent.

56. The prayer is well constructed: it contains a negative part, followed by a positive part. The Pharisee does more than is necessary; he fasts twice a week instead of once. He pays tithes on all his income, even on the herbs which were not taxed (Mt. 23, 23; Lk. 11, 42).

57. *Ouch ethelen*, he did not dare (cf. Mk. 6, 26; Lk. 18, 4; Jn. 7, 1.). The Aramaic has no word to express "to dare." Cf. J. Jeremias, *The Parables of Jesus*, pp. 139-144, regarding this parable.

58. This verse presents a few difficulties. The verb *dikaioun*, so familiar to Paul, is found but once in the gospels, namely here. The passive expresses the fact that God justifies him.

The Greek rendering attempts to translate the Hebrew preposition *min*, which takes the place of the comparative. The unusual phrasing had repercussions on the textual transmission which endeavored to render the comparative as *e ekeinos* (W H). The comparative often has an exclusive sense, for example: "Obedience to God comes before obedience to men" (Acts 5, 29). cf. also Acts 4, 19; 20, 35; Rom. 1.25. In Gn. 38, 26, the Septuagint translates the same verb *dikaiousthai* by *dedikaiotai*. Tamar is justified in comparison to me, i.e., and not me.

59. D. Buzy, *Paraboles*, pp. 270-275, exaggerates in finding here a caricature.

60. SB II, 240, who give other similar texts.

61. D. Buzy, *Paraboles*, pp. 270-282, is too exclusive in his commentary. Msgr. Cerfaux, "Trois réhabilitations dans l'Evangile." *Recueil Cerfaux*, II, 53-55, has more subtle distinctions.

62. Kataxiothete "judged worthy" in D pl lat sy; *stesesthe* "that you might seem" in D it sysc Tert.

63. Luke omits the exhortation to vigilance, but gives two exhortations to pray (Lk. 22, 40, 46).

64. E.g., Mt. 24, 42; 25, 13; Mk. 13, 35-37; Lk. 12, 37-39.

65. Cf. 1 Cor. 16, 13; 1 Th. 5, 4-8; 1 P. 5, 8.

66. Three Latin versions (a b l) anterior to Jerome attribute the canticle to Elizabeth. Nicetas of Remesiana does the same (cf. *Revue Biblique* VI, 1897), 286). The Latin translator of Origen alludes to it (*P.G.* XIII, 1817). We find

it in Irenaeus (*Adv. Haer.*, IV, 7, 1) according to an Armenian translation and two Latin manuscripts, which, however, disagree, with the text of Irenaeus, and another passage where the two Latin versions agree on the reading "Mary" (*Adv. Haer.*, III, 10, 2). All the other evidence, Greek manuscripts, versions, Fathers, attest the reading "Mary" which, from the point of view of textual criticism, is the only defensible one.

Internal criticism does not permit the attribution of the hymn to Elizabeth. Verse 48 can apply only to the mother of the Messiah. The parallelism between John the Baptist and Jesus demands that the praise of the precursor's father be answered by the thanksgiving of the mother of the Savior.

For an opinion of the Jewish roots, cf E. Klostermann, *Das Lukasevangelium* (Tübingen, 1919), pp. 378-379, 385-386.

67. Instead of *epi*, *en* is found in D lat.
68. H here inserts a comma.
69. The text shows variants. Besides our reading we find:
eis geneas kai geneas
eis genean kai genean
apo geneas eis genean A
70. Eos aionos C   pm S.
71. A simple table will show how the *Magnificat* is bejeweled with scriptural quotations in addition to those taken from Hannah (1 S. 2, 1-10), Mary (Ex. 15, 20-27), Deborah (Jg. 5), and Judith (16):

verse 46: cf. Ps. 35, 9; Si., 43, 31; Ps. 69, 31.
    47: cf. Pss. 31, 8; 35, 9; Hab. 3, 18.
    48: cf. 1 S. 1, 11; Gn. 29, 32; Ps. 31, 8; Gn. 30, 13;
        Ps. 113, 5-9; 2 S. 7, 18; Ml. 3, 12.
    49: Dt. 10, 21; Ps. 111, 9; 126, 3; Ex. 15, 11.
    50: Ps. 103, 11, 17; Gn. 17, 7.
    51: Ps. 89, 11; 2 S. 22, 28; Ex. 15, 6; Is. 51, 9;
        1 S. 2, 3, 9; Ps. 2, 1-6; Dn. 4, 37; Ml. 4, 1.
    52: Si. 10, 14; Jb. 12, 19; Ezk. 21, 31; Jb. 5, 11;
        1 S. 2, 7; Ps. 113, 7; Qo. 4, 14.
    53: Ps. 107, 9; 34, 11; 1 S. 2, 5.
    54: Is. 41, 8-10; Ps. 98, 3; Is. 63, 15.
    55: Mi. 7, 20; 2 S. 22, 51; Gn. 17, 7; 18, 18; 22, 17.

72. A comparative table will bring to light what has been borrowed from the Old Testament:

verse 68: Pss. 41, 14; 72, 18; 106, 48; 111, 9; 130, 8; cf. Lk. 7, 16.
    69: 1 S. 2, 10; Pss. 89, 25; 132, 17; 18, 3; Ezk. 29, 21.
    70: 2 K. 17, 23; Ps. 132, 17; Is. 9, 5-6; Jr. 23, 5, 6.
    71: Ps. 106, 10; Nb. 24, 8; Is. 49, 25; Ezk. 34, 28;
        Zp. 3, 15.
    72: Ex. 2, 24; Pss. 105, 8; 106, 45; Lv. 26, 42; Gn.
        17, 7; Ezk. 16, 60.
    73: Gn. 22, 16-17; Mi. 7, 20; Jr. 11, 5.
    74: Jr. 11, 5; Mi. 4, 10; Jr. 30, 8; Is. 32, 17.
    75: Jr. 31, 33; Ezk. 36, 27.
    76: Ml. 3, 1; Is. 40, 3.
    77: Is. 52, 6; Jr. 31, 34.
    78: Nb. 2, 17; Is. 60, 1-2; 63, 7; Jr. 23, 5; Mi. 3, 20.
    79: Is .9, 1; 42, 7; 59, 8, Mi. 5, 4.
73. Cf. the beginning of Jewish prayers, *supra* p. 5ff.

For the comparison between the *Benedictus* and the blessing of the priest at the incensing, cf. T. Innitzer, *Kom. zum Ev. des h. Lukas* (Graz, 1922), pp. 61-62.

74. Literally "a horn of salvation," the horn being a symbol of strength among the Semites (cf. Ps. 18, 3); SB II. 110.

75. The reference is to Gn. 22, 16-18.

76. *Pasais t. e* is missing in some Mss; *tes zoes* also occurs.

77. "The Lord" i.e., God and not the Messiah (cf. Ml. 3, 1; Is. 40, 3).

78. *Emon* C pm 122 al.

79. I.e., either the messianic era or the Messiah himself.

80. *Epeskepsato*. The future *episkepsetai* is also sound.

81. H. Schlier, art. *"anatole"* in *TWNT*, I, 355, gives another explanation, plausible in literature, more doubtful in theology, "the star coming from heaven" (cf. Philo, *Conf. ling.*, 14, who sees the Logos in Zc. 6, 12). This interpretation would conform with verse 79 and with the interpretation of Zc. 6, 12 discussed by Justin, *Dial.* 100, 4; 106, 4; 121, 2; 126, 1 and Melito.

Chapter V

JESUS AND THE NEW CULT

Though the religion of Jesus is rooted in that of Israel, Christ remains independent of the religious past. He deflected traditions in the direction of the new cult by spiritualizing them. Sacrifice became obedience and charity.

At the time when the community was drawing up the gospels, the cult, principally the Eucharist, was already animating Christian fervor and represented the hearth of Christian prayer. The liturgy of the primitive Church rooted itself in the life and teachings of Jesus. It is easy to distinguish its lineaments in the Synoptic Gospels.

The Temple

The expulsion of the sellers from the Temple at the beginning of Jesus' public life assumes the nature of a manifesto. Mark has preserved the text for us: "Does not scripture say: My house will be called a house of prayer for all the peoples? But you have turned it into a robbers' den" (Mk. 11, 17; cf. Mt. 21, 13; Lk. 19, 46). Jesus was quoting a saying from Deutero-Isaiah (Is. 56, 7) which pictures universalism as an ingathering of all peoples in Yahweh's Temple. Christ acted as the Messiah; his action was a sign of the new times in which the cult and the sanctity of the Temple are perfected in a new cult (cf. Mk. 13, 2; 14, 58; Mt. 12, 6; Mk. 7, 1; Mt. 5, 17-18).

Jesus came in person to replace the cult of the Temple, according to the misquoted statement of the false witnesses (Mk. 14, 58) which, originally, could have corresponded to John's text: "Destroy this sanctuary, and in three days I will raise it up"[1] (Jn. 2, 19), or to the form given by Mark: "And in three days I am going to build another, not made by human hands" (Mk. 14, 18). Both the witnesses and the accused gave a messianic implication to this statement. The renovation of the Temple was regarded as a sign of the expected times (Ezk. 40-48; Henoch 90, 28).

The new Temple would not be built by man's hands but would be the miracle of God's new earth. Linked to the history of salvation, the cult reached completion with it (Mt. 24, 14; 3, 2, 10), but by drawing its value and significance from the work that Christ came to fulfill. The summit of this history was reached in the death and Resurrection of Jesus. The history of Israel proclaimed and prefigured it. Jesus, polarized by the *hour* of the Father, gave to the Jews Jonah's prophetic sign, which refers to his death and Resurrection (Mt. 12, 38-45).

Baptism

The same applies to baptism. John the Baptist clearly defined the provisional import of the baptism of penance that would be replaced in the new economy by the baptism in the Holy Spirit and fire.[2]

The baptism received by Jesus was itself a heralding sign of the work of Calvary. He came out of the water, and with him came the whole world; he saw the heavens open which Adam had shut for himself and his race. Redemption was at work.[3]

But in receiving John's baptism, Jesus gave it a new significance in the work of the Cross. When speaking of his coming Passion, Jesus called it "the baptism with which I must be baptized" (Mk. 10, 38; Lk. 12, 49-50). "I am come to bring fire on the earth; and how I wish it were blazing already! There is a baptism I must still receive, and how great is my distress till it is over!" (Lk. 12, 49-50) What kindled this fire was the baptism of blood that Christ received on the Cross.

The expressions *baptism of fire, kindle the fire,* are allusions to the cult. Christ's sacrifice which fulfilled the Law and the prophets corresponds in a strict parallelism to the fire of the Jewish sacrifice, which was jealously guarded. In Christian history he is the Temple of the new cult. The trial by fire to which Jesus aspired with his whole being is the offering of Calvary in which the freely consumed, and admittedly immaculate victim, purifies our inner self and now makes it possible for us to render the new worship of the living God (Heb. 9, 14). The cultual term "baptism" signifies that Christ, once and for all, fulfilled the new and perfect cult.[4]

The eucharistic Last Supper

The same applies, with even better reason, to the *Last Supper*. The Master's instructions to prepare the meal in the upper chamber (Mk. 14, 12-17; Lk. 22, 8-13), recall the saying of Jesus preserved by John: "I am going now to prepare a place for you" (Jn. 14, 2).[5] It stresses the prophetic value of the cult, conceived as an anticipation of the end.

The Synoptics insert the Last Supper in the framework of the celebration of the Passover. It seems probable that supper and the Passover were historically linked.[6] What applies to the Temple applies to the Jewish Passover. It is fulfilled in the person of the Messiah and in the events of his death and Resurrection, ritually anticipated by the Holy Thursday supper. For the old cult Jesus substituted a new cult, the Passover of the Exodus was replaced by a Christian Easter, ritualizing the new Covenant.

The three Synoptics give us the account of the institution. Likewise, in his epistle to the Corinthians, St. Paul formulates what he received "from the Lord" (1 Cor. 11, 23-25). From a comparison of the gospel accounts it is evident that Mark's text is close to Matthew's, while Luke is independent and utilizes sources common to him and Paul. These two versions possibly represent the two liturgical traditions of Antioch and Palestine.

The relationship between Mark and Matthew is clear and may be explained by a common source. The variants are very slight and do not change the tenor of the account. Certain revisions of the text may have been brought about by liturgical use, which exerted its influence on the composition. Mark's silence on the reiteration is explained by the fact that liturgical celebrations implicity expressed it.

Luke's text[7] differs from Mark's, and even from the Apostle Paul's which he knew, because he abbreviates it or enlarges on it. Luke is at pains to insert the account in the framework of the paschal repast, which Paul does not mention. As for the bread, Luke's account agrees with Mark and Matthew. The same applies to the twice repeated eschatological perspective (Lk. 22, 16, 18; cf. Mk. 14, 25). The order of this repetition is peculiar to Pauline tradition. In Luke two chalices are mentioned, the first of which is one of the chalices of the paschal repast; it is mentioned because of the prophecy: "I shall not drink . . ." which applies to ordinary beverage. Possibly he is trying to reconcile the historical account of the Last Supper and contemporary liturgical usages, whereas Mark and Matthew only relate the second element.

Liturgical usage manifests itself in Luke's and Paul's version, over against that of Matthew and Mark, when it speaks of *the* chalice (Lk. 22, 20), " . . . for you" (idem), and in the order of the repetition (Lk. 22, 19).

Common to Mark's and Paul's tradition, and representing the primitive form, is the context of the account: Jesus took bread, prayed, and clearly explained its significance. He did the same with the wine. Then come explanatory words regarding the bread and the chalice. It must be noted that the words over the bread are common to the two traditions. Those of the chalice show a variant.[8] Finally, the eschatological perspective is common to Mark 14, 28 and Paul, 1 Cor. 11, 26.

Jesus' last meal with his own

It seems very probable that Jesus' last meal was a paschal celebration. The objections raised against this do not take the texts sufficiently into account.[9] Moreover certain difficulties disappear if we date the celebration on Holy Tuesday, as the archaic Jewish calendar and the tradition retained by the Didascalia suggest.[10]

The Passover repast began with a preparatory service.[11] The head of the household first pronounced a double blessing, the first for the solemnity, the second over the wine: "Blessed are you, Yahweh our God, King of the universe, who created the fruit of the vine." And the chalice was passed among the guests.

Then the right hand was washed. The first course was brought in, consisting of bitter herbs, of unleavened bread, of fruit juice and roasted lamb. The son asked his father what distinguished this night from all other nights. The father recounted the wonderful departure from Egypt. He quoted the words of Scripture (Dt. 26, 5-11) to recall that the unleavened bread was a reminder of the bread that had no time to rise (Dt. 16, 3); the bitter herbs recalled the days of bitterness that Israel suffered in Egypt. The roasted lamb represented the lamb each family had to slay that night and whose blood on the lintels of their houses preserved them from the exterminating angel. "So are we bound to thank, to confess, to praise, to glorify . . . him who delivered us and our brothers from Egypt and gave us that night."

After the thanksgiving for preservation in the past and in the present, the prayer reflects on the eschatological hope: "Grant us, Yahweh our God and the God of our fathers, that we may celebrate the feasts which are prepared in peace. May we rejoice in seeing our city rebuilt and in being able to serve you. We will sing our thanksgiving to you in a new canticle."[12]

After the first part of the Hallel had been sung, the second chalice was passed among the guests. The head of the household recited the blessing over the unleavened bread: "Blessed are you, Yahweh our God, King of the world, who made the earth bring forth bread."

He broke the bread and distributed the pieces among those sitting at the table. They in turn ate them with bitter herbs and fruit juice. Only at this moment did they begin to eat the paschal lamb. When the meal was over, the head of the household recited the blessing over the third chalice, which was the thanksgiving for the meal, whence the name."chalice of benediction."[13]

The meal ended with the last part of the Hallel and perhaps with a fourth chalice. Jesus sang the hymns with his own, the only prayer he seems to have said with them.

The accounts of the Last Supper amass convergent data which enable us to discover its paschal nature: the use of wine, foreign to ordinary meals (1 Cor. 11, 25; Mk. 14, 23, 25; Lk. 22, 17), a usage prescribed even for the poor,[14] the evocation of the history of salvation, signified by the elements of the meal (1 Cor. 11, 24; Mk. 14, 22), and the eschatological perspective on the kingdom of God (Mk. 14, 28; Lk. 22, 16, 18), Luke's explicit statements as the framework of his account[15] (Lk. 22, 15, 17, 19).

Two observations should be made. At the time the Synoptics composed the account of the Last Supper, liturgical usage attests the faith of the apostolic community. The new economy was inaugurated. Through the cult Christians were united to the Kyrios invisibly present among his own (Lk. 24, 3, 35, 43; cf. Jn. 21, 5, 9, 13). This liturgical use emerges from the gospel account and gives a paschal stamp to the account of the Last Supper, in accordance with the intentions expressed by Christ himself in the course of his last meal.

The Synoptic accounts are not in the least stereotyped; the versions are free and abridged. They presuppose the whole gospel of which they form an integral part and which clarify the concise formulas of the institution.

The breaking of bread[16] was a familiar gesture of Christ by which the disciples of Emmaus were able to recognize him (Lk. 24, 35); they had seen him break bread many times, as at the miraculous multiplication of the loaves (Mk. 6, 41; Lk. 9, 16). Jesus had said that he was the living bread (Jn. 6, 48, 51), he who gives eternal life. The broken bread was the bond of the community. Bread and wine recall the sacrifice of Melchizedek. They serve not only as a common bond among men, but also as a bond of communion between men and "Lord of heaven and of earth" (Mt. 11, 25).[17]

Blood signified life and played an important part in the cult (Mk. 10, 45); this liturgical usage is found in the word "shed." At Sinai part of the blood of the victims was poured on the altar of sacrifice, part was used to sprinkle the crowd. It was the sign of the Covenant between Yahweh and his people: "This is the blood of the Covenant that Yahweh has made with you, containing all these rules" (Ex. 24, 8).

The Covenant of Sinai prefigured that of Calvary foretold by Jeremias:

> See, the days are coming — it is Yahweh who speaks — when I will make a new covenant with the House of Israel (and the House of Judah), but not a covenant like the one I made with their ancestors on the day I took them by the hand to bring them out of the land of Egypt. They broke that covenant of mine, so I had to show them who was master. It is Yahweh who speaks. No, this is the convenant I will make with the House of Israel when those days arrive — it is Yahweh who speaks. Deep within them I will plant my Law, writing it on their hearts. Then I will be their God and they shall be my people. There will be no further need for neighbour to try to teach neighbour, or brother to say to brother, 'Learn to know Yahweh!' No, they will all know me, the least no less than the greatest — it is Yahweh who speaks — since I will forgive their iniquity and never call their sin to mind.[18]

The blood is shed *for many* (Mt. 26, 28; Mk. 14, 24),[19] which is an expression borrowed from Isaiah (Is. 53, 11) to signify the masses, the men of every nation (Mt. 20, 28; 24, 11, 12). Matthew alone says very explicitly "for the forgiveness of sins," following Jeremias 31, 34. He is referring here to the entirety of his Gospel.[20]

The one bread broken and the one chalice from which the Apostles drink (I Cor. 10, 16-17) express the fact that they compose God's family (Mk. 3, 35), the new people grouped around the Lord's table.[21]

Several key ideas stand out from the Synoptic accounts. The new cult is bound to the person of Christ (Lk. 17, 20-21). Jesus is the suffering Servant who fulfills the prophecies of Deutero-Isaiah (Is. 42, 6; 49, 7, 8; 53). He is the Testament of God. The history of salvation ends in him and he fulfills it in the sacrifice of the Cross, the baptism he must receive, the chalice he must drink. For this reason the apostolic Church states that Christ is our immolated Pasch. According to John, Christ's death coincided with the eating of the paschal lamb.

The sacrifice of Christ is obedience and charity, even unto death. He expiated and took away the world's sin, the obstacle to the reconciliation of men with God and among themselves; "the Son of Man came not to be served but to serve, and to give his life as a ransom for many."[23] He began the Christian community which welcomes all the children of Abraham, and in this community God's salvation is extended to all the families of the earth. The new Pasch is the culmination and total fulfillment of the promises made to Abraham.

This universal and eschatological perspective inspired Christ's tone of triumph as he went to his death (Mk. 14, 25). He knew that the love he bore towards the Father and towards men would triumph over hatred and indifference, and that he was inaugurating the kingdom in which all men are invited to God's banquet.

He is the paschal lamb who shed his blood for the sins of the world.[24] He thereby freed his people. The mystery of this efficacy lies in his perfect obedience to his Father and in the indefectible love toward men with which he accepted suffering and death. The will of the Father, the task that this will commanded him to fulfill, which were the primary object of his prayer, became the essential goal of his actions and of his sacrifice.

The eucharistic Pasch ritualizes the offering of the Cross by which Jesus freed the people from sin and the hold of the devil. The first stage of the Father's work was completed in the new and eternal Covenant, which constitutes the new Israel. It is translated into ineffable joy during the eucharistic celebrations, because the Lord in glory dwells invisibly present where his followers gather together.

Conclusion: Jesus' prayer

Heiler could justly write: "Rather does the inwardness of prayer enter on a new epoch with Jesus."[25] The reflection is correct, but it is far from taking into account all the newness and riches of the prayer of Jesus. Christ's prayer expressed the secret of his soul, of his nature, and of his mission.

Jesus was fully conscious of the mysterious bond which united him to his Father. This consciousness of an intimate union with God was clear from his infancy because it existed since the Word of God had taken possession of his human soul. At the age of twelve Jesus spoke as no other mystic ever dared speak of God. His words reveal a complete, immediate, spiritual experience which belonged to no other creature, and this sets him apart from everyone else, even his mother.

This personal communion with heaven which places him in God's world as in his very own is clearly evident in the expression *My Father* by which Christ always distinguished his filial bond from that of his disciples. He was conscious of the unique relationship which united him to his Father. Only he says *My Father*, only he received its reply: "You are my Son, the Beloved" (Mk. 1, 11) which expresses the intercommunication of his soul with the divinity, in a complete reciprocity (Mt. 11, 27).

Prayer ushered Jesus into the heart of this unique intimacy, the most personal there is. It emerged from that communion with his Father; it was truly the breath of his soul, the halting-place where the soul finds its rest, its secret, and its deepest life. Praying was natural to him. Never did Jesus experience the feeling of distance which the greatest mystics did even in their ecstasies. It will be sufficient to compare the prayer of Jesus with Paul's to measure the distance which separated Christ's own prayer from that of a privileged soul. Neither did he ever have the feeling of helplessness, misery, or anguish. Rather he knew the joy of talking with his Father in the depths of his soul. Jesus sought solitude in order to penetrate deeper into this mystery.

The sentiment of adoration is both praise and thanksgiving. Jesus stood in constant dependence on the divine will. Submission was the life of his soul: "My food is to do the will of the one who sent me" (Jn. 4, 34). The will of Jesus, relying on his Father, illumined from on high, knew neither the seduction of baser things, nor the attraction to infidelity.

Every situation, every petition always brought Jesus back to the object of his mission, the divine will, the work his Father had entrusted to him. Jesus desired nothing else. Prayer enabled him to discern and bless the plan of his Father whom he had come to serve. His petitions had no objects other than the good will of the Father and the will to act in his service. At Gethsemane Jesus found rest only in submission to his Father; this was the fruit of his prayer.

Therefore he could give thanks before a miracle, since his Father always granted what he asked, his will being entirely in accord with that of God. This submission motivated his filial and absolute trust. Never has prayer expressed this with such force, with such daring, in so absolute a manner: "Everything you ask for . . . will be yours" (Mk. 11, 24).

Jesus' prayer was "in action," it tended to action, it sought expression in action. It guided and commanded all his activity, just as it elevates all passivity. St. Luke, more insistently than all the evangelists, has shown that all the major decisions, all the intense moments always emerged from assiduous prayer. Far from isolating him from men, prayer sank him deeper into the heart of his mission (Mk. 11, 25; Mt. 5, 23-24) which was to save the world. It enabled him to discern better the meaning of his coming, to make more his own the whole history of mankind, and to give fullness and fulfillment to the expectation of his people. It enabled him to understand through actual experience his vocation as the "suffering Servant," and to satisfy the unheard of demands it implied. The Transfiguration already prepared the mystery of his death. At the hour of agony Jesus tasted the bitterness of the chalice he had to drink, but prayer enabled him to overcome the shudders of the flesh and the cowardices of human weakness, to comply with the will of God with an unconditional, heroic, and absolute submission.

The offering of Calvary was carried out "in a loud voice" (Mt. 27, 50)[26] which proclaimed before the world Jesus' filial and loving submission to his Father, the fidelity in action of what his whole life had never ceased repeating. Jesus' prayer was an offering, and his offering was a prayer. The prayer expressed the drama of the people, the struggle against unleased powers in a perspective of victory. The work entrusted to Jesus by his Father was accomplished.

PART II
Chapter V

1. O Cullman, *Early Christian Worship*, trans. A. Steward Todd and James B. Torrance (London: SCM Press Ltd., 1953), p. 72.

2. Cf. Mt. 3, 11; Lk. 3, 16; cf. Mk.: "baptism with the Holy Spirit," 1,8. O. Cullmann, *Baptism in the New Testament*, trans. J. K. S. Reid (London: SCM Press Ltd., 1950), pp. 73-80, after a patient analysis has sought to find in the verb *koluein* an allusion to the baptismal rite. He has been contradicted by A. W. Argyle, "O. Cullman's Theory concerning Koluein," *Expos. Times* (Oct., 1955), p. 17.

3. Cf. our article "La baptême de feu" *Mélanges de science religieuse* (1951), p. 290.

4. *Ibid.*, p. 292.

5. O. Cullmann, *Early Christian Worship*, p. 110.

6. The question has been discussed at length by a certain number of Protestant exegetes. For the connection between the Last Supper and the pasch, cf. J. Jeremias, *Eucharistic Words of Jesus* (N. M. Scribners, 1966) which has an exhaustive bibliography; *Klasis* and *pascha*, *TWNT*; J. Schniewind, "Das Evangelium des Markus," *NTD*.

Against associating the two are: H. Lietzmann, *Messe und Herrenmahl* (Berlin, 1955), p. 212; W. O. E. Oesterley, *The Jewish Background of the Christian Liturgy*, 1125, pp. 156-193; T. Preiss, "Le dernier repas de Jésus fut-il un repas pascal?" *Theol. Zeitschr.*, IV, (1948), 84-101; G. Dix, *The Shape of the Liturgy* (Westminster, Md., 1954), p. 50.

7. D or Codex Bezae, dc, the pre-Jerome version, the Syriac verisons suppress verses 19b and 20; cf. J. Lebreton, *The Life & Teaching of Jesus Christ Our Lord*, II, p. 236, ftnt. 1; P. Benoît, "Le récit de la cène dans Luc XXII, 15-20," *Revue biblique*, XLVIII (1939), 357-393. Cf. also the important work of H. Schurmann, *Der Paschamahlbericht*, Lk. 22, 7-14 (Munich, 1953).

8.
Mark	Paul
"This is my blood, the blood of the covenant" (14, 24).	"This cup is the new covenant in my blood" (1 Cor. 11, 25).

9. For the discussion and proof, cf. particularly: G. Dalman, *Jesus-Jeshua: Studies in the Gospels*, trans. Paul P. Levertoff, (London: 1929), pp. 86-184; SB IV, 41; II, 812; J. Jeremias, *Eucharistic Words*, pp. 15-88.

10. A. Jaubert, *La date de la Cène* (Paris, 1957). The author's thesis may modify the question of the paschal character of the Last Supper. Cf. also E. Ruckstuhl, *Chronology of the Last Days of Jesus* (New York, 1965).

11. The description is given us by the Mishna, in Pes. 10; SB IV, pp. 56-76; J. Jeremias, *Eucharistic Words*, pp. 84ff.

12. Pes. 10, 4-6; G. Daiman, *Jesus-Jeshua*, p. 9.

13. This name was not reserved for the third chalice, but was also given to the chalice over which was pronounced a prayer of thanksgiving during a solemn repast.

14. Pes. 10, 1.

15. To these indications may be added other points:
1. The Last Supper was held at night (1 Cor. 11, 23) which was the case only for the pasch, whereas the normal meal took place at the end of the afternoon.
2. Jesus stayed that night in Jerusalem, where the pasch had to be celebrated, whereas he spent the other nights outside the city (Mk. 14, 13).
3. The meal called for careful preparations which were entrusted to two disciples (Mk. 14, 12). This would not have been the case had it been a normal meal.
4. The reclining position, unusual for ordinary meals, was reserved for the paschal celebration (Mk. 14, 18; Jn. 13, 23).
5. Luke's two chalices presuppose the paschal rite (Lk. 22, 17, 20).
6. Jesus gave thanks over the third chalice and passed it around the table (1 Cor. 11, 25), and Paul explicitly calls it "the blessing-cup."
7. The Christian anamnesis (1 Cor. 11, 24) recalls the prayer of the head of the household.
8. The final hymn (Mk. 14, 26) is an allusion to the Great Hallel of the pasch.

In the opposite sense we can apply Jn. 13, 29: "some of them thought Jesus was telling him, 'Buy what you need for the festival.'"

16. "Klasis," *TWNT*, III, 726-743.

17. At Qumran, too, there was a religious repast of bread and wine. See *supra*, pp. 76-77. Cf. D. Barthélemy — T. Milik, *Qumran Cave I* (Oxford, 1955), pp. 108-118.

18. Jr. 31, 31-34. Cf. Ezk. 36, 25-30; Zc. 9, 11.

19. The expression "for many" is also found at Qumran.

20. Cf. Mt. 6, 12; 7, 11; 9, 1-8; 11, 19; 12, 31; 18, 23-35; 16, 19; 18, 18.

21. Cf. Mk. 3, 14, 16, 35; 9, 36-37; Mt. 5, 13-16; 16, 18-19; Lk. 10, 20; 12, 32.

23. Mt. 20, 28; Mk. 10, 45. Cf. Mk. 14, 21; Mt. 26, 24; Lk. 22, 22.

24. Cf. Is. 53, 4, 5, 6, 8, 10; Ex. 12, 12-13, 23, 27, 49.

25. F. Heiler, *op. cit.*, p. 123.

26. W. Grundmann, *"krazo," TWNT*, III, 900, 903.

PART III

Prayer In the Apostolic Community

A. THE ACTS OF THE APOSTLES

The book of the Acts continues St. Luke's Gospel with which, originally, it formed one single work. The two were separated when Christians wanted to have the four gospels together in the same codex. This happened around 150 A.D.[1]

Exegetes have tried to discover the sources from which the author drew. For the first part, chapters 1-15, which are composed of small literary units with no common source, Luke must have made use of a varied and detailed documentation. In the second part, chapters 15-28 — the "we" sections, where the author speaks in the plural — he may have used travel notes that he had written down for his own personal use.[2]

In this chapter we shall restrict our analysis mainly to the first part of the Acts. We shall postpone our study of the second part to the chapter on St. Paul. The first part is composed of a mosaic of episodes intended to spotlight the progress of Christianity; it was planned for the missionary use of Christians and catechumens.

It is made up of *narratives, discourses,* and *summaries.* The *narratives* are composed of a series of anecdotes and pen pictures; the *discourses* are the already stereotyped résumé of Christian missionary preaching; the *summaries* frame the narratives. These last originate from the general documentation or from Luke's later editing. They interest us more particularly here since they furnish us with valuable information on the prayer and worship of the apostolic community.

The history related in the Acts covers the first thirty years of the Church. The latest critical works fix the date of the composition of the book around 70 A.D.[3]

Exegetes generally admit the common authorship of the third Gospel and the Acts. The semantic study of the vocabulary relating to prayer corroborates this statement. There we find words dear to Luke's Gospel, as well as to the other Synoptics, e.g., *eulogein, proseuchesthai, proseuche, agalliasthai, agalliasis;* other words peculiar to the third Gospel are also found in the Acts.[4] Mark and Matthew do not use them; the only other place they are found is in St. Paul.

Chapter I

EXPLICIT PRAYERS

There are not many prayers, properly so-called, in the Acts. Only three, in fact: that of the Apostles at the election of Matthias (Acts 1, 24), that of the Christians at Peter's liberation (Acts 4, 24-30), and Stephen's at the hour of his martyrdom (Acts 7, 59).

The election of Matthias

The first prayer that the Acts has preserved for posterity is the one the Apostles addressed to heaven before proceeding with the election of a successor to Judas (Acts 1, 24-25).

> Lord, you can read everyone's heart; show us therefore which of these two you have chosen to take over this ministry and apostolate, which Judas abandoned to go to his proper place.

To whom was this prayer addressed, to God or to Christ? The question has been much discussed. It seems more likely that it was addressed to the Father. In Luke the attribute *kardiognostes* is always applied to God.[5] The title Kurios in prayer and without further clarification is addressed to God (Acts 4, 29). When it refers to Christ, he is usually named (Acts 7, 58). Moreover, in the thinking of the Acts, it is God who guides the history of salvation and who determines the choices relating to it.

Like Christ, the Apostles submitted to God everything pertaining to the work of salvation and the mission they had received to preach the gospel to the whole world. It was a solemn moment; they had to designate someone who, along with the Eleven, would collectively bear witness to Christ's Resurrection. The Apostles' prayer was an act of faith in God's primacy and in the apostolate entrusted to them.

The prayer of the community during the persecutions

More important and more significant is the prayer of the Christians who were persecuted at the time of the liberation of the Apostles Peter and John (Acts 4, 24-30). It enables us to discern the transition from Jewish to Christian prayer. There we discover an archaic Christianity, barely weaned from Judaism.[6]

It seems that Luke actually transmitted to us a typical prayer without any modifications, a prayer that furnishes us with a basic plan of prayer in the community of Jerusalem. The incident is inscribed within the context of the history of salvation, beginning with creation and punctuated with prophecies and their fulfillment. These prophecies localize and throw light on the present persecution. From them Christ's disciples draw confidence (*parresia*) to proclaim the word of God: "When they heard it (i.e., the release of Peter and John) they lifted up their voice to God all together."

> Master, it is you who made heaven and earth and sea, and everything in them; you it is who said through the Holy Spirit and speaking through our ancestor David, your servant:
> Why this arrogance among the nations,
> these futile plots among the peoples?
> Kings on earth setting out to war,
> princes making an alliance,
> against the Lord and against his Anointed.
>
> This is what has come true: in this very city Herod and Pontius Pilate made an alliance with the pagan nations and the peoples of Israel, against your holy servant Jesus whom you anointed, but only to bring about the very thing that you in your strength and your wisdom had predetermined should happen. And now, Lord, take note of their threats and help your servants to proclaim your message with

all boldness, by stretching out your hand to heal and to work miracles and marvels through the name of your holy servant Jesus. As they prayed, the house where they were assembled rocked; they were all filled with the Holy Spirit and began to proclaim the word of God boldly.

The structure of the prayer is unusual. It begins with an address to the Master whose personality is explained by two relative propositions, the first of which specifies the work of creation, while the second forms a transition to the biblical quotation and clarifies the present state of things in the light of Christ. The conclusion is introduced by a new vocative *Kurie*.[7] Without forcing the text, two parallel quatrains stand out (Acts 4, 24-26; 4, 27-30), reminders of the prayer of Hezekiah (Is. 37, 16-20).

Our text begins: "When they heard it they lifted up their voice to God all together" (4, 24).[8] The expression *eran phonen* is typical of Luke (cf. Lk. 17, 13). The emphasis of the sentence is put on *omothumadon*.[9] This expression is dear to Luke, who is the only one to use it,[10] with one exception in St. Paul (Rom. 15, 6). Among the Greeks the word meant a unanimity coming not from a common feeling but from a common cause or task in a given situation. Luke uses it for the life of the apostolic community in reference to the words of the gospel (Acts 8, 6; 20, 18) or with prayer (Acts 1, 14; 2, 1, 46; 4, 24; 5, 12; cf. Rom. 15, 6).

Harmony is not spontaneous in a community; it is a gift, a work of God (implying a *gignesthai,* as in Acts 15, 25) which is expressed in the prayer where the believers recognize the acting presence of God through Christ in the world and in the Church. The divine power was manifested in this case in the miraculous release of the two Apostles.

The prayer of the community is addressed to the *Despotes*. The word is a Grecism which is found only once in the gospels, in Simeon's *Nunc Dimittis* (Lk. 2, 29). In both these cases *Lord* contrasts with *servant* (Lk. 2, 29; Acts 4, 29). Here the word qualifies God, though elsewhere it refers to Christ (Jude 1, 4) where *Despotes* and *Kurios* are combined. *Despotes* expresses better than *Kurios* God's sovereign might and his absolute authority over all creation.[11] In the Old Testament it is often followed by a complement of plenitude *apanto*.[12] The Septuagint uses the expression less frequently than *Kurios;* it appears chiefly in post-exilic literature where Greek influence is more noticeable.[13] The word *despotes* appears particularly in prayer (Jr. 1, 6; 4, 10; 14, 13; 15, 11). It is the most frequent form of address in Josephus, from which, doubtless, it passed into Luke (Lk. 2, 29).

"It is you who made heaven and earth and sea, and everything in them" (Acts 4, 24).

This is a biblical quotation which we find in the confessions of faith of Jewish prayer,[14] expressing faith in the true God, Creator of the universe. It passed without any change into the Christian confession (Acts 14, 15; 17, 24; Re. 10, 6; 14, 7). It is constantly reappearing in the confessions of faith made by the Apostles and martyrs.[15] Even in this early state we find the links that united confessions of faith to the liturgy, confessions to martyrdom. Before the world's tribunal, the Christian testified to the faith he had received in baptism and which had been nourished by the breaking of bread.

"You it is who said through the Holy Spirit and speaking through our ancestor David, your servant" (Acts 4, 25).[16]

Here the expression *paidos sou* signifies, within the space of a few verses, both David and the Messiah. The whole Psalter is attributed to David, which is not a critical statement but a conformity to common usage (Acts 1, 16; 2, 25, 34; Rom. 4, 6; 11, 9; Heb. 4, 7). A similar introductory remark applies to any other quotation from the Psalter.

> Why this arrogance among the nations,
> these futile plots among the peoples?
> Kings on earth setting out to war,
> princes making an alliance,
> against the Lord and against his Anointed (Acts 4, 25-26).

These words of Psalm 2, 1-2 are a literal quotation from the Septuagint, which all the codices quote in perfect unanimity. Christian prayer naturally draws its inspiration from the Psalms of the synagogue, just as its faith finds the basis for its trust in the messianic prophecies. The apostolic community remained faithful to Christ's example in its utilization of the Psalter.

Understanding Scripture is a gift of the Spirit (Lk. 24, 45; Acts 4, 13). Through it we can discern in God's word the thread of the economy of salvation. It is more than an argument proving the fulfillment of the prophecies; it is the active presence of the Spirit, the power of God, to confer faith in the Resurrection of Christ.[17]

> This is what has come true: in this very city Herod and Pontius Pilate made an alliance with the pagan nations and the peoples of Israel, against your holy servant Jesus whom you anointed, but only to bring about the very thing that you in your strength and your wisdom had predetermined should happen (Acts 4, 27-28).

The prayer of the faithful applied Psalm 2 to Jesus and to those who had a share in his death. There is a continuity of action on both sides; it is the same people, in an identical spirit of hostility toward the Church, who persecute the Christians. Luke's Gospel had already emphasized this continuity between the prophets of the Old Testament, Christ, and Christians.[18]

The aorist *sunechthesan*, like the conjunction *gar*, affirm the historic reality of the prophecy fulfilled in the plots contrived against Christ. *Ep' aletheias*, which emphasizes the truth of the event, is an expression peculiar to Luke (20, 21; 4, 25; 22, 59; Acts 10, 34). The sentence contains two more of Luke's idiomatic phrases, the Hebraism *e cheir sou*, which signifies God's omnipotence, and *e Boule tou theou*,[19] which states God's plan.

The most important phrase of the pericope is *agios pais sou*, your holy servant Jesus whom you anointed (vv. 27, 30). As though to distinguish between the two uses of the word *pais*, Luke qualifies it with "holy" when applying it to Christ.

What does the epithet *pais theou*, applied to Christ by the apostolic community, stand for? Here we find ourselves at the crux of one of the most complex and most important questions of the New Testament. It is necessary to investigate what overtones the expression "servant of God" had for the Judea-Christian community.

The noun *servant* or the verb *to serve* (in Hebrew *'ebed*) includes the double concept of work and of submission. Depending on which is predominant, we have the meaning of *worker* or *servant*. The same verb can be translated by *to work* or *to obey*. These different meanings are met with both in profane literature and in religious life.[20]

In everyday life, *'ebed* signifies a man slave who has become the chattel of another.[21] This was Israel's condition in the land of Egypt.[22] Elsewhere the same word designates a person obedient to a superior, for example, the subject of a king or of a chieftain (1 S. 8, 17), a soldier conscripted for military service; the minister or messenger of a king (Gn. 40, 20, 41, 37; 2 K. 22, 12).

Far richer is the significance of the word *'ebed* in the religious domain: the servant is he who is submissive to God and who works in his service; though he calls himself servant, the pious Israelite did not use the bare, conventional form found in secular greetings; he belonged to God through the Covenant sealed at the time of his supernatural deliverance from the Egyptian yoke. God's service, therefore, has primarily a liturgical, cultual significance. But this service was not limited to a few religious ceremonies; it extends into every domain of life, the same work signifying work, service, and worship. In biblical thought there is no watertight partition between work and worship. The Jew's whole life was illumined by the light of the Covenant in which his human story had become entirely holy.

The servant of Yahweh was the people of God in their religious activity, more especially those who, in the Temple, were commissioned to celebrate the cult: the priests and Levites (Nb. 18, 7; Ne. 11, 3; Ezr. 6, 18). We should not restrict the meaning of service to ritual life; God's service is primarily a moral attitude of man towards God, which expressed itself by submission to the Torah (1 K. 8, 23; Pss. 69, 37; 102, 15). God is jealous to such a point that he will not allow his people to serve other gods.

Explicit Prayers 193

In exchange Israel received blessings and promises, protection, grace, and forgiveness.

This theology of service and of the servant of Yahweh is developed in the Book of the Consolation of Israel (Is. 40-55), in the light of its sacred history from its origins to its election (Is. 44, 1, 2, 21; 41, 8; 45, 4). It culminates in the description of the Servant of Yahweh.[23]

Beginning with the Exile, the word lost its collective meaning and was applied to a portion of the people, *a group of faithful*, those who were solicitous for the service of God;[24] the servants were the just as opposed to the wicked. Finally, the word took on an individual meaning and designated Abraham (Gn. 26, 24) Moses (14, 31), David (2 S. 3, 18; cf. Acts 4, 25), or some just man. As such, it is often found in the Psalms and the Lamentations, in which biblical meditation is most deeply felt.[25] More explicitly the word designates the king, entrusted with a special mission (Is. 37, 35; Jr. 33, 21), or the prophet as messenger of the divine will.

Four passages in particular of the Book of Consolation describe the Servant of Yahweh, in the canticles that bear his name. Who is the person designated by these poems? First of all, exegetes are divided between a collective and an individual explanation. Although the majority lean toward a single person, there is no agreement as to his name. Is it someone from the past (Moses, David), some contemporary descendant (a prophet, the author himself) or someone yet to come (the Messiah, a glorious king at the end of time)?[26]

Historically, in Hellenizing circles, post-exilic Judaism translated the Septuagint *pais* by *son of God,* and preferably interpreted it in the collective sense. Palestinian Judaism saw in the word *pais* a collectivity, the author, or the Messiah (when speaking of Is. 42, 1; 43, 10; 49, 1, 6; 52, 13). The messianic explanation remains constant regarding Is. 42, 1; 52, 13; the last text being applied to the last judgment.[27]

The New Testament reflects the thinking of Palestinian Judaism.

It uses the word eight times only, once in speaking of Israel (Lk. 1, 54), twice in speaking of David (Lk. 1, 69; Acts 4, 25), and five times in applying it to Christ (Mt. 12, 18 = Is. 42, 1; Acts 3, 13, 26; 4, 27, 30).[28]

The texts that call Christ *pais theou* come from ancient traditions. This title is applied to Jesus more particularly in prayers or in liturgical formulas. It was never widely used in pagan-Christian circles; St. Paul never uses it. We may conclude from this that it originated in Palestine before Hellenistic influence made itself felt. It designates Christ, to whom it applies the quotations from Deutero-Isaiah,[29] which are interpreted messianically.[30]

The Christology of the primitive community was greatly influenced by the description of the suffering Servant. The prophecies throw light on the drama of the Cross. Scriptural allusions are frequent in the account of the Last Supper, and in the rest of the gospel. We find references to the suffering Servant in the eucharistic liturgy (Mk. 14, 24), and also in archaic prayer, where the expression remained until the second century.[31] Finally, Christ as the suffering Servant plays a considerable part in Christian parenesis.

However sporadic Christ's own allusions to himself may be as the suffering Servant in Mark's and Matthew's accounts, it seems that he read into Is. 53 the necessity and the meaning of his Passion, as well as the significance of his messianic mission.[32]

The sermons of the Acts show that Jesus is called servant because his whole life was a submission to the will of his Father, because he never ceased serving and blessing men in order to save them. This service met with the opposition of mankind, particularly of the great, who leagued themselves against Jesus. But from now on the Cross is the sign of salvation. The Father has glorified his servant for his service; he holds his glory from God alone.

The prayer of the Acts proves that for those Christians the supreme messianic dignity (of the Son of Man) and the absolute humility of the suffering Servant were joined together in the person of the Christ of history.[33]

The expression *pais* was used by Christian liturgy and prayer and corresponds to that of lamb *agnos,* whose biblical substratum is the same.[34] *Pais* has in itself a cultual value. For Christ, the suffering Servant, unites in his own person worship and action, work and service, without any watertight separation. His sacrificial offering is his supreme act; his whole life culminated in the sacrifice of the Cross. His Resurrection was the sign of the efficacy of his sacrifice and of his glorification by the Father. Here we find ourselves at the very heart of the Christian mystery, ritualized by the liturgy in the breaking of bread.[35]

Luke specifies that the prophecies that speak of the "kings" refer to Herod and Pilate. Both are mentioned in accounts proper to Luke's Gospel (9, 9; 23, 6-16). They typify pagan responsibility at the trial of Jesus whose place in history they fix. The *archontes* are the leaders of the priests, the very ones who, on Calvary, applied in a wrong way the prophecy of the suffering Servant to Christ on the Cross: "He saved others, let him save himself if he is the Christ of God, the Chosen One" (Lk. 23, 35; cf. *o ekklektos,* Is. 42, 1).

These allusions are brought about by the events which caused the imprisonment of Peter and John. Before the crowd which had come running to the Portico of Solomon, Peter solemnly confessed: "It is the God of Abraham, Isaac and Jacob, the God of our ancestors, who has glorified his servant Jesus, the same Jesus you handed over and then disowned in the presence of Pilate" (Acts 3, 13). The same Apostle repeated his "offense" before the *archontes* by confessing "the name of Jesus Christ the Nazarene, the one you crucified, whom God raised from the dead" (Acts 4, 10).[36] Peter's trial was a continuation of that of Jesus. It enabled the Apostle to confess Christ before earthly tribunals, certain that the Son of Man would declare himself for him before God (Lk. 12, 8).

At the trial Jews and pagans had joined together (Acts 2, 23). The mission of Christians from now on was to bear witness at the bar of the world by confessing Christ as the Anointed One and

Kyrios. The prayer of the faithful therefore implies a confession of faith:

> And now, Lord, take note of their threats and help your servants to proclaim your message with all boldness, by stretching out your hand to heal and to work miracles and marvels through the name of your holy servant Jesus (Acts 4, 29-30).

Addressing God by the word *kurie* — we met in Jesus' prayer (Mt. 11, 25; Lk. 10, 21) — is quite rare in the New Testament and is linked with the divine omnipotence which governs the world according to his designs.[37] This is Yahweh's usual title in the Old Testament. Its use proves the archaic and Palestinian character of the prayer of the faithful.

The faithful ask the *parresia* for themselves. In the Bible, this word indicates a disposition of the believer toward God in prayer, a disposition made up of confidence, liberty, and joy. The Septuagint uses it to translate two passages of the book of Job:

> Is God likely to hear his cries
>   when disaster descends on him?
> Did he make Shaddai all his delight,
>   calling on him at every turn? (27, 9-10)

The same word is also found with the same meaning of tranquil liberty before God in the second passage from Job:

> If you return, humbled, to Shaddai
>   and drive all injustice from your tents,
> if you reckon gold as dust
>   and Ophir as the pebbles of the torrent . . .
> Then Shaddai will be all your delight,
>   and you will lift your face to God.
> You will pray, and he will hear;
>   you will have good reason to fulfil your vows (22, 23-24; 26-27).

The word takes on an eschatological meaning in the book of Wisdom; it becomes the assurance of the just man at God's tribunal (Ws. 5, 1). The just man shows this calm confidence especially in prayer.[38] The *parresia* is linked with persecution in later literature (4 M. 9, 5).

In the New Testament, in addition to the Acts, the word is

used in Johannine and Pauline writings. In the Acts the *parresia* characterizes the behavior of Christians before hostile Jews or pagans; it is the courage to brave the tribunal of the world, thanks to the Lord's assistance, which is the fruit of prayer. This *parresia* accompanies the confession of faith. The word is connected with the verbs *lalein* and *didaskalein*,[39] to such a degree that *parresiazesthai* takes on the meaning of "to preach."[40]

The spoken word, continuing the testimony, presupposes the public proclamation of the gospel. Both are gifts of the divine power which surpass the resources of the servants and enable them to discern the active presence of the Spirit.

The latter is made even more evident by miracles, portents and signs (Acts 2, 19, 22), these three being on an equal footing. They are the *mirabilia* which attest the work of God during Christ's life, and which authenticate the work of the disciples as being accomplished "by the name of Jesus" (Acts 4, 7, 10):

> As they prayed, the house where they were assembled rocked; they were all filled with the Holy Spirit and began to proclaim the work of God boldly (Acts 4, 31).

This was heaven's reply to their prayer, the proof that the mediation of Jesus was efficacious; the action of the Spirit is force; it strengthens the disciples by giving them a dauntless steadfastness to proclaim the gospel.

The miracles emphasize the continuity existing between Pentecost and the Church. It is always the same Spirit working; it acts with and through the community to confound or to convince.[41] It guides and unifies the apostolic action, from the center at Jerusalem to the evangelization of pagan nations. In this activity Stephen's martyrdom illustrates in a wonderful way the state of Christianity in its clash with the world.

Stephen's prayer

Stephen's activities, bolstered by miracles and great signs (Acts 6, 8; cf. 4, 30), which are mentioned in the prayer of the faithful, show a progress in the development of the community. The account relative to the first martyr belongs to the set of documents called E by Msgr. Cerfaux which group together everything relating to the Hellenists. Thanks to these documents, we can see the continuity between the Acts and the third Gospel.[42] The persecutions of the Christians prolong those endured by the prophets of the Old Testament (Acts 7, 51).

Stephen is portrayed as filled with wisdom and the Spirit (Acts 6, 10), recalling the saying in Lk. 21, 15: "I myself shall give you an eloquence and a wisdom that none of your opponents will be able to resist or contradict."

The Hellenists' opposition to Stephen finds its significance in the perspective of the messianic persecutions. The resemblance between the trial of Jesus and that of Stephen is intentionally emphasized. Stephen's vision ("I can see heaven thrown open . . . ") (Acts 7, 56) recalls Jesus' statement before his judges. It implies a confession of the Kyrios in glory, standing as a witness before the throne of God and pleading.[43] There is a parallelism between the confession of martyr and the eschatological confession of the Son of Man, which fulfills Jesus' promise to the high priest: "The Son of Man will be seated at the right hand of the Power of God" (Lk. 22, 69).[44] At the same time it marks a break with Jewish limitations (Acts 6, 13). This confessing of Christ brings about the deacon's condemnation, just as Jesus' own messianic confession was the cause of his own death (Lk. 22, 71; Mt. 26, 65; Mk. 14, 63). Stephen's testimony is therefore juridical, religious, and messianic, all in one.

Stephen's two prayers should be explained in this context. They correspond to the last words of Jesus, which the deacon would have known through oral tradition:[45] "As they were stoning him, Stephen said in invocation, 'Lord Jesus, receive my spirit.' Then he knelt down and said aloud, 'Lord, do not hold this sin against them'" (Acts 7, 58-59).

The whole scene of the martyrdom was under the sign of the Holy Spirit who guides the Church (Acts 7, 55). The verb *epikaleo* in the middle voice became, along with *krazein*, a technical term in the Septuagint to translate the Hebrew *qârâ'*, "to invoke in prayer." In the Old Testament the subject of this prayer was God; this is still found in the New Testament[46] but rather rarely. More generally prayer is addressed to Christ as Messiah and Son of God.[47] To invoke him in prayer and worship (Acts 9, 14, 21) is a sign of salvation. The Semitic expression "to call on the name of the Lord" (Jl. 2, 32; Acts 2, 21) proves the Palestinian origin of the formula.[48]

The use of the verb *epikaleisthai* throws light on the noun *kurios* and proves the faith of the apostolic community in the messiahship and the divinity of Christ.[49] The expression "to call on the name of the Lord" is a confession that Christ is the Lord. In him is fulfilled Joel's prophecy (Jl. 3, 5; Acts 2, 21; Rom. 10, 13). From now on, the word "Lord" no longer applies to Yahweh but to Jesus, the Savior who brought salvation. In this belief Christians call themselves those who invoke the name of the Lord.[50]

It is evident that the prayer to Jesus the Kyrios derives from the same Jerusalem tradition as Stephen's vision with which it must be related; the title of Kyrios therefore corresponds to Christ's manifestation in messianic glory.[51] Stephen's prayer is a confession of faith (cf. Rom. 10, 9-13). To the martyr it was, as it were, an anticipation of the judgment which saves those who call on the name of the Lord (cf. Acts 4, 12), according to Christ's promise (Lk. 22, 69). This is the first time we find a prayer addressed directly to Christ (cf. Acts 7, 59-60, where "Lord" designates Christ).

At the heart of this prayer we find faith in Christ the Kyrios associated with worship of God. As in the case of Paul, Stephen's confession expresses what the vision revealed to him.[52] Glorification by the Father is heaven's reply to the testimony which Jesus gave "in front of Pontius Pilate" (1 Tm. 6, 13; cf. Acts 4, 24). The parallelism is clear; the deacon invokes the Kyrios in the same way that Christ had invoked the Father.

It is in his name that the Christians were baptized, that they met for the breaking of bread, or that they confessed the name of the Lord. Before pagans and Jews, before princes and magistrates, Christians, like Stephen, proclaimed the same faith that made witnesses of them before making them martyrs. Stephen's prayer continues the confession of the liturgy in expressing the meaning of his bloody offering. As in Christ's case, Stephen combines prayer and action in one and the same sacrifice.

We might call Stephen's passion the first acts of Christian martyrology, preluding those of the primitive Church. We shall see the influence this account had on martyrological literature.

PART III
Chapter I

1. Introduction to the Acts of the Apostles," Jerusalem Bible, p. 195ff.
2. The most recent works on the question of sources are: L. Cerfaux, "La composition de la première partie du livre des Actes," *Recueil Cerfaux*, II, pp. 63-91; J. Jeremias, "Untersuchungen zum Quellenproblem der Apostelgeschichte," *ZNTW* 37, (9137), pp. 205-221; P. Benoît, "Remarques sur les sommaires des Actes," II, 42-V, in *Aux sources de la Tradition chrétienne* (*Mélanges Goguel*), pp. 1-10; W. L. Knox, *The Acts of the Apostles* (Cambridge, 1948), pp. 16-39.

Recent bibliography on the Acts will be found in: "Les problèmes du Livre des Actes d'après les travaux récents," *Analecta Lovaniensia et Orientalia* (Louvain, 1950), ser. II, fasc. 17. Since then H. Greeven has collected the studies of M. Dibelius on the same question in M. Dibelius, "Aufsätze zur Apostelgeschichte," *Forsch. Rel. u. Lit. des A. u. N.T.*, 42 (Göttingen, 1951). Cf. the recension of A.D. Nock in *Gnomon*, 25 (1950), pp. 497-505.

For prayer in the acts, see Ph. Menoud, *La vie de l'Eglise naissante*, (Paris, 1952), pp. 44-48.

3. J. Dupont, *Les problèmes du Livre des Actes*, p. 21.
4. E.g., *ainein* (Lk. 2, 13, 20; 19, 37; 24, 53; Acts 2, 47; 3, 8, 9).
   Klasis (Lk. 24, 35; Acts 2, 42).
   klan (Lk. 30; Acts 2, 46; 20, 7; 27, 35.
5. Cf. Acts 15, 8; Lk. 16, 15; Likewise Jr. 17, 10; Ps. 7, 10.
6. In order to situate this prayer and the problem it raises it is important to refer to L. Cerfaux, "La première communauté chrétienne à Jérusalem," *Recueil Cerfaux*, II, 125-156.

J. Dupont in *Revue biblique*, 62 (1955), p. 45 limits this prayer to the Apostles.
7. G. Delling, *Der Gottesdienst im N.T.* (1952), p. 115.
8. After *akousantes* codex Bezae adds *kai epignontes ten tou Theou energeian*, "and they recognized the force of God." It is an explanatory clause which seems to introduce the prayer that follows.
9. J. Nielen, *Gebet und Gottesdienst im N.T.*, pp. 147-149 has well pointed out the importance of this expression.
10. Cf. Acts 1, 14; 2, 46; 4, 24; 5, 12; 7, 57; 8, 6; 12, 20; 15, 25; 18, 12; 19, 29.
11. K. H. Rengstorf, *Despotes*, *TWNT*, II, 44.
12. Cf. Jb. 5, 8; Ws. 6, 7; 8, 3; Si. 36, 1; cf. 1 Clem. 8, 2; 20, 11; 33, 2; 52, 1.

13. E.g., 3 Esd. 4, 60 [19]; Tb. 3, 14; 8, 17; Jdt. 9, 12; Dn. 3, 37; 9, 8, 15-17, 19.
14. Ex. 20, 11; 2 Esd. 9, 6; Ps. 146, 6. Cf. also Gn. 1, 1; Is. 37, 16; Jr. 32, 17.
15. *I Clem.* 59-61; *Didache* 10, 3. Irenaeus states: "Faith in one God, the Father almighty, Creator of heaven and earth, of the sea and all that they contain" (*Adv. Haer.*, v, vj, v). Further on, we shall study the use of this formula in the acts of the martyrs.
16. The text of the first part of the verse is in very bad condition. B A E, 13, 15, 27, 29, 36, 38 give the reading *o tou patros emon dia pneumatos agiou stomatos D. paidos sou eipon.*
But this construction is not correct and gives no acceptable meaning. Nowhere in Scripture is it said that God speaks by the Holy Spirit. It does say that God speaks through the prophets (Acts 3, 18; Lk. 1, 70; Heb. 1, 1), or that the Spirit speaks through the mouth of David (Acts 1, 16; Mt. 22, 43).
Irenaeus, in the Latin text, seems to correct the given reading: qui per Spiritus Sancto ore Patris nostri, pueri tui dixisti. One difficulty is suppressed, but there still remains the unusual statement that God speaks through the Holy Spirit. Codex Bezae improves the text a little by writing: *os dia Pneumatos agiou dia tou stomatos lalesas D paidos sou.*
Torrey believes that this untranslatable text arises from a faulty translation of the original Aramaic, which ended by producing "an incoherent farrago of words" (C.F. Torrey, *The Beginning of Christianity*, IV).
Ancient and modern commentators have tried to remedy this situation by surgical operations. Hilary and Augustine suppress *pneumatos agiou;* D Pesch Boh Didymus suppress *patros emon;* Ps. Chrys. Preuschen suppress both. It is possible that *pneumatos agiou* may be a gloss.
Loisy retains the Vulgate text; qui Spiritus Sancto os Patris nostri David, pueri tui, dixisti. Zahn reconstructs the sentence in a similar way *o dia pneumatos agiou dia tou stomatos lalesas D. paidos sou.*
Cerfaux applies *paidos* to Christ by reading: *o dia stomatos tou patros emon D. dia pneumatos agiou peri paidos sou eipon.* Recueil *Cerfaux*, II, p. 141, n. 2.
17. The important problem of the exegesis of the Old Testament by the New has been studied many times. Let it suffice to refer to: L. Cerfaux, "L'exégèse de l'Ancien Testament," *Recueil Cerfaux*, II, pp. 205-217; C. H. Dodd, *The Old Testament in the New* (London, 1952), and *According to the Scriptures* (London, 1953).
18. E.g., Lk. 4, 24; 11, 47-51; 12, 11; 21, 12-15; 13, 34-35; Acts 7, 51.
19. Cf. Lk. 1, 66; Acts 11, 21; 13, 11; Lk. 7, 30; Acts 2, 23; 20, 27.
20. J. Jeremias, *"pais," TWNT*, V, 653-713.
21. E.g., Gn. 20, 14; 24, 35; 30, 43; 32, 6.
22. Cf. Ex. 20, 2; Dt. 5, 6; 6, 12.
23. Cf. Is. 42, 1-6; 49, 1-6; 50, 4-9; 52, 12 — 53, 12.
24. Pss. 34, 22,23; 35, 27; Is. 65, 8-14; Ml. 3, 17-18.
25. E.g., Pss. 19, 12-14; 31, 17; 109, 28; 119, 17, 23, 38; 143, 2.
27. The account of J. Jeremias, *TWNT*, 664-672, is wisely moderate.
27. Jeremias, *op. cit.*, V, p. 697.
28. The Aramaic substratum of *pais* in Mk. 1, 11 and Lk. 3, 22 is disputed. O. Cullmann, in *Baptism in the New Testament*, pp. 17-18, sees the Hebrew *ebed* in it.
29. Cf. Is. 42, 1-6; 49, 6, 52, 13 — 53, 12.
30. This stand is rather common. J. Jeremias, *op. cit.*, p. 701; L. Cerfaux, *Recueil Cerfaux*, II, pp. 139-140.
31. *Didache* 9, 2-3. The expression is also found in Clement of Rome, where

it is already beginning to have the meaning of *child* of God (1 Clem. 59, 2); this meaning seems clear in the Martyrdom of Polycarp, 14, 1.

32. Mt. 12, 18; cf. Mk. 8, 31; 9, 31; 10, 33; 14, 24; Mt. 26, 28; Lk. 22, 20; J. Jeremias, *op. cit.*, pp. 709-710.

33. A table will enable us to better understand the continuity of the borrowings:

Acts 3, 11ff.	Acts 4, 5	Acts 4, 24-31
3, 13, 26; cf. Ex. 3, 6		
pais Jesus		4, 27, 30
.....		
"the same Jesus you handed over" (Is. 53, 12) *paredokate*		
"and then disowned" *ernesasthe* (cf. Mt. 10, 33)		Acts 7, 35
Pilate		4, 27
dikaion (Lk. 23, 47)		
agion		4, 27, 30 Acts 2, 27
(Is. 53, 11)		Acts 7, 52
3, 17	4, 5, 9: *archontes* cf. Lk. 23, 35	4, 26
3, 18, 21 *christon*		4, 26
4, 5 *sunachthenai*		4, 27
4, 13 *parresia*		4, 29

In Peter's sermon we find the expression *pais* in a context evoking Jewish prayer since it calls on the God of Abraham, of Isaac, and of Jacob (Ex. 3, 6, 15) as do the prayer of Manasseh and the *Shemone Esre*.

The allusions to Isaiah in all these texts are numerous; Jesus is the *pais* (Is. 52, 13), he is delivered up (Is. 53, 12), the Just (Is. 53, 11), the stone scorned by the builders (Is. 52, 14 — 53, 5).

Peter uses the word *arneo* which means denial (Mt. 10, 33; Lk. 12, 9; cf. 8, 45; 9, 23). This technical term proves that we are really dealing here with a confession at the trial opened before Pilate.

Lastly, the prayer of the community corresponds to the whole episode related in the Acts, Peter's sermon, the arrest by the rulers, the confession of faith with complete confidence (*parresia*).

34. Already seen by O. Procksch, "*Agios*," *TWNT*, I, 103, and by H. Schlier, "*Amnos*," *ibid.*, I, 343. Same conclusion in O. Cullmann, *Baptism in the New Testament*, pp. 17ff.

35. Cf. J. Nielen, *Gebet und Gottesdienst* ..., p. 150 and note.

36. Arraigned before the Sanhedrin, Peter once again confesses the name of Jesus. Already before the people he had confessed "Jesus, the same Christ you handed over and then disowned in the presence of Pilate" (Acts 3, 13; 4, 27). Thereby, the person doubtlessly entered into every confession of faith. Cf. Justin, *Dial.* 76, 6; 85, 2. Cf. also O. Cullmann, *Early Christian Worship*, trans. A. Stewart Todd and James B. Torarnce (London, 1953), pp. 15-16.

37. W. Foerster, "*kurios*," *TWNT*, III, pp. 1086-1087.

38. E.g., Jb. 22, 27; Pss. 37, 4-11; 50, 1-3.

39. Acts 4, 29, 31; 9, 27; 18, 26.

40. Acts 9, 27; 14, 3; 18, 26; 19, 8.

41. L. Cerfaux, *Recueil Cerfaux*, II, pp. 164-166.

42. *Ibid.*, II, pp. 170-174.
For a critical study of Stephen's speech, cf. W. Mundle, "Die Stephanusrede, Apostelgeschichte 7: Eine Märtyrerapologie," *ZNTW*, 20 (1921), p. 137; M. Dibelius, "Zur Formgeschichte des N.T.," *Theol. Rundschau, N.F.*, 3 (1931), p. 234.

43. L. Cerfaux, *Recueil*, II, p. 170, states that in Stephen's confession "the primary object of the testimony, Christ's resurrection, is forgotten." However, it seems implied in the vision of Christ in his glory, to which we could compare that granted to Saul on the road to Damascus.

44. Text deliberately modified in Lk. 22, 69 if we compare it with Mk. 14, 62. Commentators who ask themselves why Christ is *standing* pose a false problem. Luke polishes the text so as to emphasize, by the position of the heavenly Witness, his role as confessor for those who confess him before men (Lk. 12, 9).

45. Cf. Acts 7, 59; Lk. 23, 46; Acts 7, 60; Lk. 23, 34.

46. E.g., Acts 2, 21; 1 Pt. 1, 17; 1 Cor. 1, 2.

47. Cf. Acts 7, 59; 9, 14, 21; 22, 16; Rom. 10, 12-14; 1 Cor. 1, 2; 2 Tim. 2, 22.

48. Cf. A. Klawek, *Das Gebet zu Jesus*, pp. 40-45.

49. K. L. Schmidt, "Epikaleo," *TWNT*, II, 501. The argument has also been formulated by J. Nielen, *Gebet und Gottesdienst* . . ., p. 163; J. Horst, *Proskynein*, pp. 193-194.

50. Cf. Acts 9, 14, 21; 22, 16; 1 Cor. 1, 2; 2 Tim. 2, 22; cf. Ps. 2, 6-11. J. Nielen, *Gebet und Gottesdienst* . . ., pp. 163-164, supposes that the expression was originally a count of indictment against Christians, and therefore originated from their adversaries.

51. L. Cerfaux, *Recueil*, I, 44; A. Klawek, *Das Gebet zu Jesu*, pp. 43-45.

52. Acts 7, 56. We find there the same messianic term "Son of Man."

Chapter II

THE PRIMITIVE CULT

While Christian prayer continues that of the Temple and the synagogue,[1] it must not mislead us regarding the newness of Christianity, which broke with the ancient rite. The focus of primitive prayer is to be sought in the eucharistic assemblies. The liturgy shaped personal prayer and gave it its own stamp.

Description of the assembly

The oldest part of the Acts, (Acts 2, 42, 46-47)[2] gives us a description of the first Christian community. The primitive text may have been extended by the addition of verses 43-45, which obviously break the rhythm and the unity of the description. The reasons for this insertion will be studied later.

> These remained faithful to the teaching of the apostles, to the brotherhood, to the breaking of bread and to the prayers (v. 42).
>
> They went as a body to the Temple every day but met in their houses for the breaking of bread; they shared their food gladly and generously; they praised God and were looked up to by everyone. Day by day the Lord added to their community those destined to be saved (vv. 46-47).[3]

Everything leads us to believe that the author is here reporting an already settled tradition. He makes use of technical terms whose meaning it is important to determine. Within the interval of a few verses, we find the verb *proskarterein* used twice in two different senses.[4] When the verb refers to prayer, it takes on the meaning of "to apply oneself, to be assiduous" (Acts 1, 14; 2, 42). This shade of meaning is further strengthened by the adverb *omothumadon* (Acts 4, 24).[5]

This fidelity of the community to prayer (adoration, praise, petition) manifests its docility to the precepts of Christ. Like Jesus, the Apostles had their eyes fixed on the Father who guides the community, particularly at decisive moments: the coming of the Spirit, the election of Matthias (Acts 1, 14; 2, 4). The new believers followed the same practice (Acts 2, 42). Prayer was a preparation for the community of life and labor in fidelity to the mission common to all of them.

The worship of the primitive community was led by the Apostles (Acts 6, 4). It was composed of four elements which the text joins in pairs: preaching and ministry, breaking of bread and prayers. These complement and do not oppose each other.[6]

First to be named, the *didache,* qualified by the liturgical term *proskarterountes,* appears as an element of Christian gatherings. In the gospel, the *didache* designates the doctrine of Jesus which contrasts him with the scribes and Pharisees.[7] In the Acts, the word is stereotyped to express exclusively "the doctrine of the Lord," which the Apostles transmitted as they received it with the faithfulness of eye-witnesses.

The teaching here does not refer to the *kerugma* or proclamation of the message to unbelievers, but to the catechetical instruction of already baptized converts (Acts 2, 41; cf. 20, 7). This preaching, of which we have an example in the episode of Paul at Troas, had as its subject the words and examples of Jesus. It must also have explained the Scriptures in the light of Christ and his fulfillment of the messianic promises. The readings from the Bible in the synagogue may have been the model for this kind of homily.[8] We have seen that Christian prayer was noticeably steeped in Scripture. An example of this was the use of Psalm 2, mentioned above (Acts 4, 25-27).

The *koinonia*[9] is an expression dear to Paul but missing from the gospels. It may signify either a centripetal relation of the community participating in one and the same reality,[10] or a centrifugal action in which the common good is shared.[11]

Here the word is taken in an absolute sense. It means a centrifugal action because of the centripetal verb *proskarterountes* and because of the three other, active elements which make up the cult. This Hellenistic word, laden with biblical overtones, should be compared with *koinos* (Acts 2, 45; 4, 32) and to *koinonos, koinonia* proper to Paul (1 Cor. 10, 16, 18). In the context of the cult, the word seems to mean a concrete act of the community, an offering, a distribution of food, which leaves us to suppose that the faithful made an offering linked to the breaking of bread for the benefit of the assembly.

The expression *klasis tou artou* is found only in St. Luke (Lk. 24, 35; Acts 2, 42). It is never used, any more than its corresponding verb, to refer to ordinary bread.[12] The reference here, then, is definitely to the breaking of a special bread, especially in the context that describes the primitive cult. Some exegetes even suppose that we are dealing here with a password, used to conceal the mystery of the Last Supper from the uninitiated.[13] Emphasized by the repetition of the article, the breaking of bread is a technical term designating the Eucharist.[14] Taken in itself, the expression recalls the rite which began the Jewish meal, when the head of the household broke bread for his guests.

What is the meaning of the Greek *proseuchai* used in connection with the breaking of bread? The article seems to indicate that we are dealing with set prayers that formed part of the cult, an essential element of the communal life of the first Christians. These prayers were said by the Apostles in the name of all. This was one of their functions during the liturgical gatherings (Acts 5, 4). They may have been freely inspired by the condition and needs of the Church.[15] They transcribed the riches of Jewish prayer into Christian form. The faithful poured new wine into the old wineskins.

Verse 46 is the natural continuation of verse 42.[16] Luke had already used the expression *kath' emeran* in his Gospel for the daily teaching of Jesus in the Temple (Lk. 19, 47; 22, 53), in the *Our Father* for daily bread; lastly, in the parable of Lazarus, the poor man, it characterizes the continuity of the days of sumptuous fare (Lk. 16, 19). These different meanings seem to come to light in the present text.[17]

Translators often do not take sufficiently into account the rhythm that *te . . . te* gives to the sentence: "They went as a body to the Temple every day but met in their houses for the breaking of bread; they shared their food gladly and generously" (Acts 2, 46-47). In either case, in the Temple as in the Christian assemblies, we are dealing with religious gatherings; the Christians shared the food that was distributed to them by the community and which came from the common pooling of their possessions (Acts 2, 45b).

The expression *kat' oikon* designates private dwellings, doubtless placed at the disposal of the community (Acts 5, 42; cf. 12, 12). It was in this way that the disciples had already gathered in "the upper room where they were staying" (Acts 1, 13; 2, 1), doubtless in the very place where the risen Christ ate a piece of grilled fish before them on Easter Sunday (Lk. 24, 36-43). The same applies to the Pauline communities.[18] On his return from prison, Peter "went straight to the *house* of Mary the mother of John Mark where a number of people had assembled and were praying" (Acts 12, 12).

The breaking of bread, which set itself over against the cult of the Temple, here means the celebration of the Eucharist.[19] *Metelambanon trophes,* on the contrary, designates a true meal organized in private homes from communal offerings, during which the faithful celebrated the Last Supper (1 Cor. 11, 20, 34).[20]

The characteristic note of these brotherly meals was joy, *agalliasis,* and simplicity of heart, *aphelotes*. The first noun took on a technical meaning in the liturgical celebrations of the primitive community. In the Septuagint, the word translates the religious joy of those who celebrate the works of God on behalf of the community and of the individual (Ps. 50, 14). The word evolved toward an eschatological meaning to express the joy of the final goal, anticipated in the cult.[21]

Linked to a meal, this joy took on a more precise and religious significance It was already implied in the noun *parresia* which we met before in the prayer of the community (Acts 4, 29). O. Cullmann justifies this liturgical joy by the memory of the meals the Apostles shared with the risen Christ (Acts 10, 41), reported by both Luke and John in their Gospels. The explanation is correct, but would gain in depth if, in addition, we associated the breaking of bread to all of Christ's meals, which in St. Luke recall the messianic banquet to which the poor and sinners are invited. We must now analyze their biblical components.

Religious meals and the breaking of bread

The book of the Acts is a continuation not only of the life of Jesus but also of Israel's history. The young community called itself *ekklesia,* because it was conscious of being the successor to the church in the desert, described in Deuteronomy. The picture of the first community throws light on the gift of the Spirit in this new Pentecost, which replaces and fulfills the promises of the old Pentecost. The eucharistic meals, too, are connected with those which, in the Old Testament, played an important role in the religion of Israel.

The book of Exodus recounts the ratification of the Covenant. In the "Yahwistic" tradition (Ex. 24, 1-2; 9-12), the Covenant is confirmed by a meal eaten in the presence of God:

> Moses went up with Aaron, Nadab and Abihu, and seventy elders of Israel. They saw the God of Israel beneath whose feet there was, it seemed, a sapphire pavement pure as the heavens themselves. He laid no hand on these notables of the sons of Israel: they gazed on God. They ate and they drank (Ex. 24, 9-11).

The "Elohistic" tradition (Ex. 24, 3-8) describes the ratification of the Covenant by the sprinkling of blood in the presence of the people at the foot of the mountain. Both rites inaugurated

Israel's entry into the community of the Covenant; the communion sacrifice or the sprinkling of the altar and of the people with the victim's blood sealed the bond with the God of the Covenant.[22]

We must compare these with the offerings made by the king on the occasion of his coronation; they were intended to seal the union between the anointed, Yahweh, and his people. Feasts were the occasion of royal liberality and of "great rejoicing."[23] The royal Psalms delight in singing of the king's munificence toward his subjects.

The transfer of the Ark and the dedication of the Temple were solemnized by a communion sacrifice, after which David distributed food to the people that they might share in the festivity which celebrated God's presence in the midst of his people (2 S. 6, 17-19). Solomon did likewise (1 K. 8, 62-66). There even was a room close to the altar of sacrifice intended for banquets (1 S. 9, 22; Jr. 35, 2; cf. 1 Ch. 15 - 16).

We also find the elements of God's presence, of reunion of the community and of joy, in religious feasts and observances which often date back to primitive rites. The same is true of the firstfruits of men, animals, and the fruits of the earth which were offered either to ensure God's protection over all their possessions, or to recognize God's right over everything and every being.[24] The sacrifice of the firstfruits of the flock is found in the Passover, that of the firstfruits of the crops in various agricultural feasts. Every sacrifice of the firstfruits was the occasion for meals of rejoicing (Dt. 16, 10-12), which are also found in post-exilic times (Tb. 2, 1).

Differing from the firstfruits, the tithe was a very old observance (Gn. 14, 20; 28, 22).[25] Originally it was the recognition of God's ownership of all things. The tithe later lost its meaning of sacrifice and became a simple tax. Its purpose for existence was to support those who had no lands of their own, first of all, the Levites, then the poor. The tithe was also connected with a meal of rejoicing (Dt. 12, 6-7, 11-12, 17-18; 14, 22-27). Every third year the tithe reverted to the poor (Dt. 14, 28-29).[26] We find the same rejoicing at the feast of Tabernacles (Ne. 8, 9-12).

On the occasion of sacrificial ceremonies and feasts, arrangements were made in favor of the poor, i.e., those who owned no property, Levites, widows, orphans, strangers, and slaves. The sabbatical year,[27] the seven-year cancellation of debts, and the third-year tithe clearly favor the poor who had their place also at the communion meals.

The reason for this attentiveness toward the disinherited was that poverty represented an insult, as it were, to the bounty of God who dispenses the gifts of the earth. Deuteronomy recalls that Israel's state in Egypt was that of a stranger: "Remember that you were a slave in Egypt" (Dt. 16, 12). For this reason strangers, widows, and orphans were to have a share in the feast of Weeks, or Pentecost.[28] We find traces of this in apocryphal literature (Test. XII Za. 5-7).

The prophets who announced messianism portrayed it as a new Exodus. They proclaimed that the poor, the *anawim* would take part in the feast; they would participate in the messianic kingdom at God's banquet, where they "will receive as much as they want to eat" (Ps. 22, 26). The "songs of the Servant" delineate the Messiah in the guise of an outcast (Is. 53, 4, 7). This hope nurtures the prayer of the Psalms, as it underlies the fervor of the *anawim*. Psalm 22, which describes the trials of the Messiah, proclaims at the same time the joy of the messianic banquet (Ps. 22, 27).

Meal and Passover

The Jewish Passover ritualized the wonderful liberation of God's people from Egyptian slavery. God did not create a new rite but gave a new meaning to the old one. The distinct parts of the paschal rite, the sacrifice of the lamb and the eating of unleavened bread, date back to a former double feast, or to a single feast with a twofold aspect,[29] the offering to God of the firstfruits of one's flock and crops. Deuteronomy clearly establishes the connection between the firstfruits and the Passover. The consecration of the firstborn of men and animals goes back to the sacrifice of the paschal lamb (Ex. 13, 1-2, 11-16; Nb. 3, 13; 8, 17). The paschal celebration combined the memory of the trials of Egypt and gratitude for deliverance, and had therefore a two-fold significance. But the theme of rejoicing, long held in the background, did not become dominant until after the Exile (Dt. 16, 12; 26, 1-11; Ezr. 6, 22). The Chronicler relates how king Jezekiah purified the Temple, re-established the cult, and solemnly celebrated "the feast of the Unleavened Bread." There was "great rejoicing" for seven days while the Israelites "praised Yahweh with all their might." The cost of this festivity was borne by the king (2 Ch. 30, 21-26). The same applies to king Josiah (2 Ch. 35, 1-9; particularly vv. 7, 8, 17).

Rabbinical Judaism interpreted the paschal meal in an eschatological sense; it became the figure of the new liberation awaited by the nation.[30] Before the institution of the Eucharist, Jesus presented the Passover as the figure of the kingdom to come. Luke alone reports the saying of Christ: "I tell you, I shall not eat it again until it is fulfilled in the kingdom of God . . . I tell you, I shall not drink wine until the kingdom of God comes" (Lk. 22, 16, 18). The other two Synoptics likewise evoke the eschatological perspective.

The eucharistic Pasch, which will be perfected in the ultimate kingdom, itself completes the figure of the communion meals which sealed the Covenant of Sinai. From now on, it is the blood of Jesus that seals the new and final Covenant (Lk. 22, 20; cf. Mt. 26, 28; Mk. 14, 24; 1 Cor. 11, 25). All the accounts, then, are unanimous in seeing in the Last Supper the fulfillment of the promises and of the prototypes. The allusion to Exodus 24, 8 is clear: "Then Moses took the blood and cast it towards the people. 'This' he said 'is the blood of the Covenant (cf. Mk. 14, 24, *touto estin to aima tes diathekes*) that Yahweh has made with you, containing all these rules' " (cf. Jr. 31, 31).

In the expectation of the consummation of the kingdom, the Last Supper is the pledge of the eschatological banquet. Here too

St. Luke alone relates the promise of Jesus: "And now I confer a kingdom (*diatithemai* and *dietheto*)[31] on you, just as my Father conferred one on me: you will eat and drink at my table in my kingdom, and you will sit on thrones to judge the twelve tribes of Israel" (Lk. 22, 29-30).

The eschatological banquet

The liturgical meals, like the paschal celebration, proclaim the messianic and eschatological blessings through the very overtones which enrich its original theme in the course of Israel's history. Already this theme appeared in the prophets through the imagery of a banquet. In Deutero-Isaiah, Yahweh invites the people to messianic happiness, depicted in the literary garb of a banquet:

> Oh, come to the water all you who are thirsty;
> though you have no money, come!
> Buy corn without money, and eat,
> and, at no cost, wine and milk (Is. 55, 1).

The invitation is addressed to the poor, to whom Yahweh gives his attention. This oracle serves as a prelude to the banquet of Wisdom in a passage, inspired by Isaiah, from the book of Proverbs:[32]

> Wisdom has built herself a house,
>   she has erected her seven pillars,
> she has slaughtered her beasts, prepared her wine,
>   she has laid her table . . .[33]
> 'Who is ignorant? Let him step this way.'
>   To the fool she says,
> Come and eat my bread,
>   drink the wine I have prepared! (Pr. 9, 1-2, 4-5)

The cult developed the theme of the messianic banquet (Ps. 23, 5) around the liturgical celebrations of firstfruits, Passover, and pentecost, as we have already studied. The royal psalms, sung during the Passover, express the rejoicing of this feast (Pss. 116—118). Psalm 16 serves as a prelude to this eschatological vision when death itself will be overcome (cf. Acts 2, 26). The same is true of Psalm 22 whose influence is evident in the apostolic Church.

This eschatological interpretation of the liturgical banquet is found particularly in apocalyptic literature. The Apocalypse of Isaiah gives us a remarkable description of the messianic banquet (Is. 25, 6-12):

> On this mountain,
> Yahweh Sabaoth will prepare for all peoples
> a banquet of rich food, a banquet of fine wines,
> of food rich and juicy, of fine strained wines.
> On this mountain he will remove
> the mourning veil covering all peoples,
> and the shroud enwrapping all nations,
> he will destroy Death for ever.
> The Lord Yahweh will wipe away
> the tears from every cheek;
> he will take away his people's shame
> everywhere on earth,
> for Yahweh has said so.
> That day, it will be said: See, this is our God
> in whom we hoped for salvation;
> Yahweh is the one in whom we hoped.
> We exult and we rejoice
> that he has saved us;
> for the hand of Yahweh
> rests on this mountain.
> Moab is trodden down where he stands
> as straw is trodden in the dung pit;
> as there he stretches out his hands
> like a swimmer stretching out his hands to swim.
> But Yahweh curbs his pride
> and whatever his hands attempt.
> Your arrogant, lofty walls
> he destroys, he overthrows,
> he flings them in the dust.

This description anticipates the parable of the wedding feast found in the gospels (Mt. 22, 2-10; Lk. 14, 16-24). Apocalyptic literature localizes the messianic banquet on Zion which, with the Temple, is the dwelling-place of Yahweh. The imagery implies a memory of the covenant meal of the seventy ancients at Sinai (Ex. 24, 1-2, 9-10). Elsewhere the feast takes place in the Temple or at Jerusalem (Pr. 9, 1; 4 Ezr. 8, 52).

With a slight change of key, the banquet theme evolved toward

The Primitive Cult

that of a wedding, which celebrated the union of Yahweh with his people. This marriage symbolism enabled the prophets to enrich the theology of the Covenant. Announced by Hosea and Jeremiah, the wedding theme found its supreme expression in the Canticle of Canticles:

> I come into my garden,
> my sister, my promised bride,
> I gather my myrrh and balsam,
> I eat my honey and my honeycomb,
> I drink my wine and my milk.
> Eat, friend, and drink,
> drink deep, my dearest friends (Sg. 5, 1).

"My dearest friends" are the Israelites, more particularly the poor (Is. 55, 1-2), who are invited to enjoy the blissfulness of the new days. The same theme is found in the New Testament, both in the parables (Mt. 22, 1-10) and in the Apocalypse, where the marriage supper of the Lamb combines the triple theme of wedding, banquet, and paschal lamb (Re. 19, 9).

By placing the messianic rejoicings in the framework of a new Exodus, the theme of banqueting interacts with that of the abundance of paradise in a restored Eden, the place of the universal ingathering. The seventy ancients of the banquet of the Covenant are interpreted as representing "all the nations of the earth."[34] The manna and the miraculous water of the desert intimate the new, wonderfully fertile land where the poor are the guests of God.

The book of Joel, which plays a major role in the Acts, orchestrates this liturgy of hope, and describes the restoration of Israel in the tones of an era of paradise, preceding by an outpouring of the Spirit (Jl. 2, 21-27). To the vision of abundance, the prophet joins the theme of rejoicing, of a plentiful feast where men will be filled and will praise the name of Yahweh for having accomplished there wonders on their behalf. We again find this theme in the multiplication of the loaves that accompanies the new Exodus (Jn. 6, 32-33), the miracle at Cana (Jn. 2, 1-11, and the miraculous draught of fishes (Jn. 21, 1-14).

Finally, a last theme interacts in apocalyptic literature with that of the eschatological meal, that of the *Son of Man* (Dn. 7, 13). Standing before the high priest, Jesus applies the prophecy of Daniel to himself (Mk. 14, 62). The repast is not only partaken of in the presence of Yahweh, but with the Messiah. We have new testimony of this in the documents found at Qumran. This is how the Apocalypse of Henoch describes the feast: "The Lord of spirits will dwell with them; and they will eat with this Son of Man; they will take their places at his table for all ages" (62, 14). The same assertion is found in Luke: "I confer a kingdom on you, just as my Father conferred one on me: you will eat and drink at my table in my kingdom" (Lk. 22, 29-30). St. John's Apocalypse, in turn, takes up the theme of apocalyptic literature: "If one of you hears me calling and opens the door, I will come in to share his meal, side by side with him" (Re. 3, 20; cf. also 14, 14-16).

The meals of Jesus

The biblical substratum of the various themes analyzed, which intertwine to describe the coming of messianic times, enable us to take better into account the allusions scattered throughout the gospels, and to place the description of the apostolic community in its proper perspective. The typology of the New Testament presents the eschatological events as fulfilled in Christ, events which the Old Testament was content to project into the future. The meals of Jesus, particularly in Luke's Gospel, take on a religious meaning. They fulfill the prototypes of the ritual repasts which foretold the messianic banquet.[35]

The presence of Jesus at these meals confers a messianic significance on them. This is obvious in St. John's Gospel, which relates as its very first miracle the sign of water changed into wine at the wedding feast of Cana. Through it Jesus manifested his messiahship and inaugurated the nuptial joy of God and mankind.

When the tax collector, Levi, heard Christ's call, he "held a great reception in his house, and with them at table was a large gathering of tax collectors and others" (Lk. 5, 29). Mark and Matthew specify that these "others" were "sinners" (Mk. 2, 15; Mt. 9, 10). The Pharisees were scandalized and said: "Why do you eat and drink with tax collectors and sinners?" Jesus replied that, according to the messianic promises, he had come for the sick and sinners. This was not a mere condescending gesture; it went to the very heart of Jesus' mission. He came to remove the barriers between sinners and God, between whom he restored communion (Lk. 5, 32), sealing it by a religious act.

The adversaries went further: "John's disciples are always fasting and saying prayers, and the disciples of the Pharisees too, but yours go on eating and drinking. Jesus replied, 'Surely you cannot make the bridegroom's attendants fast while the bridegroom is still with them?'" (Lk. 5, 33-34)

Christ put an end to the time of waiting; he stated that he was fulfilling the prototypes, making them real by his presence. In Jesus' reply the themes of the messianic meal, of rejoicing, and of wedding are interconnected.[36]

There was the same opposition to John's disciples, whose importance and way of life are better known through the Qumran documents. "For John the Baptist comes, not eating bread, not drinking wine, and you say 'he is possessed.' The Son of Man comes, eating and drinking, and you say, 'Look, a glutton and a drunkard, a friend of tax collectors and sinners'" (Lk. 7, 33-34).

Once again we meet the expression Son of Man. In his reply, Jesus emphasizes the fact that he condescends to eat with publicans and sinners. For Luke this was precisely Jesus' mission. As though to throw light on the place sinners have in the kingdom, the evangelist continues his account by describing the meal at the house of Simon the Pharisee. While at table Jesus allowed a sinful woman to enter the room and justifies her before his host. The forgiveness of her sins signifies the welcome of this sinner into the messianic community. The same reproach of welcoming sinners and eating with them, which runs like a leitmotif throughout Luke's Gospel, introduces the three parables of mercy peculiar to the evangelist: the lost sheep, the lost drachma, and the prodigal son (Lk. 15, 1-32). These parables shed light on the messianic mission of Jesus. He came to break down the barriers that separate men from God — barriers often erected by the Pharisees themselves (cf. Mt. 23, 13) — that separate the just from sinners, and to restore the community of all the prodigal to the Father.

The messianic banquet is not a privilege reserved for the children of Israel, but for those who welcome the Messiah. On this condition they will share the eschatological banquet with Abraham, Isaac, and Jacob. One's dispositions while on earth, therefore, has its repercussion even in eternity:

> Once the master of the house has got up and locked the door, you may find yourself knocking on the door, saying, "Lord, open to us" but he will answer, "I do not know where you come from." Then you will find yourself saying, "We once ate and drank in your company; you taught in our streets" but he will reply, "I do not know where you come from. Away from me, all you wicked men!"
>
> Then there will be weeping and grinding of teeth, when you see Abraham and Isaac and Jacob and all the prophets in the kingdom of God, and yourselves turned outside. And men from east and west, from north and south, will come to take their places at the feast in the kingdom of God (Lk. 13, 25-29).

In addition to concern for sinners and pagans, Luke was preoccupied with the poor, another element of the messianic promises.[37] The poor will be filled in an era of paradise plenty. This is the meaning of the petition in the *Our Father* for daily bread (Lk. 11, 3) and of the multiplication of the loaves which throws light on the meal of the poor. In both accounts it is said: "They all ate as much as they wanted" (Lk. 9, 17; Mt. 14, 13-21; Mk. 6, 30-44; Jn. 6, 1-13; Mk. 8, 1-9; Mt. 15, 32-39).

Among the evangelists Luke is the only one to give us the *logion* that the poor should be invited to a feast: "When you give a lunch or a dinner, do not ask your friends, brothers, relations or rich neighbors, for fear they repay your courtesy by inviting you in return. No; when you have a party, invite the poor, the crippled, the lame, the blind" (Lk. 14, 12-13). This paradoxical choice of guests, in sharp contrast with the usual procedure, will be rewarded "when the virtuous rise again." The parable of the invited guests which follows this saying as though to illustrate it, shows what God's attitude is toward the eschatological meal (Lk. 14, 21).[38]

The parable of the rich man who feasted "magnificently every day" (*kath' emeran;* cf. Acts 2, 46), while Lazarus, the poor man, could not satisfy his hunger (cf. Lk. 15, 16), clarifies for us the reversal brought about by the gospels in the scale of values and of social classes. The poor man goes "to the bosom of Abraham," meaning the place of honor at the side of the patriarch (Lk. 16, 19-31).[39]

Jesus' Last Supper with his disciples, from this point of view, takes on a new light. It is the sacrament of the eschatological expectation, founded on the mystery of Christ. The Twelve who were there represent the new Israel; around them the messianic community is being prepared. There is continuity from the beginning to the end of the life of Jesus, from his first to his last meal. The first miraculous sign at Cana and the multiplication of the loaves foretell the sacrament of Communion which will be the last sign.[40] In a wonderful progression these "signs" prepare the "hour" of sacrifice, the hour of supreme service where, in the rending of the Cross, the ingathering is being prepared.

Whereas Matthew and Mark place the kingdom where the disciples will drink the new wine in a distant, eschatological future (Mt. 26, 29; Mk. 14, 25), Luke describes the same kingdom as an earthly reality that is near at hand: the Eucharist inaugurates the true Pasch of the kingdom. Luke deliberately revises the text handed down by Mark and suppresses the new wine. He confines himself to the statement that Jesus will drink no more wine in his earthly state. "In insinuating that Jesus will eat and drink again in the kingdom, he was no doubt thinking of the meals that were to take place after the Resurrection."[41] For him, the inauguration took place between the paschal meal and the apparitions of the risen Christ. The meals eaten after the Resurrection fulfill the promises of all the earthly meals by uniting, around the eucharistic table, the faithful who communicate with Jesus in the true sacrifice of the Lamb.

What the Apostles only dimly perceived on Holy Thursday is made clear to them at the meals they share with the risen Christ. They were to remain deeply affected by them (Acts 10, 41), so much so that they later referred to them. Luke tells us that their joy was so great that they forgot to eat (Lk. 24, 41).

The meals with the risen Christ are by no means opposed to those of our mortal life. The death and Resurrection of Christ are inseparably linked in the faith of the disciples. The Risen One had instilled this into the companions of Emmaus: "You foolish men! So slow to believe the full message of the prophets! Was it not ordained that the Christ should suffer and so enter into his glory?" (Lk. 24, 25-26) The language of Peter and of the gospels shows to what an extent the Apostles were conscious of how the entire life of Jesus, from his baptism to his resurrection, fulfilled the messianic prophecies.

The scriptural premises, which we have tried to explain, throw light on the descriptions in the Acts where the life of the apostolic community is reported. This community was conscious of being the successor to the community in the desert. The name it borrows from Deuteronomy, *ekklesia* (Acts 5, 11; 7, 38; 8, 1), designated among the Jews the solemn assembly of the chosen people (Dt. 23, 1-9). Chronicles and Esdras apply the same word to the gatherings assembled by the king to celebrate either his coronation or the Passover, which were occasions of great rejoicing.[42]

The Church was inaugurated by the outpouring of the Spirit which, according to Joel's prophecy, filled "the entire house," open to the world. In Deuteronomy's teaching, the feast of Weeks or Pentecost was one of universal rejoicing to which Levites, strangers, orphans, and widows were invited (Dt. 16, 11), in memory of Israel's condition in Egypt. Under the impulse of the Spirit, the messianic community carried out the community of goods to the letter so that there might be no more poor. As in ancient Israel, the enthronement of the Kyrios in glory was accompanied by the serving of food and festivities at which the poor were God's guest.

If it be true that Acts 2, 43-45 are a later addition to the primitive text, their author wished to describe the fervor with which Christians took Christ's teaching on feeding the poor very literally, in order to give the messianic community concrete expression. Christian experience proves to what a degree the first Christians understood the demands of the gospel. Their faith, founded on the fulfillment of the messianic promises, was not ethereal but daily relived the examples given by the Lord. Their resemblance to the Qumran sect is striking in the matter of community of goods.[43]

These spiritual dispositions of the primitive community crystallized around the breaking of bread. This was a thanksgiving for the Resurrection of Christ, the invisible presence of the Risen One at the gathering of his followers, continuing the former repasts, the promise and firstfruits of universal ingathering at the eschatological banquet. The joy of the assembly was further accentuated by the secret hope that the Kyrios would return during one of these eucharistic meals.[44]

The rejoicing of the faithful during these liturgical meals was not, therefore, the effect of wine, as Peter sharply comments, but was the work of God. The question is accurately circumscribed by the word *aphelotes,* a characteristic expression of St. Luke. It underlines the spiritual, unequivocal origin of their exaltation.[45] Christians, following the counsel already given to the Jews for communion meals (1 S. 1, 14), carefully avoided any excess. At Corinth, St. Paul was obliged to check abuses when the pleasures of eating and drinking took precedence over the Spirit.

The expression *ainein theon,* dear to St. Luke is found precisely in those texts that speak of the *ekklesia* of the desert and recount the transfer of the Ark, both in Chronicles (1 Ch. 16, 36) and in Psalm 22, where we find both *ekklesia* and eulogy joined together: "You are the theme of my praise in the Great Assembly"

(Ps. 22, 26), followed immediately by the characteristic verse: "The poor will receive as much as they want to eat" (Ps. 22, 27). In Luke, this praise begins with the advent of Christ (Lk. 2, 13); it expresses the joy of the disciples when Jesus solemnly entered Jerusalem (Lk. 19, 37), and perhaps at the memory of the prophetic resurrection of Lazarus. The third Gospel ends on this same note in the Temple (Lk. 24, 53). From then on, it passed to the Church where it punctuates the joy and faith of the messianic community.[46]

Conscious of being the community of the desert which God sustained from day to day, the Church of Jerusalem remembered the counsel of Deuteronomy: "Let there be no poor among you" (Dt. 15, 4; cf. 7-11), which explains Paul's indignation when the poor were scorned at Corinth during the liturgical functions (1 Cor. 11, 17-22). In the Jerusalem community, the prescription of Deuteronomy was followed to the letter (Acts 4, 34). Whatever be the redactional origin of the summary which twice relates the common sharing of goods (Acts 2, 44-45; 4, 32, 34-35),[47] the way of life of the young Church shows to what an extent the liturgy was integrated into their everyday life.

The breaking of bread is rich with all the biblical overtones which, during Israel's religious history, had burdened the religious value of the meals. When instituting it, Christ had united in its sacramental reality the riches of the elements and the diversity of plans which the typology of the Old Testament had made available. Until the end of time, it will remain the prototype of the eschatological banquet which Christ will share with his followers in the Kingdom.

PART III
Chapter II

1. We have already discussed the cult of the synagogue pp. 66-72. Cf. J. Nielen, *Gebet und Gottesdienst . . .*, pp. 73-86.
2. P. Benoît, "Les sommaires des Actes," *Aux sources de la Tradition*, pp. 2, 4. L. Cerfaux, *Recueil*, II, pp. 71-73, takes the same point of view, at least for Acts 2, 46-47.
3. Codex Bezae has a slightly different text: *pantes de prosekarteroun en to iero kat'oikous epi to auto klontes.* For *laon* it substitutes *kosmon.* We have here

The Primitive Cult

a description of the apostolic community whose value and importance is increased by its archaic character.

4. The study of this has been made by E. Schürer, in *Sitzungenberichte der preussischen Akademie der Wissenschaft* (1897), p. 214. The term can be applied to people (to attach one's self to someone, Acts 8, 13; 10, 7), and to things (to apply oneself to ... to give oneself to ... to persevere in ... Acts 1, 14; 2, 42; 6, 4; cf. Mk. 3, 9; Rom. 12, 12; 13, 6; Col. 4, 2.

5. Cf. *supra*, p. 189.

6. Here we part company with E. Jacquier, *Actes des apôtres* (Paris, 1926), pp. 86-87.

7. Cf. Mt. 7, 28; 22, 33; 16, 12; cf. Jn. 7, 16; 18, 19.

8. Cf. *supra*, p. 66.

9. The word *koinonia* has been studied many times. It is sufficient here to mention J. Y. Campbell, "Koinonia and its Cognates in the N.T.," *Journal of Bibl. Lit.*, 51 (1932), p. 352; H. Seesemann, *Der Bebriff Koinonia im N.T.* (Giessen, 1933); F. Hauck, "*Koinonia*," *TWNT*, III, 804-810; H. Bolkestein, *Wohltätigkeit und Armenpflege im vorchristlichen Altertum* (1939), p. 431; Bo Reicke, *Diakonie, Festfreude und Zelos* (Uppsala, 1951), pp. 25-26.

10. 1 Cor. 1, 9; 2 Cor. 13, 13; 1 Jn. 1, 3, 6, 7.

11. Rom. 15, 26: the collection; 1 Cor. 10, 16: the Eucharistic communion; 2 Cor. 8, 4: a charitable undertaking; 2 Cor. 9, 13 and Ph. 1, 5: the offering; Heb. 13, 16: the common pooling of resources. Cf. Bo Reicke, *op. cit.*, pp. 25-26.

12. Exegetes have not finished discussing the meaning of the word *Klasis* in St. Luke. Some see in it the Eucharist, others only a blessing. Among the latest works we may mention J. Nielen, *Gebet und Gottesdienst im N.T.*, pp. 227-229, who refuses to see there the Eucharist; J. Behm, "*Klasis*," *TWNT.*, III, 729, who is led to find the Last Supper in it.

13. J. Jeremias, *Eucharistic Words*, pp. 133-134.

14. Moreover, it is sufficient to compare Acts 2, 42 and 2, 46 where the breaking of bread is clearly distinguished from ordinary meals. We find the same position in S.C. Gayford, "Church," *Dict. of the Bible*, I, p. 428; G. Delling, *Der Gottesdienst im N.T.*, p. 125.

15. It is sufficient to refer to the prayer of the community, Acts 4, 24-30. Clement of Rome's prayer gives us yet another example (*1 Clem*, 59-61).

16. Benoit, *Remarques sur les sommaires des Actes*, pp. 4-6.

17. We find more of Luke's phrasing: *omothumadon*, already met with, *kat'oikon* (Acts 5, 42), an expression which Paul applies to local churches (1 Cor. 16, 19; Col. 4, 15; Phm. 2), *aphelotes*, which is not found in the Septuagint and is used only here.

18. Cf. 1. Cor. 16, 19; Rom. 16, 5; Phm. 2, Col. 4, 15.

19. P. Menoud, *La vie de l'Eglise naissante*, pp. 35-43; "Les Actes des Apôtres et l'Eucharistie," *Revue d'histoire et de philosophie religieuses*, 33 (1953), pp. 23-26.

20. It is sufficient to refer to 1 Cor. 11, 26-34. It is also stated in the *Didache*, 10, 1.

21. Pss. 96, 11; 97, 1, 8; 126, 2, 5; Is. 12, 6; 25, 9; *Test. XII, Jud.*, 25, 5; 18, 14. Cf. R. Bultmann, "*Agalliasis*," *TWNT*, I, 19.

22. W. Eichrodt, *Theology of the Old Testament*, I, p. 157.

23. E.g., 1 S. 11, 15; 2 S. 6, 19; 15, 12; 1 K. 3, 15; 4, 20.

24. W. Eichrodt, *op. cit.*, I, pp. 152, 153. On the existence of this concept among primitive peoples, cf. W. Schmidt, *Der Ursprung der Gottesidee* (Munich, 1912), I, p. 165; II, pp. 473, 858, 895; III, pp. 125, 281, 288, 368.

25. It is enough to refer to the study of O. Eissfeld, *Erstlinge und Zehnten im A.T.* (Göttingen, 1917).

26. Josephus (*Antiq.* 4, 240-243) and the Talmud interpreted this text as a supplementary tithe for the poor to be paid every three years. The Greek version of Tobias actually mentions three tithes (Tb. 1, 6), the first to be paid for the levites, the second for the sanctuary meal, the third for the poor. This text testifies to a later usage.

27. Cf. Ex. 23, 11; Lv. 25, 6; Dt. 14, 28-29.

28. Originally a purely agricultural feast, and known to the Canaanites. It never attained the national character of the Pasch and lasted only a day. It celebrated God's generosity and became Pentecost, after the name coined by the Septuagint. Its symbolism is found in the Christian Pentecost.

29. W. Eichrodt, *Theology of the Old Testament,* I, pp. 121-122.

30. Cf. e.g., J. Bonsirven, *Le judaïsm palestinien au temps de Jésus-Christ* (Paris, 1935), II, pp. 122-123.

31. We have the same root as in *diatheke*. This play on words in Luke is not accidental, as Bo Reicke, *Diakonie, Festfreude und Zelos,* pp. 156-157, who has been our guide here, justly remarks.

32. This has been studied by A. Robert, "Les attaches littéraires de Proverbes I-IX," *Revue biblique,* 43 (1934), p. 374.

33. This text has often been interpreted by the Fathers as a Eucharistic figure, e.g., Cyprian, *Epist.* 63, 5.

34. K. H. Rengstorf, "*Eptra*", *TWNT,* II, 630-631.

35. For a question so often studied it is sufficient to refer to: E. Lohmeyer, "*Vom christlichen Abendmahl,*" *Theologischer Rundschau,* 9 (1937), pp. 276-312; O. Cullmann, "La signification eschatologique de la Cène," *Revue d'histoire et de philosophie religieuses,* 16 (1936), pp. 5-22; Y. de Montcheuil, "Signification eschatologique du repas eucharistique," *Recherche de science religieuse,* 26, (1936), 1-43.

36. The incident is immediately followed by the episode of the disciples plucking the ears of corn on the Sabbath. Here the eschatological repast and the eschatological Sabbath are found linked together. Cf. H. Reisenfeld, *Jésus transfiguré* (Copenhagen, 1947), pp. 322-326.

37. J. Daniélou has neglected this element in the article of *Maison-Dieu* No. 18 treating of the repasts of Bible and their meaning. He included it in his book *Essai sur le mystère de l'histoire* (Paris, 1953), entitling it "Le repas des pauvres."

38. Luke alone specifically mentions that the guests are "the poor, the crippled, the lame, the blind." Mt. 22, 9, its parallel text, is not specific.

39. A remark of J. Jeremias, *Gleichnisse,* p. 132.

40. This remark was made by L. Bouyer, *The Fourth Gospel,* trans. Patrick Byrne (Westminster, Md., 1964) p. 70.

41. P. Benoît, "Le récit de la Cène dans Lc. 22, 15-20," *Revue biblique,* 48 (1939), 389; F. X. Durrwell, *The Resurrection,* trans. Rosemary Sheed (New York: Sheed, 1960), pp. 156-159.

42. *Supra,* p. 24.

43. Cf. e.g., G. Vermès, *Discovery in the Judean Desert* (New York: Desclée, 1956), pp. 45-46. Cf. also W. Grossouw, "The Dead Sea Scrolls and the New Testament," *Studia Catholica* (1951), pp. 289-299.

44. O. Cullmann, *Early Christian Worship,* trans. A. Stewart Todd sees and James B. Torrance (London: SCM Press Ltd., 1953), p. 14, in the liturgical use of the prayer "Maran atha" a reminder of Jesus' apparition on the day of his Resurrection, a prayer for its renewal at the moment of the Lord's Supper, and

an intimation of his final *parousia,* which must also take place within the framework of the messianic repast.
  45. Bo Reicke, *Diakonie, Festfreude und Zelos,* p. 204.
  46. Cf. Acts 2, 46; 3, 8, 9,; 4, 21; 11, 18; 13, 48; 21, 20.
  47. P. Benoît, "Les sommaires des Actes," *loc. cit.,* pp. 2-4.

Chapter III

THE OTHER FORMS OF CULT AND PRAYER

The Eucharistic Supper is the center and the goal of every gathering, assembled by the Spirit in the name of the Kyrios. It is the act of the community living under the moving force of the Spirit. It is also at the center of the other liturgical elements: baptism, confession of faith, manifestations of the Spirit, and Christian prayer.

The baptismal rite is intimately linked to the breaking of bread. The two rites complete each other, as Paul and John will prove. The baptism of water enables the Apostles to extend to the people the messianic outpouring of Pentecost (Acts 2, 38) and the remission of sins. But for the author of the Acts, the outpouring of the Spirit does not ordinarily accompany baptism; it precedes or follows it (Acts 8, 15; 9, 17; 10, 44; 11, 15; 19, 1-6). We already see this dissociation in the third Gospel (Lk. 3, 21).

We can detect an elementary baptismal liturgy in the Acts. The minister of baptism called for a confession of faith by asking a preliminary question concerning, it would seem, Christ. The Jerusalem Bible has this footnote to Acts 8, 37: "V. 37 is a very ancient gloss preserved in the Western Text and suggested by the baptismal liturgy 'And Philip said, "If you believe with all your heart, you may." 'And he replied, "I believe that Jesus Christ[1] is the Son of God."'" Like the Eucharist, and for the same reasons, baptism brought about a burst of joy in its recipients, e.g., the eunuch of the queen of Ethiopia (Acts 8, 39) and Paul's gaoler (*egalliasato,* Acts 16, 34).[2]

The imposition of hands[3]

Several examples in the Acts join prayer to the imposition of hands. The gesture has many meanings. An example of this was the institution of the seven deacons: "They presented these (seven candidates) to the apostles, who prayed and laid their hands on them" (Acts 6, 6).

In the Old Testament, the imposition of hands was a ritual gesture by which a man transmitted his own characteristics to an animal (Lv. 1, 3-4), or to other men, such as the Levites (Nb. 8, 10), who represented him in the worship of the Temple. To this first meaning another and very kindred one was that of consecration, of setting apart. Finally, we find Moses laying hands on Joshua in order to transmit to him on God's behalf an office and "the spirit of wisdom" (Nb. 27, 18; Dt. 34, 9).

In the case of the deacons, the imposition of hands established them in their office. From parallel situations in the Old Testament we might deduce that the rite was more probably performed by the Apostles than by the community. The prayer accompanying the imposition of hands appealed to God who dispenses gifts in the government of the Church. There was nothing magical about the rite; it was subordinated to God's good will.

The same rite, always linked with prayer, is found associated with baptism in the episode of the Samaritans (Acts 8, 15-17):

> When the apostles in Jerusalem heard that Samaria had accepted the word of God, they sent Peter and John to them, and they went down there and prayed for the Samaritans to receive the Holy Spirit, for as yet he had not come down on any of them: they had only been baptised in the name of the Lord Jesus. Then they laid hands on them, and they received the Holy Spirit.

The Acts here insistently distinguish between the gift of the Spirit and baptism. Despite the gift of miracles, Philip was incapable of bestowing the Spirit too. The prayer of Peter and John expresses submission to the Father of the gifts. The verb *proseuchomai*, dear to Luke, implies this disposition of prayer as an attitude of life. The verb *epipipto*, to fall upon, to come down, marks both the violence of the irruption and the entire liberty of its initiative.

Prayer and the imposition of hands were followed by an external manifestation of the Spirit. In Luke, the coming of the Spirit primarily refers to ecstatic gifts, of tongues, of prophecy, without being limited to these. More inward but no less real was the believers' entry through the Spirit into the messianic Church.

The rite of the imposition of hands is also found when Barnabas and Paul were sent off as missionaries (Acts 13, 1-3):

> In the church at Antioch the following were prophets and teachers: Barnabas . . . One day while they were offering worship to the Lord and keeping a fast, the Holy Spirit said, "I want Barnabas and Saul set apart for the work to which I have called them." So it was that after fasting and prayer they laid their hands on them and sent them off.

As in the Old Testament, here we find prayer and fasting linked together, on two separate occasions (Acts 13, 2, 3). The gospels had already taught the efficacy of this association. Fasting accompanies the Lord's liturgy (*leitourgia*). This is the only time the Acts uses this word. In both religious and secular usage, the verb and noun always express a collective undertaking: the service undertaken on behalf of the community. Their secular usage tends to fade before their cultual use. The Septuagint uses *latreuo* as well as *leitourgeo* for the sacred service the priests render to God in the Temple.[4] This meaning is later found in Luke's Gospel to characterize Zechariah's office (Lk. 1, 23).

The word *leitourgia* here signifies a public service rendered to the Lord and designates the Christian cult, paralleling that of the Old Testament; in any case it includes communal prayers presided over by prophets and doctors. Does it refer to the whole cult as described above (Acts 2, 42)? It is difficult to say.

Prayer and the imposition of hands implored God's grace for the two missionaries chosen by the Holy Spirit to preach the gospel. It is clear from the text that the prayer (*proseuchomai*) in question expresses the entire submission of the laborers to the task and to God's will (cf. Acts 14, 26; 15, 40). The imposition of hands continues the grace of Pentecost; the new missionaries were to widen the universal mission of the Apostles.

Prayer and charismata

At Pentecost, the Apostles were heard by all peoples. According to a Jewish tradition based on Exodus 20, 18, the voice of God was heard by every nation when the Law was promulgated on Sinai.[5] The gift of the Spirit seemed to restore the unity lost at Babel, and Pentecost was its retort. It was a preparation for the universal mission of the Church. The action of the Spirit in the Church was manifested by charismata, among which figure the *glossolalia* (the gift of tongues) mentioned twice (Acts 2, 11; 10, 46): "Jews and proselytes alike — Cretans and Arabs; we hear them preaching in our own language about the marvels of God . . . They could hear them speaking strange languages and proclaiming the greatness of God."

In both cases the gift of tongues brought about an ecstatic prayer of praise and thanksgiving.[6] Whether he uses the verb or the noun, Luke wishes to express the same idea; the Apostles proclaimed the wonders of God. The *megaleia* (a word used only here) translates for the Septuagint the great deeds of God in salvation history. The verb *megalunein* is frequently found in the Psalms (12, 4; 104, 24). St. Luke's Gospel, which is the only one to use it, has it translate Mary's thanksgiving for the magnificence of God's salvific plan. The expression alludes to the traditional doxology,[7] which Paul and the Apocalypse developed.

Between the Pentecost of the Apostles and that of the first Gentiles there is continuity and relationship. St. Peter noted this (Acts 10, 47). The gift of tongues, being as it were a sign of the Spirit received before baptism, indicated to the Apostle the place

The Other Forms of Cult and Prayer

of pagans in the messianic community, since they share in the same Spirit.

The charisma of *glossolalia*, which was manifested within the community, was addressed not to the assembly but to God. It localized personal prayer within the very framework of the congregation and of collective prayer, as though to affirm their complementary nature.

Public and private prayer

The Acts speak mostly of community prayer. It is difficult to make out the rhythm of this prayer and of the Christian cult. The description of the early Christian life (Acts 2, 46) suggests that the liturgical gatherings were held daily. Later, there appears the solemn character of the day following the Sabbath. This was the paschal day, even if it had not yet received that name (Acts 20, 7).

Cultual prayer and private prayer mutually support each other. The major concerns of the community, evangelization and persecution, were an incitement to improvised prayer (Acts 20, 36; 21, 5). Men like Stephen (Acts 7, 59-60), Peter (Acts 10, 9), and Paul (Acts 9, 11) who stand out as men of prayer were attentive to the Spirit who was guiding the Church, events, and men.

CHAPTER III

1. Cf. Acts 2, 38; 8, 16; 10, 48, 19, 5.

Acts 8, 37 shows several variants in MSS. and in the Fathers: Irenaeus and the Vulgate omit *Christon* after *Iesoun*. Instead of *exestin* E gives *sothesei*.

The authenticity of this verse is feebly supported by the documents. It is included by E 15, 27, 29, 36, 60, Codex Athos 184, Vulgate, Irenaeus and Cyprian. It is omitted by almost all the majuscules A B C H L P, by the majority of minuscules, and by all the eastern translations. All the critical editions omit ti. It consists of a very ancient gloss, anterior to Irenaeus, retained in the T occ. and derived from the baptismal liturgy.

2. O. Cullmann, *Baptism in the New Testament*, pp. 73-80 has tried to deduce from the use of the verb *koluei* in the baptism accounts (Acts 8, 36; 10, 47; 11, 17) the apostolic usage of infant baptism. His proof seems specious.

3. The imposition of hands and of the hand has been studied many times. J. Coppens, *L'imposition des mains et les rites connexes dans le N.T. et dans l'Eglise ancienne* (Paris, 1925). Older than this is J. Behm, *Die Handauflegung im Urchristentum* (Leipzig, 1911); more recent and rather systematized: N. Adler, *Taufe. u. Handauflegung* (Munich, 1951).

4. Cf. Ex. 28, 35; Nb. 4, 39; Ezk. 40, 46; Jdt. 4, 14.

5. SB II, 604.

6. J. Behm, "*glossa,*" *TWNT*, I, 721. Cf. F. Kohler, "Quelques mots sur la glossolalie des Actes et de la Ire épître aux Cor.," *Revue de théol. et des questions rel.,* 20 (1911), pp. 525-554; S. Lyonnet, "De glossolalia Pentecostes ejusque significatione," *Verbum Domini,* 24 (1944), pp. 65-75; J. Dupont, *Gnosis,* (Paris, 1949), pp. 204-210.

7. Other allusions to the doxology of God are found in Acts 11, 18; 14, 27; 15, 4, 12; 21, 20. We find it also in the third Gospel, Lk. 2, 47; 10, 17. We might compare it with the idea of *umnein* in Acts 16, 25.

Chapter IV

CHARACTERISTIC NOTES OF APOSTOLIC PRAYER

The book of the Acts enables us to assist at the birth of Christian prayer in the very heart of the Jerusalem community, which drew heavily on Israel's piety, but was already conscious of what constituted its newness.

Jewish fidelity

Early Christianity was not yet weaned from the Jewish cult. The Apostles continued to frequent the Temple.[1] The Portico of Solomon was a customary meeting place (Acts 5, 12; cf. 3, 11), perhaps because specific memories of Christ were associated with it (Jn. 10, 23). It faced the Mount of Olives. Moreover, to break with the Temple would have meant banishment from Jewish society and therefore a total break with Israel, whom the Apostles wished to bring to Christ. The Judeo-Christians would not leave the Temple until the Jews drove them out. Nevertheless, the sanctuary of Jerusalem stood for no more than the figure of the new cult incarnated by Christ, and the Jews were well aware of this ambiguity (Acts 6, 13-14).

Like Jesus, the first Christians had to repeat twice a day the confession of faith in the one and only God, the *Shema,* whose traces are still found in Christian prayer. St. Paul began his preaching at synagogue gatherings; we can follow his footsteps through Salamis, Iconium, Thessalonika, Beroea, Corinth, and Ephesus.[2]

Peter and John even complied with the daily rhythm of prayer; they went to the Temple at the ninth hour (Acts 3, 1).[3]

The forms of Jewish prayer are found again in Christian prayer. The confession of faith, roughly sketched and implicit in the *Shemone Esre,* would be made explicit and become structured in Christian faith and piety (Acts 4, 24; 14, 14; 17, 24ff). Although less developed than in St. Paul, biblical doxologies do appear in the Acts (Acts 4, 24; 14, 14; 17, 24; o poiesas . . .).[4]

The Psalms and the songs of the suffering Servant in particular, together with the Jewish synagogue cult, served as models and themes for Christian prayer; they gave it their special stamp. The analyses we have made of these thus far are sufficient proof of this. It would be easy to multiply examples. The quotation that Acts 3, 13 borrowed from Exodus 3, 6, 15 is given with the variant *ton pateron emon* instead of *tou patros sou,* as in the prayer of Manasseh and the *Shemone Esre;*[5] it is a tribute of gratitude to the synagogue. The same applies to the expression *pais,* whose influence on the apostolic community we have already seen regarding faith and prayer, both of which were illuminated by the prophecies of the suffering and triumphant Messiah.

The influence of the Psalter is no less evident, whether it concerns the cornerstone rejected by the builder, the King-Messiah, or the Creator of heaven and earth.[6] Prophets and Psalms throw light on the messiahship of Christ who, through suffering, became the Kyrios. They enable us to see the wonderful progression of salvation history, where persecution itself proves that Christians are the inheritors of the promises.

The newness of Christian prayer

Though the Church was conscious of inheriting all that was of value in the Jewish past, though she constantly repeated the prayer of her youth in the Psalms, the newness lies in the mediation of Christ, the hinge of the two Testaments. All prayer from now on must lean on him if it is to rise to the Father.

The break with the prayer of the synagogue was virtually accomplished when the Apostles were no longer satisfied with going up to the Temple for the ritual prayers, but congregated in their own houses "for the breaking of bread." Christ was the very heart of the cult, of the baptismal liturgy and of the Eucharist. All prayer, liturgical or private, passed through him. Catechumens were baptized in his name (Acts 8, 16, 37-38); the breaking of bread was celebrated in his invisible presence. He was the suffering Just One, the Son of Man, the Messiah foretold by the Scriptures. The drama of salvation found its climax in his person, Passion, and death, and its denouement in the glory of his Resurrection. The outpouring of the Spirit was proof of this exaltation of Jesus (Acts 2, 33) and of the inauguration of his kingdom.[7]

Apostolic Christology is based on the mystery of his Resurrection, which made Jesus Messiah and Lord. Stephen saw him in the glory of God, prayed to him, and entrusted his soul to him, as Jesus had entrusted his to the Father. The Resurrection is the central subject of apostolic preaching.

The testimony of the Apostles took on a juridical solemnity; it was, as it were, a re-examination of the trial under Pontius Pilate (Acts 4, 25-30). The allusion to Pilate points to the future confessions of faith. It was a confession of faith in the risen Christ, in the face of an unbelieving and often hostile world. Persecutions were perceived as continuing those which brought Jesus before the Roman tribunal and condemned him. The messianic era continues.[8]

The matter is clearly expressed in the prayer of the faithful at Jerusalem. The disciples discerned the continuity of this history in which the prophets of the Old Testament, Christ, Christians, witnesses and persecuted, plead the same case before the world's tribunal.

Stephen's messianic confession of Christ is written in the same way as the trial of Jesus. It affirms the same faith. It continues and actualizes the confession of faith already proclaimed by the liturgy of the Lord in joy and thanksgiving. More than this, Stephen addressed to Christ the prayer reserved for God alone.

Persecution is only one particular case; the essential, the main preoccupation of the Apostles and the faithful was to walk the road of salvation and to proclaim it to the world. The Spirit set up beacons along the road of evangelization; the charismata bore witness to this. Christians had their eyes fixed on Christ in glory; their concern was to remain submissive to the Spirit who guides the missionary movement of the Church (Acts 13, 1-4; cf. 16, 6; 19, 21; 20, 22). Liturgical or private, the prayer of the primitive community was essentially seeking and finding God's work, the insertion of the community and of everyone of its members into the plan of salvation.

Jesus continued to live in the heart of his community, as he who unified prayer, who was the soul of both communal and personal prayer. If the faithful prayed in the name of Jesus (cf. Acts 2, 21; 7, 58; 9, 14, 21), it was because, first of all, they met in his name (cf. Mt. 18, 19-20). Their prayer was the sign and the fruit of their unity around the same Lord, through the action of the one and same Spirit. What Paul was to expound as doctrine, the first Christians of Jerusalem were already living in their faith. They knew that their unity with him and between themselves was the condition of their relationship with the "Father in heaven." Prayer gushed from a living faith as an experience of the spiritual life. It was the flame born of fire.[9]

The new cult

In his study, *Messe und Herrenmahl*, Lietzmann tried to set two irreducible eucharists against each other, one created by the primitive community commemorating the meal shared with the risen Christ (Acts of the Apostles), the other celebrating the Last Supper and the death of Christ of which the Apostle Paul was author. The latter would finally have supplanted the other by an unconscious choice of the Church.

As for the Acts, our investigation now enables us to take a firmer stand against Lietzmann's hypotheses. The book of the primitive community describes the breaking of bread as a meal of joy. This joy sprang from gratitude for the Lord's Resurrection and from the presence of the risen Christ at the meal of his followers, and lastly from the confident expectation of the eschatological ingathering, made all the more vivid because the faithful imagined it to be imminent.

We must compare the first meal eaten with the risen Christ with the Last Supper. There is an incontestable continuity between the account of the institution of the Eucharist in the third Gospel and the breaking of bread, not only in the terms used but in the reality of the elements. There death appears as the road that leads to glory (Lk. 24, 26). If the breaking of bread is essentially the sacrifice of the resurrected Lord, can we say that his Passion and death are absent from it in the Acts? We grant that their place was not emphasized. But who would dare claim that the celebration of the Eucharist in the Acts ignores Christ's prophecy during the Supper of Holy Thursday, which Luke's Gospel alone relates: "I shall not drink wine until the kingdom of God comes" (Lk. 22, 18).

The accounts of the Last Supper in the Synoptics can only be explained by comparing them with the liturgical usages of the primitive community which is related in the Acts, and whose entire genesis is given us by the evangelists.

By putting the breaking of bread back into the context familiar to Luke, the meals of the disciples, which accompanied the celebration of the Eucharist, fulfilled the first phase of the messianic promises with their different elements: joy and thanksgiving for the succession of *mirabilia* culminating in Christ's Resurrection; gathering around the invisible Christ; the expectation of the worldwide reunion to which the poor and sinful are guests at God's feast.

CHAPTER IV

1. Cf. Acts 2, 46; 3, 1, 8; 5, 42; 21, 27; cf. also Lk. 24, 53; Mk. 14, 49.
2. E.g., Acts 13, 5, 14, 43; 14, 1; 17, 1, 10; 18, 4, 7, 19, 26; 19, 8.
3. For what pertains to the Sabbath, we refer the reader to J. Nielen, *Gebet und Gottesdienst* . . ., p. 88. Cf. also the pertinent remarks of O. Cullmann, *Early Christian Worship, op. cit.*, p. 9, n. 1.
4. C. Larcher, "Le symbole des apôtres," *Lumière et Vie*, 2, pp. 15-28, tries to

prove that no Creed existed in the Old Testament. Is he not basing himself on too rigid a definition of the confession of faith, a definition such as we obtain from the Apostles' Creed? Could we not say the same thing of the New Testament? Is he not extrapolating a concept which will take centuries of Christianity to become a "sound, precise, strict statement of the doctrines of faith?"

5. Remark made by L. Cerfaux, *Recueil Cerfaux*, II, p. 140.

6. Cf. Ps. 118, 22; Acts 4, 11; Ps. 2, 1; Acts 4, 25; Ps. 146, 6; Acts 4, 24.

7. R. Koch, *Geist und Messias* (Vienna, 1950).

8. L. Cerfaux, *Recueil*, II, pp. 166-174, has pertinently analyzed "testimony during the persecutions."

9. J. Nielen, *Gebet und Gottesdienst* . . ., pp. 24, 28.